THREE THOUSAND SIX HUNDRED
GHANIAN PROVERBS
(FROM THE ASANTE AND FANTE LANGUAGE)

Compiled By
J. G. CHRISTALLER

Translated By
KOFI RON LANGE

I.C.C. LIBRARY

Studies in African Literature
Volume 2

The Edwin Mellen Press
Lewiston/Queenston/Lampeter

PN
6519
.A625
T8613
1990

Library of Congress Cataloging-in-Publication Data

This book has been registered with the Library of Congress.

This is volume 2 in the continuing series
Studies in African Literature
Volume 2 ISBN 0-88946-234-8
SAfL Series ISBN 0-88946-725-0

A CIP catalog record for this book
is available from the British Library.

The Edwin Mellen Press
Box 450
Lewiston, New York
USA 14092

The Edwin Mellen Press
Box 67
Queenston, Ontario
CANADA L0S 1L0

The Edwin Mellen Press, Ltd.
Lampeter, Dyfed, Wales
UNITED KINGDOM SA48 7DY

Printed in the United States of America

THREE THOUSAND SIX HUNDRED
GHANIAN PROVERBS
(FROM THE ASANTE AND FANTE LANGUAGE)

CONTENTS

Translator's Preface

When J. G. Christaller published his book - "Twi Mmebusem Mpensa-Ahansia Mmoaano -- A Collection of Three Thousand And Six Hundred Tshi Proverbs" in 1879, he stated in the Preface: "To add a translation and explanations to the proverbs has not been possible to the Editor for the present. Perhaps at some later time the Editor may find leisure to translate a selection of them with a short commentary." Christaller didn't find the leisure to do this.

Now - over a hundred years later - I have found the leisure to translate his collection of Twi proverbs into English. Doing the translation over the past ten years has been a privilege, joy and tremendous learning experience for me.

The proverbs have been copied in their original form with the exception of the diacritical marks, which have been omitted. The ẹ and ọ have also been changed to ɛ and ɔ respectively.

It is my hope that by publishing the original Twi with an English translation the great wealth of these Ghanaian proverbs will prove to be a helpful source for those preaching the Word of God.

Special thanks go to my relatives who helped in the typing and proof reading of this book: Lu Lange, Judy King, Roxie Vaassen, Suzanne Lange, Chris Lange and Doris Lange.

Abetifi-Kwahu, February 1985.

© Fr. Kofi Ron Lange

Preface

Proverbs are short, popular, often used sentences expressing some practical truth, the result of experience and observation. In the Tshi, the prevalent language of the countries lying on the Gold Coast between the rivers Assinie and Volta, and inland, there is an extraordinary exuberance of such pithy sayings. The language of the Negroes of the Gold Coast on the whole is highly figurative. As many ideas are expressed by a homely image, so facts or themes of discussion are usually compared with, elucidated by, or judged after certain precedents or self-evident truths substantiated by proverbs. In their public assemblies and transactions, political and judicial, the arguments of the speakers, the statements of the plaintiff and the defendant, the questions and decisions of the judges, are interwoven with proverbs held out and received as convincing proofs of the soundness of the opinions set forth by the speaker.*) Hence one of the proverbs (No. 2859) says: "When a matter (for public and formal discussion, or, as the usual term is, a palaver) comes, then proverb-making comes." And so much accustomed to the use of proverbs are the natives, that even the chief points of the savings of European governors or other officials, either by their interpreters or by other people who afterwards relate what was uttered by them, are cast, as it were, into the mould of native proverbs that are not even known to the European speaker. Yea there are instances of proverbs being referred back as far as the time of creation, interwoven in a certain mythical story, as if the Creator himself and the first men had acted upon the principles contained in the proverbs put into their mouth. - In the

* Of such public transactions the Editor of these Proverbs possesses many hundreds of pages written down by native assistants or by himself from their dictation.

common intercourse of daily life also, proverbs are frequently resorted to, as being more likely to produce effect than circuitous argument, and setting disputable things right, as it were, with one stroke. - "A proverb is the wisdom of all and the wit of one." (Trench.)

That a collection of proverbs like the present will be of no common value for all students of the language in which they sprang up, or of the peculiarities of the people who use them, needs no proof. They contain almost inexhaustible materials for the grammar and dictionary, and still more for those who aspire to a sound and thorough knowledge of the Negro mind. So the printing of this Collection has been undertaken not only for the benefit of the Natives who are able to read and write their own language and who will be glad to find them together, but also for the benefit of the Europeans who have to deal with the Natives as missionaries , rulers , magistrates or judges, not excepting the merchant, if his pursuits allow of sufficient time being spent on gaining a real acquaintance with the people.

To add a translation and explanations to the proverbs has not been possible to the Editor for the present. Not a few of the proverbs given would lose much even in the best possible translation; many would require a good deal of explanation. Perhaps at some later time the Editor may find leisure to translate a selection of them with a short commentary. Meanwhile this collection points out 268 proverbs that have been translated and explained by the Rev. H. N. Riis in his "Grammatical Outline and Vocabulary of the Oji Language, Basel, 1854," page 111-136, and 92 more that are found translated in the Editor's "Grammar of the Asante and Fante Language called Tshi, Basel, 1875." The former have the letter R. and the number of each in Mr. Riis' collection added to them, and the latter in a similar way the letters Gr. and the paragraph or page of the Grammar where the proverb and its translation is to be found along with some elucidation of its grsmmatical structure. J. Zimmerman's "Grammatical Sketch of the Akra or Ga Language, Stuttgart, 1858", on page

158-177 contains 220 proverbs in Ga with their translation in English and explanatory remarks. As the Ga, though a decidedly different language, has largely borrowed from the Tshi, and the territories of both languages are conterminous, we find among those 220 proverbs more than 80 identical with ours, to which we have added the letter Z with the number of each in Mr. Zimmerman's collection.*) Thus about 440 of our 3680 proverbs may be said to be already translated, and for the rest the student of the language must be referred to the Editor's "Dictionary of the Asante and Fante Language" (to be printed in 1879) or to the help of native interpreters.   I may add something about the way in which the present Collection of Tshi proverbs has been obtained. When Mr. Riis had finished his collection, he was forced in 1850 to quit the field; but other missionaries continued to collect materials of the language and especially proverbs. They were taken down by the missionaries themselves from the oral communication of certain elders or of other old and younger people, or they were written by native assistants who increased their own previous knowledge by learning from experienced countrymen. Thus a number of different collections being obtained, the Editor strove to unite them in alphabetical order, so that it may now be easily ascertained whether any proverb occasionally met with is already contained in this collection or not, Naturally there occur many different readings, some of which have been retained in full, whilst others, indicating the variations found in local use, are put in brackets (see the note on page 1). They require of course to be read judiciously, and will, I trust, present no difficulty to the studious reader. The Editor certainly does not assume to have said the last word on the subject of these variations, but hopes that others will find out the preferable readings and reject

* Omitted references of this kind are the following:
Our No. 159. 341. 447. 468. 499. 542. 557. 596. 606. 704. 777.
Z.'s No. 160. 215. 40. 67. 167. 29. 121. 56. 164. 101. 15.

all that are merely corruptions. Competent critics are requested to cross out what they reject and to substitute better reading where they have any, so that, if at any later time a new edition were to be printed, the best reading may be secured as far as possible.

In the alphabetical arrangement of these proverbs the formative (nominal or verbal) and pronominal prefixes of the initial words, or the separately written pronouns before the first nouns, and in a few cases a not essential particle at the head of the proverb have been disregarded and the order is in general the same as that of the words in the Dictionary. So f. i., when the consonants b, d, g, by the nasal prefix m or n or n (which serves to form the plural of certain nouns and the negative of verbs, Gr#18) have, by way of assimilation, been changed into m, n, n, the words are still to be sought for under b, d, g, just as done in using the Dictionary. Slight deviations from the strict order have been admitted where it seemed advisable to unite proverbs bearing closer relation to each other.

The Editor has had the greater part of the proverbs in this collection read or explained to him by Natives; as to the rest, doubts and obscurities hover still about some of them, chiefly those collected by the Rev. S. Suss (either at Akropong from the mouth of Agyakwa, one of the elders, or at Gyadam, Akem, from the mouth of an Asanteman), and by Jonathan Palmer Bekoe, a native of Akropong, They are indicated by the letter S. or B. put after them.

Origin of the Proverbs. As in other languages, the author of most proverbs is not known. Many proverbs are introduced by the words: "The Tshi people" or "the elders made it a proverb saying:"...Sometimes a proverb is expressly ascribed to a certain tribe, as, the Asantes, the Akems, the Fantes. Of some proverbs, however, the author is still known, and his name, if not forming an integrant part of the proverb, is added in parenthesis.

Dialect. The proverbs are given in the dialect in which they were first penned down, most of them in the

Akuapem, some in the Asante or Akem dialect, only a few in the Fante dialect. On the territories and comparatively slight differences of these dialects, see the Editor's Grammar page XIX. 185-194.*)

We cannot enter into the distinction of general and historical proverbs, nor into the discussion of the requisites by which it is decided whether a given sentence deserves the name of proverb or not, A few may have crept in, to which the character of proverb may be disputed. To the Editor's knowledge this has been done only in two cases: No. 243 "Nobody is satisfied for another" is only an explanation of No. 286 "Nobody drinks the medicine for the sick one"; and No. 319 "Nobody gathers riches (and) lays them up in As ante and stands boasting of them in Akuapem" has been given as a proverb by one native (with the meaning of "Hic Rodus, hic salta!") and objected to by another, though he could not show a sufficient reason for contesting its right to be called a proverb.-

We add a few remarks on the use that may be made of this collection in school-teaching.

1. The proverbs may serve for instruction in the Tshi language in various ways. a. They may furnish grammatical, especially syntactical, examples for the instruction in Tshi Grammar. b. They may serve for exercises in Orthography. c. In Akem schools they may be written in the Akem dialect, whereas in Akuapem schools the Akem dialect of some may be turned into Akuapem. In Fante schools they may be written in Fante. d. In higher schools they may help to educate the interpreter in various languages, by turning them into English, Ga, Adanme &c. - Of course only such will be picked out as may best serve some practical purpose.

2. Regarding the objects mentioned in, or the doctrines expressed by the proverbs, part of them may be selected and systematically grouped together. a. Proverbs may be selected in which God, or the so-called fetishes,

---

* In the Asante and Akem dialects we distinguish the 1. and 3. pers. plur. of the personal pronoun by putting an apostrophe before the 3. pers. ('ye-); cf Gr. 58#Rem. 2.

or soothsayers and wizards are mentioned; others, in which the general state and condition, the fate and destiny of man are spoken of; othes, in which man's head, ace, eye, ear &c. are mentioned; others, in which certain domestic or wild animals, plants and minerals, land and water, rain and wind, sun, moon and stars, day and night, the year and its seasons, or other objects of nature and art are spoken of. b. Other proverbs are taken from, or refer to, the domestic, social and political life and conditions of the people: dwellings (houses and towns). care of the body (food and drink, clothing and ornaments, washing, sleeping); family life (marriage, husband and wife, parents and children, old and young people, health and sickness, death and burial); social intercourse (relations, friends and foreigners, benefactors and enemies); occupations: agriculture (plantations and their produce, palm-wine and palm-oil); hunting and fishing; handicraft (weaving, dying, tanning smith's, carpenter's or joiner's, and potter's trade &c.); money; weights and measures; trade; travelling; music; plays; - in public life: king and officials, people and subjects, persons of high and low rank, masters and slaves, rich and poor, wealth and poverty, property and debts, crimes and punishments, dissension and unity, judicial proceedings and reconciliation, war and peace, welfare and ruin. c. Other proverbs refer to the intellectual conditions and faculties of man, speak of wisdom and foolishness, learning and rudeness, state what is reasonable or not, and pronounce maxims of prudence. d. Others contain or furnish moral rules and principles and may be arranged according to the Ten Commandments, at least the fifth to the tenth under their respective virtues and opposite vices. (Teachers will find a help towards arranging the respective proverbs under their proper headings in "The Doctrines of Christian Religion, based on Dr. Luther's smaller Catechism, by Dr. Kurtz, translated into Tshi, Basel, 1872" 76-130.) e. Other proverbs point to affections or states and dispositions of body or mind, as, pleasure and pain, happiness and misery, cheerfuless dejection, rejoicing and lamentation, hope and fear, courage and cowardice, rashness and caution.

3. Other kinds of exercise for schools may consist in the explanation and manifold application and illustration of proverbs, and in the comparison of proverbs with each other. Often one proverb contradicts or limits another; the understanding and judgment of pupils may well be exercised by examining the measure of truth and the weight to be allotted to the one and the other. This will often be most effectually done by comparing them with Scriptural truth. -

In what manner a good number of proverbs may be turned to account in the preaching of the Word of God before the heathen, need not be expounded here.

May this Collection give a new stimulus to the diligent gathering of folk-lore and to the increasing cultivation of native literature. May those Africans who are enjoying the benefit of a Christian education, make the best of this privilege; but let them not despise the sparks of truth entrusted to and preserved by their own people, and let them not forget that by entering into their way of thinking and by acknowledging what is good and expounding what is wrong they will gain the more access to the hearts and minds of their less favoured countrymen.

SCHORNDORF, February 1879

J. G. Christaller

Postscript to the Preface

The empty space of this page permits two additional remarks.

1. In H. Rowley's "Africa Unveiled" (London, Society for Promoting Christian Knowledge, 1876) the author (on page 230-235) shows six prominent causes of the failure of that form of Christianity which was introduced by the Portuguese in Southern Guinea (Congo, Angola &c.) and Eastern Africa (Quilimane Mozambique &c.) soon after their discovery of those countries. We cope and are confident that none of these causes are at work or are likely to uproot Christianity as it is in our days being planted in the countries of the Gold Coast. But to quote what Mr. Rowley, who himself has been a missionary in those parts of Eastern Africa, gives as the 2d cause, will not be out of place here, because his words on the one hand agree with the last words of our Preface, and on the other hand warn against accommodation to heathenish notions. He says: "The (Roman Catholic) missionaries were guilty of an unholy accommodation of Christian truth and observances to heathenish superstitions and customs. Christianity, be it said, is only a sword against that which is evil; it is conservative of all that is good wherever it may be found. It is the greatest unwisdom in missionaries not to make use of all that can be possibly utilised in what the heathen believe and do. There are many customs amongst the heathen that should be sanctified, not destroyed, and their imperfect conception of a truth, if rightly used, may aid the missionary greatly in leading then to accept the truth in its fulness. But, from all accounts, the Portugese, in their desire to make converts, sacrificed both Christian principle and morality in many of the accommodations which they made to the prejudices of the heathen."-

2. The real number of proverb in this collections wIll be reduced from 3680 to about 3600, if those among them which occur repeatedly, only in a different form, be counted only once. The references to identical proverbs of different numbers, or to proverbs which have similar meanings or in which the same or similar expressions are found, may, by those who use the collection, be increased beyond the extent to which such references are already embodied in the work.

SCHORNDORF, April, 1879.

J. G. Chr.

Guide to Pronunciation

The letters used in the Tshi Language sound as in Dr. Lepsius'
Standard Alphabet.
The Vowels form two classes: I. a ɛ ɔ, e ọ;
                                                  II. a̰ e o, i u,
a ā, 1) full, sounds as in "far", short and long;
      2) thin (a̰), before i, u, full e, e, o, gya,
nyã, tw̌a, as in "fat" or (in Fante) as e in "prey";
ɛ ɛ̃, ɔɔ̃ , as in "let, there, not, nor"; e ẽ, o õ,
1) in cl. II. full as in "bed, fate, -note";
2) in cl. I. diminished, approaching to i, u; i ī,
u ū, as in "fill, field, pull, true".
ã ẽ ī õ ũ, are nasal; ă ě ĭ ŏ ŭ are very short. á é ... ḿ ń
ń have high or middle tone, à è ..lowtone. Diphthongs sound
according to their single letters: ae ãe ai ɛe ei ɔe oe oi ui;
aw ɛw ew iw ɔw ow uw.

Consonants and consonantal combinations are:
p b m f w, t d n s r, k g ṅ h, y;
ky gy ny hy ; kw (gw) ṅw hw; tw̌ dw̌ ṅw fw̌ w̃.
ṅ=ng in "sing"; hy=x; w̌=wy; in tw̌ the sound
sh (and in dw that of zh) is mixed up with palatal t (d) and w̌;
in fw̌ the f is produced with the tongue and both lips, which
are formed nearly as for whistling.

Cf. A Grammar of the Asante and Fante Language called
Tshi, Basel 1875, pag. 1-7 and (on the difference of the
Akan and Fante Dialects) pag. 185-196. - The tones inherent
to the single syllables (see Gr. # 25) are only exceptionally
marked in single words, clauses, or whole proverbs.

1. Ɛba a, ɛka oni.

   If anything (either good or bad) comes to you, it affects your mother.

2. "Ɛba a, mebɔ ano (:*miso ano, misom)" ne - "Ɛtoto a, mesan", - wɔn mu hena akyi (:afa) na wowɔ? - Mewɔ "Ɛba a, mebɔ ano" akyi.

   When trouble is coming, I prevent it, and when it is entangled, I disentangle it. Which of these two do you prefer? I prefer, When it is coming, I prevent it.

3. "Ɛreba, ɛreba" na ɛyɛ hu; na enya ba a, ɛnyɛ hu bio.

   "It is coming, it is coming," makes you afraid, but when it actually comes, it is no longer fearful.

4. "Mereba, mereyɛ ansa" na ɛmaa ɔkwakuo dua kaa hɔ.

   "I am coming, I am doing something first," made the monkey's tail remain.

5. Womma ntɛm a, woma oguan.

   If you do not come on time, you pay for it with a sheep.

6. Ɔba a ɔbɛyɛ yiye, wonnya no (:wɔnyɛn no) kɛtɛ-pa so nko.

   The child which will do well in life is not reared only on a good mat.

7. Ɔba sɛ ɔse, na(nso) ɔwɔ abusua (:mmusua).

   A child may resemble his father, but he belongs to the mother's side of the family.

8. Ɔba nsu a, womma no nufu?

   If the baby does not cry, do you not breast feed him?

9. Wo ba kɔ sumana so na ɔwɔ ka no a, wuntwa ho nkyene, na woyɛ no (:hɔ) aduru.

   If your child goes to the rubbish heap and a snake bites him, you do not cut off that part of the body, but you apply medicine to it.

10. Wo ba ne to (:gu) wo serɛ so a, wode baha (:mposae) na eyi (:ɛpopa), na womfa ɔsekan ntwa (na wuntwa nkyene). Cf. 569.

---

* The words in brackets with two dots before them may be put instead of the words preceeding them; those without the two dots may be added or left out.

When your child's excreetment falls on your lap, you
remove it with dry plantain fibres, you do not cut off
the soiled flesh.

11. Wo ba saw asa-bone a, se no sɛ: wo asaw nyɛ fɛ; nse no
sɛ: ɔkra, tete gu mu. B.

If your child dances indecently, tell him: "Your dancing
is not good," don't tell him: "Darling, dance with all
your might."

12. Wo ba sisi wo kora ba a, enye; nanso wo kora ba sisi
wo ba a, enye. R.262.

If your own child deceives the child of your fellow-
wife, it is not right; and if the child of your fellow-
wife deceives your child, it is also not right.

13. Ɔba bone nnim kasakyerɛ.

The bad child does not take correction.

14. Ɔba-dueduefo nto ne na funu.

The wandering child does not meet the dead body of his
mother before it is buried.

15. Ɔba-gyigyɛfo na ɔma ɔbayifo adidi no da adi.

The adversary brings to light the sorcery of the witch.

16. Ɔba-nyansafo, wobu no bɛ, na wɔnka no asɛm.

We don't tell the wise man things in plain words, we
speak to him in proverbs.

17. Ɔba-werefo nte aduru.

The person who is not on good terms with you does not
collect herbs for you.

18. Ɔba biara te sɛ deɛbɛn ara, na wugyae aware gyae aware
a, wo anim mma onyam.

However beautiful a woman is, if she is often divorced
she loses the respect of men.

19. Ɔba ho yɛ fɛ a, efi ne kunu.

The beauty of a woman is attributed to her husband.

20. Ɔba na onim kunu.

The pregnant woman alone knows the husband (and father
of her baby).

21. Ɔba nyinsɛn na wanwo ba a, ɔwo banin.

When a woman conceives and does not give birth to a
girl, she gives birth to a boy.

22. Oba twa bomma (:Obea twa akyene a.s. yɛ kyɛm) a,
etweri barima dan mu.

Even if a woman makes a talking drum, she keeps it in
a man's room.

23. Obea kɔ aguare na wamma ntɛm a, na osiesie neho.

When a woman goes to take her bath and stays a long
time, it is because she is making herself beautiful.

24. Obea ne ne kunu asɛm, obi nnim mu.

Nobody knows the secrets that exist between a husband
and a wife.

25. Obea tenten so abɛ a, ɔnwam di.   R.208.

When a tall woman carries palm nuts, the hornbill
eats them.

26. Mma-dodow kunu yare a, ɔkɔm na ekum no.

When a man who has many wives is sick, he dies of
starvation.

27. Mmea nhina yɛ bako.

All women are alike.

28. Mmea nnyae anka aguare, na ahohow ho bɔn.

Women should stop using lime in their bath water because
even the red ant (which lives in the lime tree) stinks.

29. Mmea pɛ nea sika wɔ.

Women like to be where there is money.

30. Mmea se: wo he yɛ fɛ! a, ɛne ka.

If women say you are handsome, it means you are going
to incur debts.

31. Aba a wɔde bɔ ofie aboa no wɔmfa mmɔ wuram' de.   Z.21.

The stick with which one beats a domestic animal should
not be used in beating a wild animal.

32. Babi asɛm a wɔka serew no na wɔka su wo babi.

What is said in one place makes people laugh and in
another place it makes people cry.

33. Babi yɛ sum na wɔde sika pe hɔ a, ɛhɔ tew.

If a place is dark and then money is scattered there,
it becomes light.

34. Ɔbaeankɔr' a, wɔfrɛ no aboa bi (:akoa bi).

If someone comes and does not return to his home town, he
is called an animal (slave).

35. Bafan se: ɔreyɛ ne na (:odi ne na aboro): onnim sɛ ɔresɛe
ne to.

The crippled child says he is hurting his mother; he doesn't
know he is hurting his own buttocks.

36. Bafoɔ, wowɔ adeɛ a, wɔnkɔ afoɔ.

Big man, if you were wealthy, you wouldn't have gone out
to loot.

37. Abaguade yɛ wo dɛ a, wo afuw yɛ ketewa.

If you like to get your share of the money from helping to
settle cases, your farm will always be small.

38. Bagya afɛre, kotobankye afɛre.

If "bagya" is disgraced, so is the wild casava.
(Ɔbako, Ɔbakofo ...see Ɔbiak ...445.459.

39. Bakoma, wodi no wɔn na gya ho, na wonni no obi ne na de ho.

A person of high rank shows his pride at his mother's fireside and not at another man's mother's fireside.

40. Ban kata asɛm so.

The fence conceals the secrets of a household.

41. Abane betu a, efi yam'.

The destruction of a stone house comes from within.

42. Ɔbankye de, wɔnka no adwobaw.

The cassava has no climbing strings to tie around a supporting
stick.

43. Abanoma nsen ɔba-pa.

A step-child is not better than one's own ohild.

44. Banu ko (a), nea etia no basa yɛ ɔpatafo.

If two persons are fighting, the third person is the peace-maker.

45. Banu so dua a, emmia.

If two person's carry a log, it doesn't press hard (on their
heads).

46. Banu wea kɔ kutu mu.

A tree bear belonging to two persons goes into one cooking pot.

47. Ɔbarima mfe ntasu nto fam' na ɔmfa n ano mfa.

A man does not spit on the ground and then pick it up with his mouth.

48. Ɔbarima (mu) nni akakra.

Among men none are small.

49. Ɔbarima nse ne yɔnko barima se: mefwe wo.

No man tells another man, "I will beat you."

50. Ɔbarima, woyɛ no dɔm ano, na wɔnyɛ no fie.

Courage is shown on the battlefield, not in the house.

51. Mmarima nni ho a, mmabasia yi wɔnho kyerɛ.

When men are not present, women show their nudity.

52. Basafawa nni biribi a, ɔwɔ abɔnsam'. S.

Even though the cripple has nothing, he can at least clap his hands.

53. Batafoɔ ogya, ago wɔ akyi.

The trader's fire draws others from afar.

54. Batafo se: ɛnyɛ n'ano, ɛnyɛ n'ano; na (ɛyɛ) n'ano ara nen. R. 115. Z. 200.

The wild boar keeps saying it is not his mouth, but it is his mouth.

55. Batiri nna babi na woatwa wo ba-bɔne ti akɔtɔ ho.

There is no other shoulder somewhere else on which you can put the head of your own bad child after you have cut it off.

56. Abayɛm-mone nti na kokosakyi ba di bini.

The vulture's baby eats dung because of poor home training.

57. Bayerɛ ammɔ a, yennunu no; aba ne sibere so.

When a yam doesn't grow well, we don't blame it; it is because of the soil.

58. Bayerɛ (ɛre)nyɛ 'ye, na ɛyɛ dufudufu.

A yam which hasn't grown is deficient in quality.

59. Ɔbayifo ba wu a, ɛyɛ no yaw.

Even if a witch's child dies, it makes her sad.

60. Ɔbayifo ɔrekɔ e! ɔbayifo ɔrekɔ e! na wonyɛ ɔbayifo a, wuntwa wo ani. R.42.

The witch is going! The witch is going! but if you are not a witch you don't turn around to look.

61. Ɔbayifo kum wadi-wamma-me, na onkum wama-me-na-esua.

The witch kills "he ate and he did not give me', but she does not kill, "he gave me too little."

62. Ɔbayifo nsuo, obiako nnware.

It is not only one person who bathes in the witch's water.

63. Ɛbɛ ne bɛ bi nsɛ a, wɔmfa nto ho mmu.

If two proverbs are not similiar, one is not used to explain the other.

64. Abɛ bere a, woso fa, meso fa. R.218.

When the palm nuts ripen, you carry half and I carry half.

65. Abɛ biako na ɛsɛe nsa. R.1.

It is only one bad palm tree that spoils the whole lot of palm wine.

66. Abɛ de ne mpopa na ɛyɛ ɔbarima.

The strength of the palm tree is in its branches.

67. Abɛ dɔm ara ne ne mpopa.   Cf.2624.

The army of the palm tree is its branches.

68. Abɛ ho nni nam a, wɔtwɛre no saara.

Even though the peel of the palm nut has no pulpy substance in it, it is stripped off all the same (and the oil is extracted).

69. Abɛ mpopa nnim 'manni.
Ɔbea ... see 18-30.

The prickly branches of the palm tree do not show preference even to friends.

70. Abebɛw a ɔbɛn ni na ɔwe abebɛserɛ.

The grasshopper which is always near its mother eats the best food.

71. Ɔbɛdɛw mu nni ankyeafo.

There is no distinction among the common baskets made of palm branches.

72. Obedi-ama-wo, owom' na oyε wo (:εyε wo).
    He who seems to be for you may be working against you.

73. Abεdwea gyae pene (:apinsi), na wo ba ne kwabεten.
    Little palm tree, stop crying, your child is the
    tall palm tree.

74. Abεdwea pε nkwa a, na εbata (:obra odum.
    If the young palm tree wants to stay alive,
    it grows next to the odum tree.

75. Befua-koro, wontwεre no mperennu (:mperεnsa).
    One palm nut can not be peeled twice.

76. Befua-kyim, wogye no afonom'.
    The blood soup made of one palm nut is shared
    in little drops.

77. Begye-a-egye, wode biribi na ese.
    "I will get it because I can," one says with a
    reason (based on experience).

78. Wobεn asu a, na wote sε ɔkotɔ bɔ waw.
    If you come near the river, you will hear the crab cough.

79. Abεn nyε dε a,(na) etua ɔnipa ano. R. 132.
    Even though the sound of the horn is not pleasant,
    it is still blown by a man's mouth.

80. Bεn-nedaw na wode to foforo ho sen.
    You make a new arrow by comparing it to an old one.

81. Benkum guare nifa, na nifa guare benkum
    The left hand washes the right and the right washes
    the left.

82. Ɔbεnkyε, wobεnkyε oni (:ɔdesani) a, ɔde wo yε osua.
    If you go too near your relatives, they will not
    respect you.

83. Obenya-adeε kara nky(ri) biribi.
    The soul of a rich man has no taboos.

84. Bepo-dwuma, obi nfwε obi to.
    People working on the slope of a mountain do
    not look at the buttocks of one another.

85. Ɔberan nni biribi a, ɔwɔ nhyɛso.
    If the strong man has nothing else, he can at least
    command others.

86. Ɔberan nkyere beran.
    One strong man does not catch another strong man.

87. Mmerante abien te nsu ho a, egu.
    If two selfish young men sit next to a pot of water, the
    water spills out on the ground.

88. Mmerante-bo yɛ sika a, anka nnipa nhina anya bi pɛn.
    If youthful pride were wealth, then every man would
    have had it in his lifetime.

89. Wobere di, na wɔmmerɛ mma wɔn yɔnko.
    What people get by hard work they don't get for their
    neighbors.

90. Bere annu annu a, ɛtra.
    If an opportunity is not taken when it comes, it
    passes away.

91. Mmere di adannan.
    Times keep changing..

92. Berebu nyɛ nwene-na a, anka apatiperɛ da nnua abien so?
    If the building of a nest were easy, would the little
    "apatiperɛ" bird roost in the fork of a tree?

93. Ɔbereku-nam, wodi no hyew.
    The "obereku" bird should be eaten hot.

94. Aberekyi se ɔbɛdan guanten a, tuntum mpa mu da.
    If the goat says it will become a sheep, there will
    always be black spots on its body.

95. Aberekyi se: obi nnantew nkowu.
    The goat says: "Nobody willingly walks to his own death."

96. Aberekyi se: nea ɛbɛba aba dedaw.
    The goat says: "What will come has already come."

97. Aberekyi se: nea abogyabum wɔ no, ɛhɔ na adidi wɔ. R.138.
Cf.498.

The goat says: "Where there is blood, there is plenty
of food."

98. Aberekyi se: woatɔ me na woantɔ me.

The goat says: "They bought my mother, not I."

99. Aberekyiba, woma no so kɔ soro a, wogya no berɛw.

However high you lift the kid goat, you place it gently
on the ground.

100. Aberewa a onni se no, n'atadwe gu ne kotokum'.

Even if the old woman has no teeth, her tiger nuts
remain in her own bag.

101. Aberewa fwɛ akokɔ, na akokɔ fwɛ aberewa.

The old woman looks after her hens and the hens look
after the old woman.

102. Aberewa kɔ asu a, ɔbɛba, na ne ntɛm na yɛrepɛ.

When an old woman goes to fetch water she will return,
but we want someone who will return quickly with the
water.

103. Aberewa nim ade a, onnye ne ban.
(Aberewa ano yɛ den a, ogye n. b.)

If the old lady knows so much, let her make her own fence.
(If the old lady is quarrelsome, she makes her own fence.)

104. Aberewa, wo ano yɛ den a, gye wo ban! R.236.

Old woman, if you are quarrelsome, make your own fence!

105. Aberewa nsampana yiye. S.

The old lady doesn't wear properly the rag that is tied
about one's chest when mourning for a close relative.

106. Aberewa atomdeɛ ne fane.

The old woman's meat is vegetables.

107. Wobese mako a, ɛfefɛw, na wubu so a, na ewu.

If you collect peppers one by one, the plant grows well;
but if you break the stem, it dies.

108. Besebese na ɛma ɔtɔn.
Abetia... see Abɛdwea...74.

Grumbling causes the slave to be sold.

-9-

109. Abew nhyɛ da.

Misfortunes do not have set times for coming.

110. Abew mmew akoa nko.

Misfortunes do not come only to slaves.

111. Ebi da wo anom' na woto bi a, ɛben.

If you have some food in your mouth, and you are roasting something, it becomes well roasted.

112. Ebi akyi wo bi.

There is something better somewhere.

113. Ebi anyɛ wo dɛ a, ɛma ebi yɛ wo nwene (:ma ebi nyɛ wo nw.).

If something doesn't please you, it makes everything else bitter to you.

114. Obi bɛma wo aduan adi a, na ɔde ampesi di wo adanse. =405. R.206.

If someone is going to prepare really good food for you, he gives you "ampesi"-boiled yam first.

115. Obi abɛsɛburow mma (:nyɛ yiye) a, wɔmfa wɔn anan ase akumsuman nkɔfa mu (:ase).

If someone's corn planted in the second rainy season does not grow well, no one passes through it with a destructive amulet on his feet.

116. Obi bɔ wo dua se: ma onwu! a, ɛnyɛ yaw sɛ ose: ma ohia nka no!

If someone curses you saying: "Let him die", it is not as painful as saying, "Let him become poor."

117. Obi bɔ wo awerɛkyekye suman na ɔde nkɔmmɔ due wo ano a, na wannya papa bi anyɛ wo.

If someone makes a comforting charm for you and later only besmears your mouth with mere words to make things turn out well, he has not really helped you at all.

118. Obi abusude yɛ obi akarade.

One man's curse is another man's fortune.

119. Obi busuyɛfoɔ ne bi nipa-pa.

One man's enemy is another man's friend.

120. Obi ade dɔso a, wɔmfa mpampa na ɛfow. =128.

However rich a man is, it is not right to plunder his things with big pans.

121. Obi ade-dedaw kɔ obi nsam' a, ɛyɛ no foforo.

When an old thing belonging to one person gets into another man's hands it is a new thing to him.

122. Obi dehye kɔsom a, na wɔfrɛ no afana. R.250.

When a member of the royal family goes somewhere to serve, she is called a slave.

123. Obi dɔ wo a, na ɔ(fa kwan) ba wo fi.

If someone loves you, he comes to visit you in your house.

124. Obi dɔ wo a, ɔfrɛ wo asanom.

If someone loves you, he invites you for a drink.

125. Obi dɔ wo a, ɔserɛ wo hɔ ade. R.68.Gr.#276,2.

If someone loves you, he asks a favor from you.

126. Obi afom akum a, wo nso mfom nnua!..
Obi mfa..mfi... see 136-178.

If someone kills an animal by accident, you do not skin it by accident!

127. Obi frɛ wo Sɛwose a, mpɛ ntɛm nserew; ebia wo agya yɛ ɔbonnatofo.

If someone says you are the very image of your father, do not laugh too quickly, perhaps your father is a womanizer.

128. Obi afuw so a, womfa mpampa na ɛfow (:ɛnyɛ mp. na wode fow). Cf.120.

However big anyone's farm is, it is wrong to plunder his crops with a big pan.

129. Obi fwɛ obi anim na ɔnom sasin. Cf.262. 696. 1183.

One drinks the dregs of palm wine out of regard for the giver.

130. Obi gyina obi 'mati na ohu guam'.

You can see the inside of an assembly by standing on the shoulders of someone.

131. Obi akoa de Ahima a, wonhima no kwa. R.203.

Even though someone's slave is called "Punishment", still he isn't punished without a reason.

132. Obi akoa di pereguan na woma asuasa tɔ no a, oyi kaw
sua ma wutua.

If a slave is worth thirty six dollars and you buy him
for twenty seven dollars, he will incur a debt of nine
dollars which you have to pay.

133. Obi akɔnnɔde ne dompo nsono.

The intestines of the wild dog are someone's favorite
food.

134. Obi kwan nkyɛ na esi bi de mu.

One man's way does not go far without meeting another's.

135. Obi kyɛ wo ade a, (na) woda n'ase.

When someone gives you a present, you thank him.

136. Obi mfa* aberekyi nto guanten ho. Gr.p.154.

You can't compare a goat with a sheep.

137. Obi mfa obi ade nhoahoa neho. Cf.302.

No one boasts about what belongs to someone else.

138. Obi mfa ɔbomu nhow gya so.

Nobody takes a whole animal, not yet skinned, and
smokes it over a fire.

139. Obi mfa ade-kɔkɔ nsisi bayifo. R.248.

Nobody can deceive the witch with something red.

140. Obi mfa ade nkoyi mmusu wɔ kurotia, na ɔnsan nkɔfa bio.

No one puts a propitiatory offering at the entrance of
a village and then goes back again to take it away.

141. Ɔbi mfa adidi mfa adepɛ. (Agyakwa.)

No one can be a glutton and still become rich.

142. Obi mfa dɔkonsin kwankyen mmisa nea otwaa so.

One does not pick up a piece of kenkey from the roadside and then ask for the person who ate the other piece.

143. Obi mfa fɛre nkodwa Ampɔforo (:Ampɔfowa).

No one shakes hands with Ampɔforo (a leper) out of
respect for her.

---

* The m,n,ñ of neg. verbs in No.136—240 are exceptionally
treated (in the arrangement) as the consonants with which
the words begin.

144. Obi mfa fɛre nkyia ɔkwatani.
No one shakes hands with a leper out of respect.

145. Obi mfa fɛre nware obi nɛ nua a ne pam pɔw. =163.
(Kwasi Kurommɔ Tabiragyee, ɔwɔ Akyem Boats).
No one, because of respect, marries someone's sister
who has a deformed waist.

146. Obi mfa ohia ntow adotebɛ.
No one fells a palm tree which has taken firm root
in the ground because of poverty.

147. Obi mfa ohia nsi apempem.
No one should use his poverty under the pretence of
a righteous claim to force others to give him sympathy.

148. Obi mfa ahina hunu mu nkyerɛ ɔpanyin.
One does not show the inside of an empty pot to an elder.

149. Obi mfa nhoma nto nsu mu nkɔ ahemfi.
No one puts an animal's hide in water and then goes off
to the chief's palace.

150. Obi mfa hyirew ntiw nea watɔ wuram'.
No one takes white clay with him while he is pursuing
a person who has fled into the bush.

151. Obi mfa akokɔ nan ase ade mfa nkɔto akokɔfwerew nan
ase. Cf.397.
No one takes the small piece of cloth that is tied
around a chicken's leg and puts it on the leg of
a wood-hen.

152. Obi mfa kokuroko nni amim.
One should not oppress with one's size or strength.

153. Obi mfa koma-bone nkɔ Anum.
One does not go to Anum with a bad temper.

154. Obi mfa nkwadasɛm nsisi kontromfi. R.234.
You can not deceive the baboon by tricks.

155. Obi mfa amanne a wahu ntutu kaw.
No one should use his troubles as an excuse for not
paying a debt.

156. Obi mfa n'afuru mmutuw buropata so na ne mfɛfo ntwetwe
mfa n'ase.

No one uses his own belly to cover up corn drying on a
rack and then lets his friends take the corn from under
him.

157. Obi mfa ne kore-takara (:ɔsansa-takara) nkɔsesa opete-
takara.

Nobody exchanges his eagle feathers for the feathers
of a vulture.

158. Obi mfa ne nan abien nsusuw asu. Gr.p.154. Z.51.

Nobody measures the depth of a river with both of his
legs.

159. Obi mfa ne nsa benkum nkyerɛ n'agya amamfo so.

Nobody points to the ruins of his father's house with
his left hand.

160. Obi mfa ne nsa nto bi anom' na ɔmpae n'atifi.

Nobody puts his hand in someone's mouth and then hits
him over the head.

161. Obi mfa ne se mmobɔ adwe mma ne yɔnko.

Nobody cracks palm kernels with his own teeth for his
neighbor.

162. Obi mfa nea wawu suman nka sɛ: ma me nkwa ne akwahosan!

Nobody takes a dead person's amulet and says to it: "Give
me life and health!"

163. Obi mfa aniwu nware ne yɔnko nuabea a ne pim wɔ pɔw. =145.

One does not, because of bashfulness, marry a friend's
sister who has a knot on her clitoris.

164. Obi mfa ɔpanyin (=ɔhene) nhyɛ adanse.

An elder (chief) is not called to witness.

165. Obi mfa asamanfo ntwa mpasua. Z.210.

One does not count on the dead in getting ready to
fight a battle.

166. Obi mfa asɛmpa nyɛ nsɛmma-nsɛmma.

One does not treat an important matter as a small matter.

167. Obi mfa osigyafo na n'apɛde nka mu.

No one goes to bed with an unmarried woman without giving her something.

168. Obi mfa toamum mfa nkosers nno.

Nobody takes a gourd without an opening in it to go and beg for palm oil.

169. Obi mfa ntwaho nsisi komfo.

Nobody can deceive the fetish priest by dancing in a wheeling around fashion.

170. Obi mfi bea akyi ntu ne tam.

No one can take the loin cloth off a woman without her knowledge.

171. Obi mfi aboa no anim mmo hama.

Nobody makes a rope in front of an animal (he hopes to catch).

172. Obi mfi agyama so mma fam' mmepɛ okotokoro.

No one comes down from the "agyama" tree and then looks for a forked stick.

173. Obi mfi kwan mu na n'anom' asɛm nsa.

No one returns from travelling and has nothing to say.

174. Obi mfi Kyebi nkɔto Pannɔ adewa-dwom so.

One does not go from Kibi to sing "adewa" songs at Pannɔ.

175. Obi mfi Nsaba a wotɔ nipa taku ne damma mma Kwanyako mmesu sɛ: me nko menam.

One does not come from Nsaba where a slave is sold for seven pesewas and cry out to the person he meets on the way: "I am walking alone."

176. Obi mfi suguasɛn ho nhuane neho.

No one comes from the washing pot scratching himself.

177. Obi mfi tan akyi nsie ɔba.

Once the husband has given gifts to his wife when she has given birth to a baby, he does not need to give gifts to the child.

178. Obi mfi awoe mmegye feam.

No one comes from where she has just given birth and goes to fetch an amulet to bring about the quick delivery of a child.

179. Obi mfiri sono so nkɔbɔ aseredoa bo. Cf.300. R.174.

One does not stop pursuing an elephant to go and throw stones at a small bird.

180. Obi nfwɛ kuru anim mfa dua nwɔ mu.

No one cares for his sore and then pricks it with a pointed stick.

181. Obi mfwɛ (:nhu) tumm ntiam'. R.195.

Nobody looks at something black and then steps on it.

182. Obi nfwefwɛɛ ɔdabere na ade nkyɛe da.

No one ever kept looking for a sleeping place until dawn.

183. Obi nhintaw mmɔ waw. Gr.p.154.

No one goes to hide and then coughs.

184. Obi nhintaw mpun ahina.

No one cleans his water pot with smoke while hiding.

185. Obi nhintaw nsɔ gya.

No one hides himself and then lights a fire.

186. Obi nhinti prɛko (:dakoro) mmɔ ahina.

No one breaks the water pot the first time he stumbles.

187. Obi nhu bi kwaberan nhuruw nsi. R.65. Gr.p.155. Z.125.

Nobody jumps for joy on seeing somone else's strong slave.

188. Obi nhu 'ha tokurum' biribi nwu.

No one sees something in the bat's hole and dies.

189. Obi nhu ankana nkita n'ankana nnya n'ankana na onse sɛ: mihui a, ankana. Cf. 203.1558.1835.

You should not see fortune and seize it and let it go and then say, if I had known I would have seized it.

190. Obi nhu ne nsono ho mfe.

No one sees his own intestines and vomits.

191. Ohi nhu nimdee nko ayi (ase) na ɔ(kɔ or bɛ) sore a, waserew.

Anybody with any sense doesn't go to a funeral and then laughs when he gets up to leave.

192. Obi nhu onipa dakoro nse no sɛ: woafon! Gr. p. 154.
(Yenhunu nipa dako yɛnse no sɛ:w.)

You (we) don't meet a person for the first time and then tell him, "you have lost weight."

193. Obi nhu onipa awia na anadwo ɔnsɔ kanea nfwɛ n'anim.

You don't see a person in the daytime and then at night light a lamp to look at his face.

194. Obi nhyɛɛ da nwoo panyin pɛn.

No one has ever yet fixed a particular day to give birth to an important person.

195. Obi nhyɛ kontromfi na (:mma) onni son (:osɔn aba).
Cf. 237. Gr. p. 155.

Nobody forces the monkey to eat the fruit of the tamarind tree.

196. Obi nhyɛ neho ntu sa.

Nobody forces himself to bet.

197. Obi nhyira (:nnɔ) ne tamfo (:ne busuyɛfo).

One does not bless his enemy.

198. Obi nhyira yɛ obi nnome.

One man's blessing is another man's curse.

199. Obi nka nkyerɛ ɔsafo sɛ ɔmfa ɔpodo (ahina) nsi ho (:asafree).

You don't have to tell the palm wine seller to set his pot down at the place where palm wine is sold.

200. Obi nkae ne wuda mfon.

You shouldn't become thin by always thinking of the day when you will die.

201. Obi nkari peredwane nna afa.

Nobody pays the bridal price of thirty six dollars for a woman and then sleeps alone.

202. Obi nkasa nwe 'sa. Cf. 2394. 2375. 2417.

You don't talk while drinking palm wine.

203. Obi nkita nanka nnyae nanka na onse sɛ:mihui anka!
Cf. 189. 220. 1558. 1835.

One should not seize fortune and let fortune go and then
say, "if I had known I would have seized it."

204. Obi nkɔ obi akura nkyerɛ n'ase.

You don't go to your neighbor's village to tell him his
origin of birth.

205. Obi nkɔ obi kurom' nkɔfrɛ neho sɛ: Agyeman.

Nobody goes to someone else's town and calls himself,
"Savior."

206. Obi nkɔ obi kurom' nkokyerɛ neho sɛ: meyɛ ɔdehye.

No one should go to someone else's town and brag saying,
"I am a member of the royal family."

207. Obi nkɔ ahua na ɔnka nkwan.

The one who goes begging for food does not taste it,
(to find out whether it is good or not).

208. Obi ankɔ na obi amma a, anka yɛbɛyɛ dɛn ahu sɛ ɔkwan mu nye?

If someone didn't go and someone didn't come, how would
we get to know whether the road is safe or not?

209. Obi nkɔ asaman nsan mmɛka abibisɛm.

No one goes to the land of the dead and comes back
telling fairy tales.

210. Obi nkɔ asu so ntware kwarifa (-fua).   Cf. 371.

No one goes out on the river to catch a rat.

211. Obi nkɔfwɛ sikakɛse anim mmua nna.

No one should be so concerned about his money that he
dies of starvation.

212. Obi nkonnyaa sɛ Ɔpare anya.   Cf. 294.   Z. 113.

No one ever got things like Ɔpare.

213. Obi nkose sɛ: putuw nhyew! putuw hyew a, yehua bi adi.
Cf. 326.

No one says, "Let the yam hut burn!" When it has burned,
we will scrape some of the roasted yams and eat them.

214. Obi nkotew bisekyim mfa mfra bisetoro nkɔton mma ne manni.

No one picks good cola nuts and mixes them with bad ones and then sells them to his own countrymen.

215. Obi nkɔtoa ɔhahini wɔ ne bon ano na onse sɛ: wo ho bɔn. R. 21.

No one goes to the hole of the stink ant and tells him, "you stink".

216. Obi nkɔtoto mman nnu ho nkɔserɛ kobi mmɛka brɔdeɛ-dwo.

No one roasts herrings and puts them aside and goes out to beg for stink fish to eat with roasted plantain.

217. Obi nkɔtra wuram' nkɔyɛ mumo mfa mma ofie.

No one goes to the bush to do evil things and then brings them home.

218. Obi nkɔyɛ akokɔfwere adwuma nkɔnom nsamerewa nsuo) (:nnyae mmɛnom samina nsu). Cf. 290, 395.

The one who does the work of the bush fowl does not drink "nsamerewa" water (soap water).

219. Obi nkukuru ɔpanteu mfa mmɔ kahiri mfa nsoa ne nana mma.

One does not use the python as a head pad on which he will carry his grandmother's children.

220. Obi nkura n'ankara,...see 203, 1558. 1835.

No one has his fortune in his own hands...

221. Obi nkwati (:nkwae, nnyaw, nsiane) kokurobeti mmɔ pɔw. Gr. #237c.Z.115.

Nobody ties a knot without the thumb.

222. Obi nkwati Tanno nkɔ aka ase.

No one attends the ordeal to decide the guilt or innocence of someone without first calling on the fetish Tanno.

223. Obi nkyerekyere nyansa-kotoku mfa nkɔto adakam' mmegyina adiho nse (no) sɛ: kyerɛ me asɛm!

No one should collect wisdom in a bag and put it in a box and then stand in the street and say, "Teach me wisdom".

224. Obi nkyɛn nea wawu nna.

No one surpasses the dead in sleeping.

225. Obi nkyɛnemu yɛ ɔtra-na.

It is difficult to stay with someone who is not your relative.

226. Obi nkyerɛ obi sɛ: tɔ nkyene di. R. 29.

You don't tell anyone to buy salt and eat it.

227. Obi nkyerɛ abofra onyame. Z. 71.

No one teaches the child about God.

228. Obi nkyerɛ agyinamoa akrɔmmɔ. Gr. p. 68.
(Obi nkyerɛ agyinamoa apakyi mu fwɛ).

No one teaches the cat how to steal. (No one teaches the cat how to look into a calabash.)

229. Obi nkyerɛ ɔkɔmfo ba akɔm.

Nobody teaches the child of a fetish priest how to dance the fetish dance.

230. Obi nkyerɛ nkwankwasɛm-di na ɔnkyerɛ nnɔn.

Nobody teaches someone to behave proudly without at the same time teaching him to walk in a proud manner.

231. Obi nkyerɛ ampan (:ɔpantweanini) ba akɔmfo-hyɛ.

One does not teach the child of a bat how to tumble topsy turvy.

232. Obi nkyerɛ ɔsansa ba aguare nkyerɛ no nkurase kwan nka ho.

One does not teach the hawk's child how to bathe and not also teach him how to catch mice.

233. Obi nkyerɛ ɔsebɔ ba atow.

Nobody teaches the leopard's cub how to leap.

234. Obi nkyerɛ ɔtomfo ba atono; onim atono a, (na) Onyame na ɔkyerɛɛ no.

Nobody teaches the blacksmith's son how to forge, if he knows how to forge, then it is God who taught him.

235. Obi nkyerɛ akokɔtan mmutuw aba (:nkesua) so.

Nobody teaches a hen to sit on her eggs.

236. Obi nkyere katakyie mmua n'ano mmisa no ofie asɛm.

No one catches a strong man and forces him to talk about domestic affairs.

237. Obi nkyere kwagyadu mma onni nsron. Cf. 195.

NO one catches the babies of a monkey for them to eat
the fruit of the tamarind tree.

238. Obi nkyere ɔkwatakyi (:kwaberan) nto dom ano (nko ntɔ).

No one catches a warrior in the front line of battle.

239. Obi nkyi koko na onni ne mma.

No one has an aversion to the hen and then eats her chicks.

240. Obi nkyi pete nni ne nkesua.

No one detests the vulture and then eats her eggs.

241. Obi mmaa bafan ne na due da.

One does not forever give consolation to the mother of
a crippled child.

242. Obi amma me amo a, merema meho amo. R. 198.

If no one congratulates me, I'll congratulate myself.

243. Obi mme mma obi. Cf. 286. Gr. p. 154.

No one is satisfied for another person.

244. Obi mme Memeneda na ɔmme Kwasida.

No one is well fed on Saturday as well as on Sunday.

245. Obi mmɔ kokora ntow mu atuo.

No one shoots his gun while he is hiding from the enemy.

246. Obi mmu dua nnyaw so ba.

One does not chop down a tree without also picking up
some of its fruit.

247. Obi mmua n'ano nni fo. R. 187. Gr. p. 155.

The one who is innocent does not remain silent.

248. Obi mmuna ntra sum mu.

One should not be gloomy and then sit in the dark.

249. Obi ne amim nsɛw kɛtɛ nnae nsene da.

One does not make his bed with a bully and ever outdo
him in sleeping.

-21-

250. Obi ne yafunu ntwe manso (:nyɛ akaw).
     Nobody bears his stomach a grudge.

251. Obi ni ayi ase na wosu wɔn ni.
     One weeps for his own mother at the funeral of someone
     else's mother.

252. Obi nni Bɛgorɔ asɛm nnyae Ntim.
     One does not settle Begoro palavers without Ntim.

253. Obi nni ŋkwankwasɛm nsuro nnimmo (:nfwɛ n'akyi, ntie
     n'akyi).
     The person who behaves proudly should expect to get a
     bad reputation.

254. Obi nni n'akaraduan na n'anom' nhyehye no.
     Nobody eats his favorite food and burns his mouth.

255. Obi nni asɛmmone nsuro nnimmo.
     The person who misbehaves should expect to get a bad
     name.

256. Obi nni sono akyi mmorɔ huasu. Cf. 893
     The person who walks behind an elephant doesn't get wet
     from the dew on the grass.

257. Obi nni tuo nni ne nsa.
     No one shoots himself without having a gun in his hand.

258. Obi nnii dɔte-dwini na ɛmmɔɔ no da.
     Nobody ever made clay pots without sometimes breaking
     one or the other.

259. Obi nnidi mma ne werɛ mfi wu.
     One's honor does not make him forget death.

260. Obi nnidi mme nka n'akarasem. (Nni-bone-akyi, Osanteni
     akoa bi.)
     One's honor is not done justice to by telling his secret.
     (After doing evil an Ashanti becomes another man's
     slave.)

261. Obi nnidi nnu ne ho. Gr. p.154.
     No one eats so that he repents of it.

262. Obi anim' na wofwɛ nom sasin (:nsasin).
(Obi nti na wonom basin). Cf. 129. 696. 1183.

In another person's presence, one takes care to drink the
last bit of palm wine in the calabash.
(It's because of someone that you drink with a one-armed
person.)

263. Obi nim nea owu wɔ a, anka onsi hɔ ara da.

If one knew where death resided he would never enter
there.

264. Obi nim sɛ ohia behia no a, anka ɔkɔ Brofo ma 'yɛwo no.

If one knew he would become poor he would have gone to
the Europeans that he might have been born of them.

265. Obi nnim (ade) a, obi kyerɛ (no). Cf. 1407

If someone doesn't know something another teaches him.

266. Obi nnim a, ɛyɛ nyansa kyerɛ.

If one does not know, it is a warning.

267. Obi nnim bi a, onso ne nka mu.

If one doesn't know someone, he does not hold his rings.

268. Obi nnim bi ase a, ɔnkyerɛ n'ase sɛ ɔdɔnkɔ.

If one doesn't know someone's family background, he
doesn't give it as that of a slave.

269. Obi nnim bi tirim a, onni nnuammoa nsie (mmena) no.

If others are not reliable you don't unite with them in
buying a sheep in order to share the meat.

270. Obi nnim bi tirim a, ɔnsoma no aguadi.

If someone is not reliable you don't send him to do
trading.

271. Obi nnim bi tirim a, ɛnyɛ wɔnne fwento.

If someone is not reliable it is not because his nose
was lost by disease.

272. Obi nnim adekyee mu asɛm.

No one knows what a new day will bring forth.

273. Obi nnim Adwabirem' asɛm a, ɛnyɛ 'yɛnne Ti.

If one does not know the palavers of Adwabirem it is
not because he has no head.

274. Obi nnim dwonku-ko (:koro) a ade bɛkye so.
Nobody knows which hip bone will see the light of day.

275. Obi nnim akyiri.
Nobody knows the future.

276. Obi nnim n'akyi a, ɔntɔ ade.
If one does not know his financial strength he doesn't
buy things.

277. Obi nnim nea nkyene nam na ɛkɔɔ apateram mu.
No one knows where the salt has gone for it has gone
into the beans.

278. Obi nnim nea ɛsono di yɛɛ kɛse.
No one knows what the elephant ate to make it so big.

279. Obi nnim nea ɔwoo hene.
Nobody knows who gave birth to a chief.

280. Obi nnim onipa tirim asɛm.
No one knows another person's thoughts.

281. Obi nnim mpotia fufu.
No one knows how to make "fufu" from stunted yams.

282. Obi nnim tuo tirim.
No one knows the gun's thoughts.

283. Obi nnɔ ne nan ho nnɔ n'akoa nan ho.
One does not spare his feet from walking and spare
his slave's feet also.

284. Obi nnoa aduan (mfa) nkɔta nkwanta nfwefwɛ ɔmanni.
R. 19. Z. 131.
No one cooks food and sits it at the junction and then
looks for a guest.

285. Obi nnoa aduanfin mfa nkɔyɛ hɔho mma onsë no sɛ: wo aduan
yɛ me dɛ. (Okyerawuruku, ɔte Tafo.)
One does not prepare stale food and take it to the
children of the guest and then he tells you your food
is delicious.

286. Obi nnom aduru mma ɔyarefo. Cf. 243. 308. 1045.
Nobody can drink medicine for a sick person.

287. Obi nnom nsa mmɔ kora.

You don't break the calabash from which you are drinking palm wine.

288. Obi nnom nsu nsie ɔpɛ.

Nobody can prepare for the harmattan by drinking plenty of water.

289. Obi nnome nea obewu na wawu.

One should not curse a person who will die before he dies.

290. Obi nnow akoɔfwerew nnom nsuhunu. Cf. 218.

One does not weed for the bush bowl and then drink mere water.

291. Obi nnu ahome kwa.

No one sighs without a reason.

292. Obi nnuan yiye.

No one runs away from goodness.

293. Obi nnya sɛ ananse ne pare nya.

Nobody comes by things like Ananse and Opare.

294. Obi (re) nnya sɛ wɔde ne mpana (:nwewe) abesi ne na awowa. Cf. 212

No one rejects the idea that his concubine is to be brought to his mother as a hostage.

295. Obi nnya sɛ woatow bo a, akɔbɔ wo akontagye akoa tirin.

If someone doesn't get to throw a stone, he hits your slave on the head saying, "brother-in-law, take it."

296. Obi nnyae abawu (:niwu) nkodi akorasɛm.

Nobody ignores the death of her child and gets involved in a quarrel between two wives of a polygamous husband.

297. Obi nnyae duam' nko (:nkodi ntokwa).

One does not cease to be in prison by not fighting.

298. Obi nnyae n'ani bere mmere ne se.

One does not stop making one's eyes from being red (because of anger) by making his teeth red.

299. Obi nnyae nno so tare nkɔtare adwe so.

One does not stop storing palm oil and go to store palm kernels.

300. Obi nnyae sono akyi di nkodi aseredoa akyi. Cf. 179.

One does not stop running after an elephant to go and run after a small bird.

301. Obi nnyaw asuten nkɔnom ɔtare. Gr. p. 175.

No one leaves a flowing river to go to drink from a pool.

302. Obi nnye (:mfa) obi ade mfa nyɛ ne ho. Cf. 137.

You shouldn't borrow others things and make them your own.

303. Obi nnye obi ade nsɛe no.

You shouldn't borrow something from your neighbor and then destroy it.

304. Obi nnye obi amanne nyɛ ne de.

No one takes someone's troubles and makes them his own.

305. Obi nnye obi asia mma ɔnka guam'.

You shouldn't take someone's six pence and then make him stay behind in a meeting.

306. Obi nnye boafo kyɛm ntwitwam' ansa-na wase sɛ: boa me!

Nobody snatches his helper's shield and tears it to pieces and then say to him, "Help me".

307. Obi nnye bɔmmɔfo ade nni nyɛ no ahabusu.

One does not curse the hunter from whom one gets gifts of meat.

308. Obi nnye ɔyarefo aduru nnom. =286.

Nobody can drink medicine for a sick person.

309. Obi nnwen wu nnwen porɔw.

No one thinks about his death and at the same time thinks of his body decaying.

310. Obi nnwow n'akyeakyɛn gua so.

Nobody peels half ripe palm nuts in public.

311. Obi nnyin nni akura.

Adults do not eat mice.

312. Obi nnyina akono (=ɔko ano) nnwene kyɛm.

No one stands in the front line of battle and then makes a shield.

313.   Obi nnyina nkran mu ntutu nkran (:ntu nsoe).

Nobody remains standing in the path of soldier ants to pick them off his body.

314.   Obi mpata adaban abien nhye gyam'. R.72.

No one puts two pieces of iron in the fire at the same time.

315.   Obi mpatuw bereku mma ommo waw. Cf. 2643.

No one suprises the "bereku" and causes it to cough.

316.   Obi mpatuw nnya ade a onni bi no.

No one suddenly gets something he does not have.

317.   Obi mpe obi yiye.

No one wishes well for another.

318.   Obi mpe da bi nye pa na wape da bi aye bone.

No one deliberately chooses a day to do good and another day to do bad.

319.   Obi mpe ade nnu Asante na onnyina Akuapem nkamfo.

One does not display his wealth in Ashanti and then stand in Akuapem and give praise.

320.   Obi mpe sika nnu ne dan mu na o-ne no nkasa.

No one finds gold and puts it in his room and then talks to it.

321.   Obi mpo ne ti mma dwiw.

No one gives up his head to lice.

322   Obi mpra na obi nsesaw. R.154. Gr.p.171.

One person does not do the sweeping and another person picks up the sweepings.

323.   Obi nse obi se: fa wo nipa-pa sore fi me so (:na wose: fa wo nipa-bone sore me so).

One never says to a person: "Go away from me with your kindness" (and you say, "Get away from me with your badness.")

324.   Obi nse okunafo se: konom ntunkum.

No one tells the widow: "Go and drink sweet palm wine."

325. Obi nse n'aberewa se: sɔre na menfwɛ wo!

No one tells his old mother, "Get up and let me look at you!"

326. Obi nse sɛ: putu nhyew; na ɛhyew a, wowe mfudwe. Cf. 213.

No one says: "Let the yam hut burn, and when it has burned down we can eat the roasted yams."

327. Obi nse tɔrɔdɔ (:twɔrɔdɔ) mma toa.

One does not fetch the noise of the water when it drops into the pot.

328. Obi nsen fasu akotoku-se. R.231.

No one excels a wall in holding bags.

329. Obi nsen Mɛwe-mɛwe akotɔ-bɔ.

No one is greater than the one saying, "I'll eat," while he is still digging for the crabs.

330. Obi nsen ne na ne nua dehye.

The rich relative is not greater than the mother.

331. Obi nsen Yoyo nnebɔ.

No one surpasses the "Yoyo" animal in giving excretment at random.

332. Obi nserew hia.

Poverty is nothing to be laughed at.

333. Obi nsi kwaefuo nnɔ no dako.

No one can clear the bush for a new farm in only one day.

334. Obi nsiane ne kɛtɛ ho nna fam.

No one passes by his mat and goes to sleep on the ground.

335. Obi nsiw ne ntɛnne nni fɔ.

You shouldn't hold back the voice of your complaint and then expect to be acquitted.

336. Obi nsɔ gya foforo mfa nwaw ntom'. Gr.p.171.

Nobody puts snails in a newly kindled fire.

337. Obi nsɔ gya nnu ne kotoku mu.

No one starts a fire and then puts it in his pocket.

338. Obi nsɔ obi nsa nsi ne koko.

No one takes another person's hand and then strikes it
against his own breast in boasting.

339. Obi nsɔ dae nkɔ nea wobekum no. R.178.

No one has a dream showing where he will be killed
and then goes there.

340. Obi nsoma obi afirifwɛ, na anoma nkasa no. Cf.2614.
R.137.

When you send someone to check a trap, the bird shouts
at him.

341. Obi nsoma obi (:abofra) ɔsoro(na o)nhuan n'ase antweri.

No one sends a child up (a tree) and then takes away
the ladder from beneath him.

342. Obi nsoma abofra na ɔmmɛfa no so abufuw.

No one sends a child and then gets angry with him.

343. Obi nsoma abofra nfwɛ n'ani akyi.

No one sends a child and looks to see if the child is
pleased.

344. Obi nsɔre prɛko nka abirɛmpɔn banu.

No one gets up at once and provokes two strong men.

345. Obi nsum aberewa nfwɛ nea ɔbɛfwe.

No one knocks an old woman to see where she will fall.

346. Obi nsusuw sono yam' mmu ahaban. Gr.p.155.

No one measures the elephant's belly before he gathers
leaves for it to eat.

347. Obi nte bi asɛm ase a, wonnye no anyaado.

If you don't understand what someone is saying to you,
don't respond with the respectful greeting, "anyaado."

348. Obi ntew mmerɛnkɛnsono aduasa mfa nkobɔ werefo.

No one plucks thirty young palm tree leaves and gives
them to an avenger.

349. Obi ntie "su su" mmua nna.
    No one fasts just because he hears weeping.

350. Obi ntɔ ade-fefe nhintaw.
    No one buys a nice thing and then goes and hides.

351. Obi ntɔ ade na ɛnwo no.
    No one is charged interest for something he has bought.

352. Obi ntɔ akoa na ɔmmɛhyɛ no so.
    No one buys a slave to act as a restraint on himself.

353. Obi ntɔ akokonini na ɔmmɔn (:mma ɔnkɔbɔn) obi akura.
    R.41. Gr.p.154.
    No one buys a cock to let it crow in another man's
    village.

354. Obi ntɔ nantwi nammɔn. R.68.
    No one buys the foot-prints of a cow.

355. Obi ntɔ sɛn foforo nsi pata so.
    No one buys a new pot and then puts it in a shed.

356. Obi ntɔ yare nsa.
    You can not buy the power of healing diseases.

357. Obi ntɔ asum' na onsuro awɔw.
    No one jumps into the water if he is afraid of the cold.

358. Obi nto ana na onyi sɛnfoforo mmutuw. =3323.
    No one gives his genealogy by taking out a new cook-
    ing pot and turning it upside down.

359. Obi nto anansesɛm nkyerɛ Ntikuma.
    No one tells Ananse stories to Ntikuma.

360. Obi nto ntasu nto fam' mfa ne tɛkrɛma mfa.
    No one spits on the ground and then licks up the
    spittle with his tongue.

361. Obi ntow abɛ na obi mpene.
    No one fells a palm tree to let another man groan
    because of the effort involved in felling it.

362. Obi nto(w) agyan mma ɛborɔ nka no. Cf. 372.
    No one shoots an arrow and lets the poison hit himself.

-30-

363. Obi ntɔn ne kokɔbere kwa (:hunu).
You don't sell your hen without a good reason.

364. Obi ntoto namporɔwe mfa nhyɛ ne yɔnko anom' nse no
se: wo anom' bɔn.
No one roasts rotten meat and puts it in the mouth of
his friend and then tells him, "your mouth stinks."

365. Obi ntoto neho kuru nsu.
No one dresses his own sore with hot water or medicine
and then cries.

366. Obi ntra ne katiri nsom.
No one relinquishes his capital to be a servant.

367. Obi ntra ɔba anan so nnye asisiduru.
No one lays upon the thighs of a woman and expects
to get medicine for his waist.

368. Obi ntra obi serɛ so nsum no.
You don't sit upon someone's lap and then push him away.

369. Obi ntra akwannya nni akwannya asɛm.
No one sits on one side of a road and solves a problem
pertaining to things on the other side of the road.

370. Obb ntra asɛm ho nni mu abaguade, na ɔmfrɛ no saredwuma.
The arbitrator who has a share in the arbitration fee
has not wasted his time.

371. Obi ntra siw so ntiwiri kwarifua (=okisi). Cf. 210.
No one sits on an ant hill to catch a rat.

372. Obi ntu agyan na (:mma) bɔre nka mu. Cf. 362.
One does not take out an arrow and let the poison
remain in the wound.

373. Obi ntu mmerɛ nsie siw so. R.202. Gr.p.155.171.
No one plucks mushrooms and puts them on an ant hill.

374. Obi ntua obi agorɔ ka; agorɔ tua neho ka.
No one pays for someone's dancing; the dance pays for
itself.

375. Obi ntumi kokuroko tɔmma a, ɔnsensan (=onsusu so nyɛ bi).

If one is not a match for the beads of the strong man, he does not loosen them (he does not make a copy of them).

376. Obi nturu wo nkɔfwɛ atuo na wunturu no nkɔfwɛ mmɛn.

One does not carry you on his back to see guns and you do not carry him on your back to see horns.

377. Obi nturu yarefo nkɔ sa.

One does not carry a sick person on his back when going to war.

378. Obi ntutu 'mirika mfa nammɔntenten nkɔ Asante nkohu Sɛe ade nhuruw.

One does not run with long strides to Ashanti to see the chief's property and then jumps.

379. Obi ntutu 'mirika nkɔ aka ase.

No one runs to be tried by ordeal.

380. Obi ntutu 'mirika nkɔfwɛ Bosonopo ne Ayesu ntam'.

No one runs to see what is between the ocean and the Ayensu River.

381. Obi ntutu 'mirika nkɔtra kurotia nkɔserɛ amanne mfa nto neho so.

No one runs and sits at the entrance of the town and begs that troubles be put on him.

382. Obi ntutu anoma nkɔkyerɛ ɔpanyin. R.142. Gr.#258,5.

You don't pluck all the feathers from a bird and then show it to the elder (to find out its name.)

383. Obi ntwa obi ho nhyɛn ne dan.

You shouldn't overtake your neighbor in order to enter his house.

384. Obi ntwa oguan nna afa.

No one kills a sheep in atonement (to his husband or wife) and then sleeps alone.

385. Obi ntwa akokɔ ano mma akye. R.51.

No one says good morning before the rooster.

386. Obi ntwa ne kafo abobow-ano nkɔsom.

No one passes by the threshold of his creditor's house without becoming his servant.

387. Obi ntwa ne mene nhyɛ adinkra.

No one cuts his throat and squeezes out blood to use in dyeing an "adinkra" (mourning) cloth.

388. Obi ntwa poma (na ɛ)nsen (:nkyɛn) no (tenten). Gr.p.155.

No one cuts a walking stick longer than himself.

389. Obi ntwa asu Kwasida na Dwoda ɛmfa no.

No one crosses a river on Sunday and then drowns in it on Monday.

390. Obi ntwɛn Firaw ansa-na wahoro ne tam.

No one waits to reach the Firaw River before washing his cloth.

391. Obi nwo ba nto (no) Agyako na onnyae (din no akyi di) nni abaninsɛm.

No one gives birth to a child and gives him the name Agyako and then he ceases to be brave.

392. Obi nyare ntotɔ na obi nyare anomdɛw. Cf.3548.

If you do not suffer from the compulsion to buy, you also do not suffer from the compulsion to eat sweet things.

393. Obi nyare twow nhintaw guasɛn.

The one suffering from hydrocele does not hide it from the basin used for washing.

394. Obi nyare ayamka nkyɛ akyeburo mfa nsa neho yare.

No one who has a belly-ache tries to cure himself with roasted corn.

395. Obi nyɛ akokɔfwerew adwuma na ɔnkɔnom Osamere nsu.=218.

No one does the work of the red-legged partridge and then goes to drink "Osamere" water.

396. Obi nyɛ yiye nnya bone. Gr.p.154.

The one doing good does not receive evil.

397. Obi nyi akokɔ nanase ade nkɔto akokɔfwerew (:asamante)
nanase (:mma) ɔmfa ntu nkɔ wuram'.

One does not take what is tied on the leg of a chicken
and put it on the red-legged partridge's leg and then
let it run into the bush.

398. Obi nyi mmusu mfa mmusu. Gr.p.155.

No one removes trouble in order to get trouble.

399. Obi nyiyi mmerɛ mu mmoa.

No one selects mushrooms in bunches.

400. Obi pae wo atifi (:mpampam') a, ɔhyɛ wo akonmuden.
If someone hits you on the top of your head, he is
making your neck strong.

401. Obi pɛtuw pɔw ne se apɔw-mono a, etu.

If you don't clean your teeth carefully with a chewing
stick, you will knock out some of them.

402. Obi nsam' nyɛ wo nsam'. Z.211.

What is in someone's hand is not in your hand.

403. Obi se 'ɔbɛforo dunsin' a, ma ɔmforo: na ɔkoso anim
asan aba. R.160. Cf.574.

If someone says he will climb up the stump of a tree,
let him do it, for when he reaches the top he will
come down.

404. Obi se 'obehuruw tana' a, ma onhuruw, na ohuruw a,
wobehu.

If someone says he will jump over a pile of burning
wood, let him jump, when he jumps you will see what
happens.

405. Obi se 'ɔbɛma wo biribi adi' a, na ɔde ampesi di wo
adanse.=114.

If someone says he will give you something special to
eat, he will first give you boiled yam to confirm his
promise.

406. Obi se 'ɔbɛma wo fremfrem (:adɔkɔdɔkɔde) adi'na ɔma
wo sika a, na wawie wo ma.

If someone says he will give you something sweet to eat
and he gives you money, he has done it.

407. Obi se 'ɔbɛma woane (woho)' a, ɛnte sɛ woankasa wosɛn
yane so (:worekɔne).

If someone says he will go to the toilet for you, it
isn't the same as when you go yourself.

408. Obi se 'ɔbɛsoa wo' a, wunse sɛ: mɛnantew.

When someone says he will carry you, don't say, "I'll
walk."

409. Obi se "bɔ wo bra yiye" a, ɔnyaw wo ɛ.

If someone says, "Watch your conduct", he has not
insulted you.

410. Obi se: gye ntam kɔma ne yere - wugyina kurotia tɛrɛw
mu - ɛware a, na wutwa so, anasɛ ɛyɛ tia a, na wotoa so.

Someone says: "Take this cloth and give it to my wife",
you spread it out on the road, and if it is too long,
will you cut off a piece, or if it is too short, will
you add a piece?

411. Obi se "hyɛ wo sapow mu nsu" a, ɛnye ɔyaw.

If someone says: "Put water in your sponge" (take courage),
he is not insulting you.

412. Obi se'ɔka wo yafunum' kɔm' a, woma wo adatia yɛ den.

If someone says he swears by your hunger, you should
hold fast to your cutlass.

413. Obi se 'ɔkyɛn wo amirika' a, huruw fwe kwankyɛn, na fa
akyiri ne anim to no ho.

When someone says he can run faster than you, you stand
aside and leave the way open for him.

414. Obi se'n'akoa ne wo' a, (na) wanya wo (:na wahaw wo).

If someone says you are his slave, he has insulted you.

415. Obi se 'ɔmpɛ wo agoru' a, tra woho ase, na ɔkɔtɔ bɔ
pemmɔ a, ɔnsan n'akyi.

If someone says he doesn't like your game, sit down,
because when the crab falls on its back, it doesn't
turn back.

416. Obi se wo sɛ 'ɔkraman ani yɛ anan' a, ɔboa, abien yɛ nhwi.

If someone tells you the dog has four eyes, he lies, two
are only hair.

417. Obi se wɔ asɛm bi a' se no bi;na abogyesɛ yɛ nhwi.
                    (1... na onipa kyi nea ɛyɛ den).
                    (2... na owu wowu no dakoro).

     If somebody tells you something, tell him something
     also, for a beard is only hair.
                    (1... man shuns what is dif-
                     ficult).
                    (2... as for death, you only
                     die once.)

418. Obi se "wosɛ wo agya (:wo se)" a, mpɛ ntɛm nsu, na mpɛ
     ntɛm nserew: na wunnim sɛ wo agya yɛ onipa-pa anasɛ
     onipa-bone.

     If someone says you resemble your father, neither cry
     nor laugh immediately, for you don't know whether your
     father is a good or bad person.

419. Obi se "wu" a, wunya nkwa kyerɛ no.

     If someone says "death", show him life.

420. Obi asɛm ba a, na woamfa ho biribi a, wofa ntodii.

     If someone's trouble comes and you don't help him, you
     have to buy your own food.

421. Obi asɛm nware kwa.

     No one is talkative without a good reason.

422. Obi sen wo a, ma ɔnsen wo, na ɔno nso wɔ obi a ɔsen no.

     If someone excels you let him excel you, for there is
     also someone who excels him.

423. Obi sen wo fompɔw a, ɔsen wo ntasu.=2253.

     If someone has more puffed up cheeks than you do, he
     also can spit more than you.

424. Obi soa wo san ase ade a, wopa wo to ase fi adi.

     If someone loads you with something from the barn, you
     manage to get out of carrying it by sliding away.

425. Obi soɛ wo na wamfa sika ansoɛ wo a, na ɔde asɛm asoɛ wo.

     If someone lodges with you but does not pay for his
     lodging, he lodges you with troubles.

426. Obi soma wo dupɔn-tow a, tow, na tokuru dam'.

     If someone sends you to fell a huge tree, fell it,
     for it may be a hollow tree.

427. Obi soma wo no yere ko a, ɔsoma wo mpata.

If someone sends you to his wife's fight, he also
sends you to bring peace.

428. Obi tan wo a, ma onnya wo atanye.

If someone hates you, don't let him find you hateful.

429. Obi tan wo a, na ɔbɔ wo aboa ade. R.251.

If someone hates you, he insults you.

430. Obi tan wo a, na ɔfa wo yere.

If someone hates you, he commits adultery with your
wife.

431. Obi tan wo a, na ɔparuw wo mparunwoma.

If someone hates you, he makes bad remarks about you.

432. Obi tan wo a, ɛnworanwora wo.

If someone hates you, it scratches you.

433. Obi tan wo na wonom nsa a, na ɔma wo akye.

If someone hates you, he greets you as you are drinking palm wine.

434. Obi ti bo nni wo foto mu a, wommɔ no anyabuw.

If someone's purchase money is not in your purse, you
do not call him your slave.

435. Obi to wo ano a, nanso woto ne to.

If someone falsely accuses you, you also falsely
accuse him.

436. Obi to wo ano fa asamampow mu a, wosan wo ano fa hɔ.

If someone falsely accuses you in the cemetery, you
also go there and clear yourself from the accusation.

437. Obi tu gya hye wo ano a, wutu bi hye ne to.

If someone takes out a fire-brand and burns your mouth,
you also take one out and burn his ass.

438. Obi wu a, obi ka.

If someone dies, someone remains.

439. Obi yɛ ne biribi a, ma ɔnyɛ, na owu bɛn. R.60.

If someone is doing his thing, let him do it for
death is near.

440. Obi yɛ wo biribi a, mma ɛnnyɛ wo yaw; asu ayiri, han
    atew.

    If someone does something against you don't let it
    bother you. for the river overflows and then the rope
    stretching from one side to the other side breaks.

441. Obi ayi ase na wosu wɔn na ne wɔn agya.

    At someone's funeral we weep for our own mothers and
    fathers.

442. Obi yaw wo na woyaw no bi a, na he ho ayɛ no den.

    If someone insults you and you insult him, it makes
    him all the more abusive.

443. Abia nyɛ ahene bi; nanso wɔannya no a, wonsina
    kyekyerekona.

    "Abia" seeds are not really beads; but if you don't
    get any you can't string them together as precious
    beads.

444. Ebia wobedi sono na biribi hia wo; na wudi apata a,
    na dompe (:kasae) ahia wo. (Owusu Akyem).

    Perhaps you will eat a whole elephant and nothing gets
    stuck in your throat, and then you eat a fish and a
    bone gets stuck in your throat.

445. Obiako di 'wo a, ɛtoa ne yam'.

    If one person eats all the honey, he is sure to get a
    belly-ache.

446. Ɔbako kohu a, adansefo ne hena? woka kyerɛ nyansafo a,
    oregye wo akyinnye.

    If one man goes to see something, who is his witness?
    When you tell a wise man, he doesn't believe you.

447. Ɔbako nkyekye kurow.

    One man can not build a town.

448. Ɔbako mmɔ dam nkyerɛ ɔman asɛm.

    A crazy person does not tell the country something
    important.

449. Ɔbako nam hu apennuasa.

    The man who travels alone sees many things.

450. Ɔbako nam, odi toro. (As.)=457.

    When a man moves about alone, he tells lies.

451. Ɔbako yɛ odwen.

A man who moves about alone is met on the road and seized as a slave.

452. Ɔbako yɛ yaw.

To be alone is hard.

453. Ɔbako nyɛ ɔbarima.

The man who is all alone has no courage.

454. Ɔbako nyɛ kataw'.

A person who is alone does not succeed.

455. Ɔbiakofo na okum sono, na amansan nhina di.

It is one man who kills the elephant but the whole town eats it.

456. Ɔbakofo na ɔtow tuo, na ɛdɔm gu.

It is only one man who shoots the gun, but the whole army flees.

457. Ɔbakofo nam a, odi atoro.=450.

When a man moves about alone he tells lies.

458. Ɔbakofo ntwam adesae. (Agyakwa).
Ɔbakofo ntwam' ntwam' na (:mma) ade nsa.

No one can go around and around til sunset.

459. Ɔbakofo wɛre aduru a, egugu.

If only one person scrapes medicine from the bark of of a tree, it gets scattered all over the ground.

460. Bin bɔn na wuse ho a, na ɛbɔn wura wo.

Excreetment stinks and if you go near it, the smell sticks to you.

461. Bini yɛ wo tane, nanso wo nsa dam'.

Excreetment is repulsive to you, but you put your hand on it (when you go to toilet).

462. Birebire amma a, amanne mma.

If Birebire had not come, there would have been no trouble.

463. Obiri, fwɛ nea wode reyɛ Ɔbene.

Obiri, look at what is being done to Ɔbene.

464. Biribiara nyɛ yaw sɛ aniwu.
     There is nothing as painful as being disgraced.

465. Biribi anka aboya mu (:nni asanka mu) a, wɔntaforo
     mu. Cf. 2573.
     If there is nothing left in the pot, it can't be licked.

466. Biribi ankɔka mpopa a, ɛ(re)nyɛ karada. R.145.
     If nothing touches the palm branches, they don't
     make any sound.

467. Biribi nkyɛn gya kɔkɔ. R.28.
     There is nothing as red as fire.

468. Biribi nni wo nsam' a, mmua ano na mmɔfra nntiti
     akyiri. R.22. Cf.2738.
     If there is nothing in your hands, don't close them and
     and have the children scratch the back side of your
     hands.

469. Biribi (-biribi) nte sɛ Ɔbempɔn Ntiamoa a Kwakye awo
     no (Ɔb. ne Nt. a wɔnam).
     There is nothing like Ɔbempɔn Ntiamoa whom Kwakye has
     given birth to.

470. Biribi nte sɛ odwumfo a ɔwo bafane.
     There is nothing like a craftsman who gives birth to
     a cripple.

471. Biribi nte sɛ wotwa ɔpɛ abɛ na asa abere.
     There is nothing like tapping a palm tree during the
     harmattan when the wine is fresh.

472. Biribi wɔ soro a, etwa sɛ ɛbɛba fam'.
     Whatever goes up must come down.

473. Biribi yɛ wo a, nnu woho, na ebia anka nea ɛreba so.
     If something happens to you, don't be uneasy about it,
     for perhaps what is coming will be worse.

474. Wo biribi ne twea a, ankara worema no aduane fam'?
     If a female dog were your relative, would you give it
     food on the bare ground?

475. Abirika so kokoam' a, na asa.
     When running reaches a corner, then it is finished.

476. Wobisa aguaman se: wops deɛn? Ose: ɛwɔ nea merepɛ.

If you ask a prostitite: "What are you looking for?"
She says, "It is rather who I am looking for."

477. Woabisa akyeremadefo, na 'yese: 'yɛ-ne wo bɛgoro ma
ade akye.

You have asked the chief's drummers and we say: "We
will all dance til morning."

478. Wommisa Kwasi a, wonni wea.

If you don't ask Kwasi you don't eat the animal that
lives in tall trees.

479. Obisabisafo nto (:mfom) kwan.

The one who keeps asking doesn't lose the way.

480. Bisekyem ne (bise) toro ahaban, wotase no nyansafo.

Only the wise person is able to gather up both the
true cola nut leaves as well as the false cola nut
leaves.

481. "Bɔ me na memmɔ wo" nyɛ agorɔ.

"Hit me but I must not hit you," is no game at all.

482. "Bɔ me na minni"; na sɛ anka me kora ɛ?

"Hit me and I don't ward off the blow"; and what
if it doesn't touch me at all?

483. Wobo aberekyi (aba) a, (ansa-)na ohu ne wura ofi
kwan. R.78.

If you hit a goat with a stick, it finds its way
to its owner's house.

484. Wobɔ bra pa a, wote mu dɛw.

If you behave well, you enjoy the benefits of your
good character.

485. Wobɔ ahina ho a, na wuhu nea ɔkam da.

If you tap the pot, you see where it is cracked.

486. Wobɔ ayamɔnwene kan na wunya sika na woyɛ ayɛ a, na
wo din hye.

If at first you are a stingy person, and then get
money and give gifts, your bad name still spreads
around.

487. Sɛ yɛkɔbɔ ɔdom-nsu a, ɛnkɔ ɔpanyin ano.

If we are tried by ordeal, the case doesn't go
before an elder.

488. "Mabɔ no na ɔreba", wokyi.

I have beaten him and he is still coming, you don't
like this.

489. Ɔbo da ɔbo so a, na wɔfrɛ no bepɔw.

If one stone is piled on top of another, it is
called a mountain.

490. Ɔbo (ɔtwɛrebo) da nsu ase a, ogya mpa mu da.

If a flint stone is lying at the bottom of a river,
the power of striking fire never passes over it.

491. Ɔbo mu nni adoma. (Ɔbo: minni domawa.)

There is nothing soft inside a rock.

492. (Wo) bo annwo a, (wo) werɛ mfi.

If you haven't been appeased, you don't forget it.

493. Woboa akobɔfo ano (:Wɔpɔn ak.) a, wo tam (ɔamoase)
ano yɛ duru.

If you collect fugitive slaves, the corner of your
loin cloth (as the place to keep gold dust in) is
heavy.

494. Yɛboa yɛn ase na yɛmmoa yɛn na mma.

We help our own children, not our mother's children.

495. Aboa a ɔbɛba nnim waw.

The animal that is coming to be killed, does not
hear the hunter cough.

496. Aboa a ne ho wɔ nhwi fi fifiri a, wonhu.

If an animal with hair sweats, it is not noticed.

497. Aboa a ɔsebɔ antumi anni no, agyinamoa mfa no afo.

The animal which the leopard could not eat, is not
eaten by the cat.

498. Aboa aberekyi na obu ne bɛ sɛ: Adepa na wɔkata so.

The goat has a saying which goes: "A good thing is
sure to be covered."

499. Aboa bi dɔ srade a, osua prako. R.149.

If an animal gets fat, it is imitating the pig.

500. Aboa bi renka wo a, onnwen (nwen) ne se nkyere wo.

If an animal is not going to bite you, it does not
show you its teeth.

501. Aboa bi tan wo a, na one gu wo so.

If a bird dislikes you, it shits on you.

502. Aboa biako, wonyi ne ho ayan abien.

You don't take out two breasts from one animal.

503. Aboa biara nni soro a odi kube.

There is no animal in the sky that eats the coconut.

504. Aboa adanko na obuu ne be se : woanya awo wo barima yi,
na aka wo ne ye-gu.

The rabbit has a saying which goes: "If you were born a
male, then you are given impossible tasks."

505. Aboa dompo nni asumguarede nti na onam asu ho bo akoto.

Because the wild dog has nothing to sacrifice for his
soul, he goes to the river to dig for crabs.

506. Aboa agyinamoa nni biribi, nanso owo ahoehere.

The cat may have nothing else, but it certainly
has agility and swiftness.

507. Aboa agyinamoa nim se ntwemu ye de a, anka otwe ne mu
du Aburokyiri.

If the cat thought that stretching its back was so
delightful, it would do it til it reached Europe.

508. Aboa agyinamoa se: ntwemu nti na wanto akoa.

The cat says it is because of stretching its body
that it doesn't buy a slave.

509. Aboa oketew na obuu be se: Odesani me a, obo dam.

The lizard has this saying: "If man is ever fully
satisfied in eating, he becomes crazy."

510. Aboa okisi kofa n'aduan (:fa adwe) na Onyankopon tew
(:osoro pa) no so anyinam a, ogya (:odan) kyene.

If the rat goes to steal food (palm nuts), and God
flashes lightning on him, he drops it.

511. Aboa kisi nya fufu a, obedi, na ɔwoma na ɛnkɔ ne bɔn mu.
If the rat gets fufu, he will eat it, but the pestle for pounding it doesn't go into his hole.

512. Aboa ako nni nsa, nanso ɔforo dua.
A parrot has no hands but it can still climb a tree.

513. Aboa kokosakyi kasa kyerɛ obunukyerɛfo a, ɔte.=2688.
If the vulture gives advice to the hyena, he takes it.

514. Aboa kokosakyi nni tuo, na ɔtɔn asommɛn.
The vulture has no gun, but it sells ivory.

515. Aboa kokosakyi anya nehɔ se: ɔkwadu ho bɔn.
The vulture defends himself by saying: "The "ɔkwadu" antelope stinks."

516. Aboa kokosakyi se: akasadi nti na ɔka sumana so.
The vulture says it is in order to avoid fines that he stays at the dump.

517. Aboa akrampa(kokosakyi), wudi bi bin na obi nni wo de.=2690.
Vulture, you eat anybody's excreetment, but nodody eats yours.

518. Aboa akokromfi yɛ ɔbrane a, ankara onnyae atwɛrɛko da.
If the preying mantis were so strong, it would never stop fighting with its fists.

519. Aboa kurotwiamansa hunu ato nifa a, ankrana aboa bi nni wiram'.
If the leopard knew how to spring to his right side in catching its prey, then there would be no animals left in the forest.

520. Aboa kurutu, wonsi no nsɛmma.
You don't lay a snare for the "kurutu" animal.

521. Aboa ɔkwaku nim sɛ ɔkɔm bɛba nti na okiti koro ho.
Because the monkey knows that faminine will come, he gnaws off the bark of the "koro" tree.

522. Aboa akyekyereɛ nni ntama, nsoso awɔw nne no da.
Though the tortoise has no native cloth, it is never cold.

523. Aboa ameme ne homa te ho yi, omene nhoma na ommene dompe.

The animal "ameme" and its hide are both together, it can swallow the hide but not the bones.

524. Aboa nanka nim adekyee a, anka oda nwiada?

If the python knew when it was dawn, would it sleep in the day time?

525. Aboa ananse nam na oso ne dan.

The spider travels and takes his house (web)along.

526. Aboa ne nea owe wura wo wuram'.
Aboa no, s. Aboa okisi, Okraman, Kokosakyi.

It is the animal that eats grass that is found in the forest.

527. Aboa no* didi nea n'asom' dwo no. *Aboa biara.

Every animal eats where it finds peace.

528. Aboa no nhintaw nnyaw ne dua.

An animal does not hide itself and then leave its tail sticking out.

529. Aboa no kaw nea n'ano so.

An animal bites whatever its mouth reaches to.

530. Aboa no* koda ne ahema yi! *odemerefua, odompo.

The wild dog goes to sleep and day break comes.

531. Aboa no* ta yen, wubisa me se:oye onini anaa obere??
*osebo.

A leopard is chasing us and do you ask me:"Is it a male or female?"

532. Aboa apatipere se: ohoho nnim a, omanni nim. Cf.1407.

The "apatipere" bird says that if the stranger does not know, the native does know.

533. Aboa patu muna wo a, wunhu.

When the owl makes a sad face at you, you don't even notice it.

534. Aboa petebere-nyankobere na okasa: onipa wu, na wose: owu kasa na mete.

The "petebere-nyankobere" animal speaks thus: "Man dies," and you say:"Death speak, for I am listening."

-45-

535. Aboa prako nim sɛ ɔte nti na ɔnennam mfikyiri.

Because the pig knows that it stinks, it roams
about behind the houses.

536. Aboa tum wɔ hɔ yi, ne mma sa a, ɔde ne mfɛfo mma yɛ mma.

As for the animal "tum", if its children die, it takes
those of its neighbors' for its own children.

537. Aboa atwaboa se: ɔsoro ade yɛ duru (os. ade duru sare fwe
no so a, na wawu).

The grass-cutter says that what is on top is heavy. (If
what is on top falls on it, then it is dead).

538. Aboadi nti na wobɔ nkuro.

It is because of cruel treatment that people take their
cases before the chief's court.

539. Aboadi yaw nti na wukum wɔ a, ɔdan ne yam' kyerɛ wo.

The reason the snake turns over, showing its belly to
you, when you kill it, is that it is a painful thing.

540. Mmoadoma nhina benya dabere o, na apranwam!

Even if all the animals will get a resting place, what
about the toucan?

541. Mmoadoma nhina fi fifiri, na nhwi na ɛmma yenhu.

All animals sweat, but because of their hair, we don't
notice it.

542. Mmoadoma nhina foro bo; akyekyere n'kɔforo bi,
wapɔn afwe.

All animals can climb rocks, but when the tortoise
climbs one, he falls down.

543. Mmoadoma nhina kyerɛ ahoofɛ a, woyi gyahene si hɔ.

When all the animals show their beauty, the leopard
is chosen as the most beautiful one.

544. Mmoadoma (:mmoa nhina) pɛ Amiri (ɔbɔmɔfo?) kurom.

All the animals like Amiri's village.

545. Ɔboafo yɛ na.

It is difficult to get a good helper.

546. Wobobɔ wo adɔtɔ mu hama a, owia hye wo.

If you cut the thickets down from a tall tree, the
sun beats down on you.

-46-

547. Ɔbɔdamfo mfɛre a, ne mma fɛre.

If the mad man does not feel ashamed, his children do.

548. Woboa ntorewa di a, na wommene n'ahono.

If you eat garden eggs for the first time, you don't swallow the skins.

549. Ɔbɔfo a wokodi no yaw (=abɔfo) na otuo apae aka no nsa yi, na wo de, woso brɔde bɛdɛw rekɔ he?

The hunter, whom you serve as helper by providing him with food and water, has been wounded in the hand by the bursting of his gun, and you, where are you going with that basket of plantains?

550. Ɔbɔfo aboa a wofom no biara nyɛ ketewa da.   Cf. 601.

No animal that a hunter has ever missed was small.

551. Ɔbɔfoɔ anhyehyɛ toa yiye a, ɛbo.

If the hunter doesn't pack his bottle well, it gets broken.

552. Ɔbobo mmofra ho nyɛ fɛ da.   R. 245.

An evil person's children are **never** beautiful.

553. Ɔbɔfo ntɔ akoa.

A cruel person does not buy a slave.

554. Abofra a ɔkɔ asu na ɔbɔ ahina.

It is the child who goes to fetch water that breaks the water pot.

555. Abofra bɔ mmusu akron a, ɔfa mu nnum.   R. 264.

If a child commits nine crimes, he suffers for five of them himself.

556. Abofra bɔ mmusu akron a, ɔbɛfa mu asia de asane n'abusuafo.

If a child commits nine misdeeds, he will put six of them on his family (abusua).

557. Abofra bɔ nwaw na ɔmmɔ akyekyere.   R. 3.   Gr. #251d.

A child can break the shell of a snail but not that of a tortoise.

558. Abofra boapa wu a, na woboapa sie no.

If a child pretends to be dead, we pretend to bury him.

559. Abofra kɔda gya na ɔpere ho a, ne ntama hyew.

If a child goes to lie by the fire and is fidgety,
his cloth catches on fire.

560. Abofra di tɔ na ɛmmere a, na ose: wɔmfa nno nnu so!

When a child eats mashed plantain which is not ripe,
he says, "put palm oil on it."

561. Abofra mfa pereguan na ɔde sua aguadi.

A child does not start trading with a capital of
thirty six dollars.

562. Abofra foto kɛse ye ka.

If a child is entrusted with a large amount of money,
he will incur big debts.

563. Abofra nfwɛ kwansɛn ase kwa.

A child doesn't look at the bottom of the soup pot
for nothing.

564. Abofra hu ne nsa hoho(ro) a, (na) ɔ-ne mpanyim(fo) didi.

When a child knows how to wash his hands well, he eats
with the elders.

565. Abofra anhu aguadi a, n'asia nyera. R.239.

If a child doesn't know how to trade, he doesn't lose
his gold weights.

566. Abofra ka na ɛnkɔ ɔpanyin nsa, na n'aduan de, ɛkɔ
panyin anom.

A child's ring does not fit on an adult's finger, but
his food goes into an adult's mouth.

567. Abofra ketewa bi te fi-kɛse bim' a, ma no due, na
wahu amanne.

If there is only one small child in a great big house,
pity him, for he has suffered.

568. Abofra kotow panyin nkyɛn.

A child should squat beside an elder.

569. Abofra kyima wo so a, wode baha na eyi, na ɛnyɛ
ɔsekan. Cf.9.

When a child goes to toilet on you, you clean it off
with the dry fibres of the plantain tree, and
not with a cutlass.

570. Abofra ani anso panyin a, ɔfrɛ mpopa sɛ haha. R.38.

If a child does not respect his elders, he will say the name for palm branches (mpopa) through his nose.

571. Abofra ano yɛ den a, ɔde hyɛn abɛn, na ɔmfa nhyɛn woaduru.

If a child is very talkative, he uses his mouth to blow a horn, and not to blow a mortar that is used in pounding fufu.

572. Abofra benyin abofra-kokonini nkyɛ.
(Ab. nkyɛ na wayɛ mpanyinsɛm.)

If a child always likes to be with the elders, he will grow up too fast.

573. Abofra nsam' ade nyɛ hyɛ-na.

It is not difficult to fill a child's hand.

574. Abofra se 'ɔkɔfoɔ dunsin" a, . . . s. 403.

When a child says he is going to climb a tree stump...

575. Abofra se: obeso gya mu; ma onso mu, na ɛhye no a, ɔbɛdan akyene.

When a child says he will hold a piece of burning firewood, let him hold it; for when it burns him, he will throw it down.

576. Abofra se 'ɔbɛyɛ mpanyinne' a, ma ɔnyɛ, na ɛbia obenya ɔpanyin a, obi nnim.

When a child says he wants to act as if he were already a grown-up, let him do so; whether he will ever become one, no one knows.

577. Abofra sika yɛ (:te sɛ) anyankoma-gya: wotwa so a, na adum.

A child's money is like firewood of the "anyankoma" tree; when it is broken up, it soon burns out.

578. Abofra su a, wɔmmɔ no duam'.

When a child cries, he is not put in prison.

579. Abofra sua adwini-di a, ɛnyɛ ɔsebɔ-nhoma na ɔde sua.

When a child is learning to make designs, he does not practice on a leopard's skin.

580. Abofra te hɔ yi, wo ani tra wo a, wuwia ade.
If you are greedy as a child you steal.

581. Abofra nte ne na ne n'agya asɛm a, ɛyɛ mmusu.
(..., odi aduan a nkyene nnim'.) R.4.
When a child does not obey his father and mother, it brings
misfortune. (..., he eats food without salt in it.)

582. Abofra tew neho fi n'agya ne ne na ho ntɛm a, ohu ne
werɛ bo.
When a child leaves his mother and father early in life,
he learns how to look after himself.

583. Abofra twa fufu a, otwa nea ɛbɛkɔ n'anom.
When a child is eating fufu, he takes as much as he can
put into his mouth at one time.

584. Abofra yaw panyin a, ne fwene buru gu n'anom'.
When a child insults an elder, he has his nose knocked into
his mouth.

585. Abofra, woyaw panyin a, wonkye ade.
Child, if you insult an elder, you won't prosper.

586. Abofra yɛ nea ɔpanyin yɛ a, ohu nea ɔpanyin hu.
When a child does what a grown-up does, he suffers what
a grown-up suffers.

587. Abofra yɛ nea wɔnyɛ a, ohu nea wonhu.
When a child does what he is not supposed to do, he suffers
what he is not supposed to suffer.

588. Abofra yɛ yaw.
To be a child is painful.

589. Abofra nyɛ tirim kam a, ɔnsoa dadekyɛw.
If a child does not have a scar on his head, he does not
wear a helmet.

590. Abofra yem a, nankasa na ɔwo.
If a child becomes pregnant, she delivers by herself.

591. Mmofra hu kɔre a osu atɔ aboro no a, wose: ɔyɛ opete.
When children see an eagle that has been beaten by the
rain, they say it is a vulture.

592. Mmofra nkotu a, woanhu tu; mpanyin nkotu a, wotiatia
so. R.152.

When children go to pluck mushrooms, they don't know how
to do it; and when grown-ups go to do so, they trample on
the mushrooms.

593. Bogya gu wo ho a, yebisa dea aba?

When there is blood all over you, do we ask what has
happened?

594. Bogya ne asɛm.

Blood relations are what really matters.

595. Bogya, wompopa (:'yɛmpopa ntwene).

A blood relation can not be blotted out.

596. 'Mogya mpa otɛn tirimu da.

There is always blood in the head of the tsetse fly.

597. Wo abogye rewae (na mekotew hama mabɛkyekye ama wo a,
wuse 'wugya mu' ana?) na "so mu na menkotew hama memmɛkyekyerɛ
memma wo" a, woka sɛ: "woamma ntɛm a, miregya mu"?

If your jaw bone is broken (and I go to cut a string to tie
it up for you, do you say, "shall I leave it go?") and if I
say hold it and I am going to look for a string to bind
it, do you tell me, "if you do not hurry, I will let it go"?

598. Abɔhyeafo a yɛ-ne wo bɔ hye a, yedi 'motodoma.

If we both have the same border (for our farms) we both
eat green plantains.

599. Abɔm na enni ho nti na wode ntoa sua abɛ.

It is because the pots to catch the palm wine are not here
that they catch it with gourds.

600. Obɔmofo a woakum pete (a wonni ne nam), woasɛe wo atuduru!

A hunter who kills a vulture (which is not eaten)
wastes his gunpowder.

601. Obɔmofo aboa a ɔkɔ na ɔsɔ. Cf.550.

To the hunter the animal that gets away is always a big one.

602. Obommofo din bata sonnam ho.

The hunter's name is always connected with the meat of the
elephant.

603. Ɔbɔmɔfo fi wuram ba na okura mmerɛ a, wommisa ahayɔ
mu asɛm.

If the hunter comes from the bush carrying mushrooms,
you don't ask him how the hunting went.

604. Ɔbɔmɔfo kɔ wuram' ma osu tɔ afwe no, ma ntummoa keka ne ho,
ma awɔw ade no, ma ɔfwerem' awɔ no, ne nhina na yɛ due
na mede memae.

When the hunter goes to the bush and the rain beats him,
the horse flies bite him, he becomes cold, thorns prick
him, these are all included in the consolation I give him.

605. Ɔbɔmɔfo kɔtɛw dua na aboa amma a, ɔsan ba ofie.

When the hunter goes and crouches behind a tree and no
animal comes, he returns home.

606. Ɔbɔmɔfo nnim aboa yarefo.

The hunter doesn't spare the sick animal.

607. Ɔbɔmɔfo annya biribi na efi katwi (=tani).

If the hunter didn't get anything, it is because of his
spleen.

608. Ɔbɔmmɔfoɔ, woma anoma atewa biribi dii a, anka wote
n'anom' kasa-pa.

Hunter, if you would have given the "atewa" bird something
to eat, you would have heard it's sweet voice.

609. Obontu se: ɔyɛ yiye, na owu a, ɔde agyaw ne mma.

The "obontu" goat says he is prospering, and if he dies,
he leaves his children all his wealth.

610. Ɔborakɔmfo (Kwasi Ta a ɔwɔ Abiriw) se: osuro kum nti.
na wayɛ ne kɔn (tia) tia. Cf.3126. ·

Ɔborakomfo (Kwasi Ta who lives at Abiriw) says: because
he is afraid of being killed, he has made his neck short.

611. Woboro gyata a, wo tiri pa wo.

If you strike a lion, your own head will pain you.

612. Woboro amu so a, na woawie ayi yɛ.

When you stamp the ground over the grave, the funeral
is finished.

613. Aboro nye, osua na eye.
Destroying things is not good, but learning is.

614. Abosoba na ɛma ogya pae.
The club used in hitting the wedge, is what makes the firewood split.

615. Obosom a onnii guan da (no), (na) ohu guan aniwaɔ' mpe a, ose: ɛyɛ srade.
If the fetish that has never eaten sheep meat sees the matter in the corner of the sheep's eyes, it says it is fat.

616. Obosom a ɔyɛ nnam (Ob. yɛ nnam a) na odi aboade.
A fetish that is powerful recieves thank-offerings.

617. Obosom Kyerɛ nantwi, womfa mfa abonten, womfa mfa afkyiri, nso ɛwo nea wode fa. Cf.2031. 2110.
The fetish Kyerɛ's cow is not allowed to pass the streets nor the outskirts of town, but somehow there is a way for it to pass.

618. Obosom anim, woko no mperensa.
One goes to the fetish god three (many) times.

619. Obosom so, 'yɛnko no mperensa.
One is taken before a fetish three (many) times.

620. Abosom na ɛkyerɛ akomfo ntwaho.
It is the fetish gods who show the fetish priests how to wheel around in dancing.

621. Obosomaketere hyɛ ɔhye a, ɔhye.
If the chameleon wants to be burned, it will be burned.

622. Obosomaketew se: ntɛm ye (na) ɔgom ye: wututu 'mirika a wunya, wudwo wo ani nso a, wunya. R.119 Cf.1931..
The chameleon says: speed is good, and slowness is good: if you run, you get it, and if you proceed slowly, you also get it.

623. Obosomaketew wo awogyedur' a, anka ɔrebɛwo a, ne yam' mpae.
If the chameleon had medicine for giving birth, when it would be giving birth, it's belly would not burst.

624. Obosomfo (=ɔkɔmfo) ka ne nkonim, na ɔnka ne nkogu.

The fetish priest tells of his successes but not of his failures.

625. Obosomfo anom' asɛm nsae da.

The fetish priest always has something to say.

626. Bosonopo ne Ayesu ntam', wugoru hɔ a, ɔboba si wo.

If you play between the ocean and the Ayensu river you will be stoned.

627. Bosonotwe ho nnua ara ne nketewa no.

The trees you see at Lake Bosomtwe (which people expect to be big) are small.

628. Bosonotwe ankame wo nam a, wo nso wonkame no nkasanim' (=nkasae, nnompe).

If Bosonotwe doesn't refuse to give you fish, you should not refuse to give it the fish bones.

629. Abotafowa hu baha ansa-na ohu wekomma.

A small child sees the dry fibres of the bark of the plantain tree before he sees the native cloth woven of cotton or silk thread.

630. Abotafowa na ɔde fɛa ba.

A small child is the one who dies first in the family.

631. Abotan kɔtɔ: mewɔ adaye; m'akyiri twere bo, me yam' fam aban.

The rock-crab says: "I have a good sleeping place; my back leans against a rock, and my stomach embraces a rock."

632. Obotiri nyera nam mu.

The head of an animal is not lost among the pieces of meat.

633. Botɔwa fwe (ni a,) ɔsaman woraw?

If there is no musical instrument hissing, does the ghost come unexpectedly?

634. Ɔbra yɛ bɔ-na.

Life is difficult.

635. Wo bra yɛ fɛ a, na wosua wo.
     If your character is good, they will imitate you.

636. Ɔbrafo ne akyere nna.   Cf.3154
     Brafo apatiperɛ...s.2640.
     Ɔbran...Cf.85.86   Mmrante...Cf.87.88.
     The executioner and the person destined to be killed
     do not sleep.

637. Ɔbrɛfo ntɔn na ɔbrɛfo ntɔ.=1377.
     The poor man can not sell nor buy.

638. Abrobɛ mfa ne kɔkɔ a, ɛnyɛ ɔdɛ.   Cf.642.1504.
     If the pineapple doesn't become red, it isn't sweet.

639. Ɔbrɔde a woto a ɛbɛhyew no, wonoa a,ɛhow.
     The plantain which if you roast, will burn, and if you
     boil it,it is not sufficiently boiled.

640. Ɔbrɔde dwe ne nkate nnyae dɛ-yɛ da.
     Roasted plantain and ground nuts never lose their
     sweetness.

641. Ɔbrɔde dwe, wɔwe no akɔnnɔ (so).
     Roasted plantain is eaten for pleasure.

642. Brɔfere annya ammere soro, na annya anyɛ dɛ. R.77.
     A pawpaw that does not become ripe on the tree, is not
     sweet.

643. Brɔfere yɛ dɛ a, na dua da ase.
     If a pawpaw is delicious, a stick is always lying at the
     bottom of the tree.

644. Brɔfo adaworoma na yen nhina furafura ntama.
     Thanks to the white man, we all wear native cloths.

645. Brɔfo de nyansa na ɛforo po.
     Because of wisdom the white man can sail on the sea.

646. Ɔbrofotefo na ɔma oburoni yɛ ayɛ.   R.84.
     It is the one who knows English and can speak to the white
     man who induces him to give him gifts.

647. Abrɔnoma da soro, odwaɲsae da fam'.

The pigeon sleeps above, the castraed ram sleeps on the ground.

648. Abrɔnoma se: ɔkwankyerɛ yɛ mmusu.

The pigeon says: "the act of showing the way brings misfortune."

649. Ebu so a, ebu ma nea ɛyɛ ne dea.

If things are abundant, they are abundant for the owner.

650. Wubu akawa (:aka) dua a, wuwie ɔwe.

If you curse the small fish "akawa", you stop eating fish.

651. Wubu me kuma a, mibu wo kuma.

If you think I am inferior, I also think you are inferior.

652. Wubu na woammobɔ na wohyew a, ɛnhyew (:woberɛ).

If you cut down brush but don't stack it and you burn it, it doesn't burn well.

653. Wubu to ho kyekye na ɛnyɛ yiye a, wode si anim kyekye.=766.

If you double something to join it together and it doesn't go well, then you join it together by the two ends.

654. Wubu woho kokuro a, na wotwa wo nwini (:wɔde nkuma a. s. mmerenkonyan twa wo).

If you consider yourself to be great, you cut your hair, (with an axe.)

655. Wubu wo suman asumamma a, ekita wo.

If you consider your amulet a trifling thing, it will take vengenance on you.

656. Wobu kwasea bɛ a, onyansafo te ase.

If you tell a proverb to a foolish man, a wise man will understand.

657. Wurebua ada a, wunse sɛ: mikyi nkoa aduan.

If you are starving you do not say,"I despise food given to slaves."

658. Abubu-mmaba-aɲwene, ɔnwereẹ na ɔkɔɔ mu o, ɔkɔɔ mu na ɔnwenee o, obi nnim (:yennim).

The moth's house,which is made of little sticks - no one knows whether it made it before going into it or went into it before making it.

659. Abufuw te sɛ ɔhɔho, ɔntra obiakofo fi.

Anger is like a stranger, it doesn't stay in only one person's house.

660. Abufuw yɛ ɔbrammiri.
Obuntu s. Obontu 609.

Anger can make a man commit things which otherwise he would never do.

661. Aburobia ahaban kɔ kwaem' a, na aworo ahaban reba ofie.

If the leaves of the "aburobia" plant go to the bush, the leaves of the "aworo" herb come to the house.

662. Aburobua wɔ anom', obi nse no sɛ: aburobua bedi nkɔmmɔdom.

A clay tobacco pipe in your mouth, no one says: "the pipe will bring about sympathy with a suffering man."

663. Aburokyiri adaban, ɔha agyirawotwe.

European bars of iron, a hundred gold weight.

664. Aburokyiri nipa yare a, ne ho san.

If a European is sick, he recovers.

665. Aburokyiri nyɛ kɔ-na, na po(na ehia)! (:na akyiri-!).

It would not be difficult to go to Europe if it were not for the sea!

666. Aburokyiri a merekɔ, enhia me; mpoano na ehia me.

Going to Europe is not bothering me, it is just getting to the coast that is difficult enough.

667. Oburoni a onni biribi na ɔte sɛ obibini a waɦyɛ ada so.

A European who has nothing is like an African who heaps up riches.

668. Oburoni a ɔte abantenten mu, sɛ owu a, na ɔda fam'.

Even a white man who lives in a castle is put in the ground when he dies.

669. Oburoni (a ɔ)tɔn asekan na ne ti afuw.

It is the white man who sells scissors, yet his head is overgrown with hair.

670. Oburoni Kokobɔ se: ɛpo yem; sɛ ɛbɛwo dɛn o, ɛno de, onnim.

The white man's bush cat says,"the sea is pregnant," but it doesn't know what it will give birth to.

671. Oburoni annwansi wo yiye, afei hena na ɔreyɛ wo ayɛ bio?

If the white man does not sneeze to endow good luck on you, who else will do you any favor?

672. Aburow a ahoa (:Ab. hoa a), wonti ani bio.

When the corn is ready to be harvested you don't tear open the leaves any more.

673. Aburo-guane (:Aburow guannuan), wonti ani. (Amoa a ɔte Akuropɔn 1858.)

You don't take the husks off ripe ears of corn. (Amoa of Akuropɔn 1858.)

674. Aburow de ne mpɛsɛe rekum nnuadewa (=ntɔrewa).

The blossoms of the corn are obstructing the garden eggs.

675. Aburow, wɔde n'ani na edua.

It is the seed of corn that is planted.

676. Aburow (nko) dua neho a, stotɔ.

If corn plants itself, it drops at random.

677. Aburow wɔ hɔ yi, wɔyam yam a, wɔfrɛ no aburow, na wɔmfrɛ no fufu.

As for corn, no matter how much you grind it, it is still called corn, and not "fufu."

678. Burofua na ɛyɛ san.

A single ear of corn can produce a whole shed full of corn.

679. Burohono dodonku se: Wotow me kyene a, mesan meba.

The swollen corn husk says: "if you throw me away, I'll return."

680. Aburo-pata hyew a, na ɛka mmurofua ɔha.

If the shed for storing corn burns down, there still remains a hundred grains of corn.

681. Aburuburu na obuu bɛ sɛ: Ade a ɛbɛyɛ ye nsɛe.=784.

The dove gives this saying: "the thing which will be good never spoils.

682. Burum afɛ sa a, ɔbɔ aforɔte afɛ.

If the "burum" animal's friends die he befriends the "aforɔte" deer.

683. Abusua nhina yɛ abusua, na yɛfwefwɛ mmɛtema so de.

All extended families are families, but we are looking for the one where the members are closely related to one another.

684. Abusua te sɛ nfwiren; egugu akuw-akuw.

An extended family is like flowers that grow in bunches.

685. Abusua yɛ dɔm, na wo na ɔba ne wo nua.

The extended family is an army, and your own mother's child is your real brother and sister.

686. Abusua dua, wontwa.

The family tree is not cut down.

687. Obusuapanyin (:Abusuaponni) mpene kɔm.

The head of an extended family weeps because of hunger.

688. Da a ehia Opoti (Ga: Okpoti) na ehia Daye (G. Laye).

The day Opoti is in need, Daye is also in need.

689. Da a onipa begyae adidie no, na n'asɛm asa.

The day man stops eating his troubles will cease.

690. Da a wo ho nye na wo ne wo ase hyia.

The day you are not doing well you meet your mother in law.

691. Da a wotɔɔ me too Kara no, da no ara na mihui sɛ me nkwa bata me wura de ho.

The day on which they bought me as a slave and gave me the name 'Kara', on that day I saw that my life was connected with my master.

692. Da a ntoa tewe no, da no na ɔdanka boe.

On the day the calabash fell down, the powder-horn was broken.

693. Da bi a ɔtenten benya, akwatia rennya. R.15.

On the day the tall have good luck, (the same day) the short have poor luck.

694. Da-koro adwuma nyɛ adwuma.

Work that can be finished in one day is not real work.

695. Da-koro na wohu manni.

In one instant you can immediately see the native.

696. Da sɛ nnɛ nti wofwɛ obi anim nom nsasin. Cf.262.1183.

Because of the future and out of respect for a person, one drinks the last bit of palm wine from the calabash.

697. Da sɛ nnɛ nti na wonnuare ahinam.

Because of the future you don't bathe in the water pot.

698. Da sɛ nnɛ nti na woayɛ awerɛw (na wode ahuane woho.) R.57. Gr.#248,6.

Because of the future you let your fingernails grow (to scratch yourself.)

699. Woda adagyaw a, wotɔ tam-mone.

If you are naked, you will buy a cloth of poor quality.

700. Woda akuru mu a, womma Sakwa due.

If your whole body is full of sores, you are not sympathetic with Sakwa.

701. Woda na nsaseboa ka wo na wutu no to gyam' a, na woda a, wo ani kum.

If you are sleeping and a sand-worm bites you and you throw it into the fire, then if you lie down again you go to sleep.

702. Woda pata ase na nkyene porow gu wo anom' a, womporow nnu.

If you are lying under a shed and salt drops on your mouth, you do not shake it off.

703. Wodae na wosoo dae-pa a, ka kyerɛ nnipa-pa; na woso dae-bone a, ɛka wo tirim'.

If your are sleeping and have a good dream tell good people; if you are sleeping and have a bad dream keep it to yourself.

704. Wɔnna a, wɔnso dae.

If you don't sleep you can't dream.

705. Wɔnna afa mpere afa.

If you are not sleeping in a bed with some one, you don't struggle for his half of the bed.

706. Wɔanna wɔanna a, wɔnne dasu.
    Those who don't sleep have no break in their sleep.

707. Meda-ase, Afi, wonse no kwa.
    You don't say thank you, Afi, without a good reason.

708. Wodada abofra na wokaw ne nnwoma so.
    If you win over a child you bite off his cooked yam.

709. Wodada onipa na wodi n'ade.
    If you win over someone you inherit him.

710. Ɔdadafo na ogyigye ade ma ɔpempensifo.
    The deceiver gets something for an extortioner.

711. Adae rebɛto na wokoyi kyenekɛse adi a, ɔkyekye sɛ: me
    tiri ho wɔ pow?
    When the Adae Festival is coming and they take out the king's
    drum, the lizard says: "is there a lump on my head?"

712. Dagere sene fweawa adekora.
    Sealing wax is better than ordinary wax in the securing of
    things.

713. Adaka hini dea ɔdeɛ.
    The box opens for the owner.

714. Adam bere afanu a, anka wɔbɛto no (ama) pereguan.
    If the shell of a certain species of shell fish becomes
    red on both sides, they would sell it for thirty six dollars.

715. Adam mmerɛ afanu.
    The shell of a shell fish does not become red on both
    sides.

716. Damma ankɔ a, pereguan mma.
    If 2 pesewas weight of gold does not go out 4 1/2 oz.
    of gold does not come.

717. Dammefa (:Dammirifa?) firi tete, emfiri nnɛ.
    Sympathy is from the olden days, not from today.

718. Nnamfo banu goru bea bako ho a, ɛnkyɛ na ɔko ba.
    If two friends flirt with one woman, it doesn't take long
    before a fight begins.

719. Ɔdamfo nan, wɔtwe no nya. Cf.962

You pull a madman's foot slowly.

720. Medan wo ketew na mennan wo akura.

I seek the protection of your lizard but not the protection of your mouse.

721. Wodan kara-ka a, wo sika nnɔ.

If you demand payment for your debt, your money does not increase.

722. Wodan kwasea kaw a, woankasa na wututu woho.

If you demand payment for a debt from a fool, you have put off the payment of your debt.

723. Wodan wo na kaw a, wokɔto wo agya de.

If you demand payment of your mother's debt, the payment falls on your father.

724. Wodan okisi adwerɛ (:amoakua) a, ɔnnan ara da.

If you change the rat into a squirrel, it doesn't change.

725. Ɔdanka worowora-worowora a, na biribi wɔ mu.

If the powder horn makes a rattling noise, something is inside it.

726. Dankyira bɔmmɔfoɔ annya biribi, na efiri (ne nua) Bereku.

If the Dankyira hunter didn't get anything it is because of (his brother) Bereku.

727. Dankyira-ɔman abɔ, na (menne) tawasɛn! Cf.1998.

If the Dankyira state is going to ruin, then what about the tobacco!

728. Adare bɔ bo a, nankasa na etua. R.91.

If the cutlass strikes a rock, it pays (suffers).

729. Adare: mannya ayɛ, na woma asɔw amo.

Cutlass: I haven't done anything well, and you give the hoe congratulations.

730. Wo adare twa wo a, wontow nkyene.

If your cutlass cuts you, you don't throw it away.

731. Odasikyi begu wo asu a, (na) efi Agyebɔn.

If the plaything "dasikyi damages you, it is because of Agyebɔn.

732. Odawuru tuntun-sansan, yɛfwefwɛ mu nea ɔyɛ dɛ na yeabɔ.

We look where on the gong it will sound nice and hit there.

733. Wode abasatoto (:abasakyea) na ɛserɛ abofra ade.

You beg from the child by swinging him with your arms.

734. Wode berɛberɛ gua ntɛtea a, wuhu ne nsono (:ne 'merɛbo). Cf.3390.

If you skin the ant with patience, you see its intestines (liver).

735. Wode bi di a, wɔde wo di. Cf.902.

If you inherit someone, someone also inherits you.

736. Wode adare na ɛpere asase.

We fight for the land with the cutlass.

737. Wode dwen na ɛyɛ ɔpanyin a, anka obi nsen asuakwa. Wode dwoa ka...s.747.

If gray hair was the only characteristic of old age, no one would be older than the "asuakwa" bird.

738. Wɔde Ofe ho nsu na ɛnoa n'adwene.

You boil the fish caught in the River Offin in it's own water.

739. Wode guanhoma na ɛserɛ dabere.

You ask for a sleeping place with a sheep skin.

740. 'Yɛde hia na ebu Asante-tɛn.

We condemn an Ashanti because of poverty.

741. 'Yɛde hia na 'yɛde warɛɛ akyɛkyɛwa.

In times of poverty we marry a hunch-backed person.

742. 'Yɛde hia na edi akrampa aduane.

We eat food eaten by the vulture in times of real necessity.

743. 'Yɛde hia na edidi ademene (=sumana) soɔ.

In times of poverty we eat on the refuse heap.

744. 'Yɛde hia na ɛmo ntomporie (= ntampehama).

It is out of sheer poverty that women use "ntomporie" beads.

745. 'Yɛde hia na ɛwe dɛnkyɛmmoɔ.

In times of necessity, we eat the "dɛnkyemmoɔ" nuts.

746. Wode ahupo pɛ ade a, wusiane ho.

If you seek wealth in a presumptious manner you miss it.

747. Wode ka dwɔwa na wunya mu taku a, na aka dwoa-gyina.

If you are $8.00 in debt and you get five cents then it only remains a dwoa-gyina to pay the debt off.

748. Wode ka na wutua a, wo ho dwo.

If you pay your debts you get peace of mind.

749. Wɔde nkatae dodow na edi amim.

Victory comes through the covers of many gun locks.

750. Wɔde nketenkete na ɛkyekyere kurow.

It is through small things that a village is established.

751. Wɔde akokoduru na ɛbɔ kron.

Stealing is done with courage.

752. Wode kokurobeti kɔ ayi a, wɔde sotɔre bua wo (:gye wo so). R.35.

If you go to a funeral with your thumb you are received with a slap in the face.

753. Wɔde kokuroko na edi amim a, anka ɛsono bɛba ofie. R.11.

If bodily size and strength were used to oppress and cheat then the elephant could have come to the house.

754. Wɔde nkontompo ka asɛm a, wobers.

When you tell lies in stating a case, you become tired.

755. Wode nkontompo pɛ ade (mfe apem) a, ɔnokwafo de nokware (:n'anokwasɛm) gye wo nsam' (dakoro).

When you seek for a thing (for 1000 years) by the aid of falsehood, the truthful man, using truth, takes it from you in one day.

756. Wode kyɛw soa nankroma a, ɛbɛyɛ 'ye; na wode soa ti
(:wo sore na ehia).

If you put your hat on your knee, it fits just as on
your head, but it prevents you from standing up.

757. Wode akyiri gya me a, ɛnka me nko.

If you hand things over to me, you have not left me alone.

758. 'Yɛde manni dorowa to panes pa ho?

Do we compare a good needle with a native needle?

759. Wode anantenantew a, wudi wo akyiwade (:akyide).

If you travel about much you eat what you don't like.

760. Yɛde ani ketewa na yɛde hu adeɛ.

We use our small eyes to see things.

761. Wode nokware ka asɛm a, ewu.

When you speak the truth in stating a case, the matter is
quickly settled.

762. Wode nokware tutu kaw a, woboro wo, nanso wo asɛmpa
ara no woaka no.

If you truthfully (honestly) put off payment of your
debt, you are beaten but you have said nothing but the
truth of your circumstances.

763. Wode nyansa na esi ntantwee.

Through the use of wisdom they beat about the bush.

764. Wode safe to bamma ho na wudi asɛm a, wuhu ano.

If you put your keys on the swish seat while you settle
a case you will know what to say.

765. Wode sebo nhoma sua adwinni a, na wode awie.

When you use a leapoard's skin for learning leather work,
it shows you have already mastered your trade.

766. Wode si anim kyekye na anyɛ yiye a, wode to ho kyekye.=653.

If you can not join two pieces of wood by the two ends,
you do it by the sides.

767. Wode sikamono na esisi pɛwadifo.

You can deceive a hawker with ready cash.

768. Wode sono nhoma bu kotoku, na wode dɛn ahyɛm'?

You may make a bag out of an elephant's hide but what are
you going to put in it?

-65-

769. Wɔde tɛkrɛma-pa na ɛwɛn tiri.
A man protects his head with a good tongue.

770. Wode tɛkrɛma si awowa a, wuntumi mpɔn no.
If you pledge your tongue, you cannot get it back.

771. Wode wo tɛkrɛma ma ɔman na wogye a, wɔmfa mma wo.
If you give your tongue to the nation and they take it, they don't give it back to you.

772. Wode tenten sene tia a, wunya.
If you want to exchange a tall person for a short one, you get him.

773. Wode tiri ma ti wura a, koma tɔ.
If you give the head to the owner, he is satisfied.

774. Wode wo ba to Wu-a-wu a, owu. R. 124.
If you name your child "he-is-death-like" he dies.

775. Wode woho bobɔ nnua na ehia wo a, ɛnnen wo.
If you give yourself away here and there you find a ready helper when in need.

776. Wode wo kra kaw na woantua no a, ɔfa wo abufuw.
If you are in debt to your soul, and have not paid this debt, your soul gets angry with you.

777. Wode wo ani abien fwɛ toam' a, wunhu mu ade.
If you look into a bottle with both of your eyes at the same time, you can't see inside it.

778. Wode wo nsa bɛtew apem-ne-ada (:mpenna) na wotwa kotɔkoro ma wo a, wunse (no) sɛ: ɛyɛ tia.
If you are going to pull down the hornet's nest with your hand and someone cuts and gives you a forked stick for it, you should not say it is too short.

779. Wode wo nsa to yarefo aduan mu a, wudi no prɛko.
If you put your hand in a sick person's food you eat it quietly.

780. Wode wo tuo gye ɔtwe-serɛ a, ɛpae.
If you shoot the antelope's thigh it breaks open.

781. Wode wo yonko bu aboa a, ode wo bu ebin.

If you consider your friend to be an animal he considers you to be shit.

782. Wode ayaaseduru na shyɛn abɛn.

One blows the horn with a full stomach.

783. Ade a ohene pɛ na woyɛ ma no.

Whatever the chief wants is what is done for him.

784. Ade a ɛbɛyɛ 'ye nsɛe.=681.

A thing which has come to stay is indestructible.

785. Ade a enye (:ɛnyɛ (:anyɛ) 'ye) no na woyɛ no yiye.
Cf.815. R.261.

What is bad we make good.

786. Ade a enye wo wo kurom' na ste sɛ nea ɛwo wo yonko kurom na eye.

The thing which is bad in your town is just like what is good in your neighbor's town.

787. Ade a ɛwo wo kurom'a ɛnyɛ fɛ no na ste sɛ nea ɛwo obi kurom'.

That which doesn't look beautiful in your own town is just like what is in your neighbor's town.

788. Ade abien nyɛ okyɛ-na. (F. Adze abien ne kyɛ onyɛ kyɛ-na.)

It is easy to share two things.

789. Ade-bone nti na woto din mmako-'mako. Cf.2548.

In order to find evil doers, every human being is given a name.

790. Ade-bone 'yɛtono no abosiri.

Bad things are sold cheaply.

791. Ade da ho a, womfa nsusuw serɛ.

If something is lying on the ground it can not be compared to the grass which is standing.

792. Ade da (:bɛn) pata ano a, yi (no ntɛm), na mma ɛnnko akyiri ansa.

If something is lying near the edge of the roof, pick it up, quickly, and don't let it fall down before doing so.

793. Ade da pata ano a, 'yeyi; na sɛ ɛkɔ akyiri a, na 'yɛtoa
 awaduru kɔpɛ.

 When something is lying just at the edge of a shed, it
 is easily taken, but if it is way in the back we have to
 join wooden mortars together to get it.

794. Ade-foforo fɛ nti na awirikwaw de ne kɔkɔ bɔɔ n'anim.

 Because of the beauty of a new thing, the parrot put
 scarlet on it's chest.

795. Adeɛ-foforo nyɛ fɛ a, ankara ɔhemmea bɔ abia?

 If a new thing is not beautiful would the queen mother put
 on beads?

796. Ade hia ɔdɛnkyɛm a, odidi asum', onnidi kwaem'.

 However poor the crocodile becomes, it searches for food
 in the river, not in the forest.

797. Ade hia ɔdehye a, ehia no kakra.

 When a noble man lacks something, the thing is usually
 something very big.

798. Ade hia ɔhene nana a, okita tuo, na ɔnsoa akɛtɛ.

 When a chief's grandson is poor, he carries a gun but
 he doesn't carry sleeping mats.

799. Ade hia ɔkyɛmfoɔ ba a, ofua tuo, na ɔnsoa akɛtɛ.

 When a shield bearer's son is poor, he carries a gun but he
 doesn't carry sleeping mats.

800. Ade hia ɔsebɔ a, ɔwe wura (:twa).

 When a leopard is in need, it eats grass.

801. Ade na ehia Ɔkwamni nti na ɔ-ne Pekyini nam. Cf.1320.Z.207.

 Because the Akwam man is poor, he and the Pekyi man move
 together.

802. Ade nhina dan suahu.=2284.

 Every situation can be a learning experience.

803. Ade nhina nsɛe.

 A thing is not allowed entirely to go to pieces.

804. Ade nhina wɔ ne bere ne n'awiei. (Mp.)
 All things have their time and end.

805. Ade ho ade nyɛ na a, anka Krobofo frɛ kora se kyeme?
(...Okroboni remfrɛ k. se ky.)

If the appearance of a thing were not difficult to obtain
then would the Krobo's silk cloth be called a calabash?

806. Ade ho ade nyɛ na a, anka abebɛw mu nni 'mogya?

If the appearance of thing were not difficult to judge
then wouldn't the grasshopper have blood?

807. Ade ketewa na wode susuw kɛse.

It is a small thing that is taken to measure a big thing.

808. Ade nkyee a, fwɛ anim (:akyiri) fwɛ.

If it is not light (morning) look ahead.

809. Ade-pa na ɛtɔn neho.

A good thing sells itself.

810. Ade sa a, ɔkɔkɔ biri. R.209.Z.11.

In the evening even a copper colored person looks black.

811. Ade sa na osua tew a, ɔntew nhyɛ ne ba ano.

When it is dark and the monkey picks some fruits she
doesn't pick it and put it in her child's mouth.

812. Ade nsa ano.

Darkness doesn't come on one's mouth.

813. Ade te sɛ 'wo, ɛnnɔ fako. Cf.1348.

Riches are like a snake, it doesn't love only one place.

814. Ade tɔ wo ani so a, (ɛnyɛ woankasa na wuyi,) wo yɔnko
na oyi ma wo.

When something gets in your eye (it's not you who takes
it out) your friend takes it out for you.

815. Ade nyɛ a, na wɔyɛ no yiye.=785.

If a thing is bad, we make it good.

816. Ade nyɛ na wɔnkɔtow nkyene a, wɔde kɔhyɛ adaka mu?
Cf.3351.

If you have a bad thing and don't throw it away, do you
keep it in your box?

817. Ade yera a, wofi fie na ɛpɛ.

If a thing is lost, we start looking for it at home.

818. Ade yera a, wɔpɛ no akwansin.
When a thing is lost we search for it on the path.

819. Ade yera a, na ɛwɔ nipa nsam'.
When a thing is lost it is in someone's possession.

820. Wo ade bo yɛ den a, wo nnuadan yɛ berɛw (:merɛw).
If your goods are expensive, giving back what has been bought is slow.

821. Wo ade rebɛsa a, na wo ani tew.
When your riches are getting exhausted, you come to your senses.

822. Wo ade yɛ fɛ a, obi na ɔka kyerɛ wo, na ɛnyɛ woankasa na woka.
If something you have is beautiful, let someone tell you, do not say it yourself.

823. "Wo de wɔ mu, meremfa memma wo" na ɛmaa ɔdetamfo dii awu. B.
You have a share in it, but I will not give it to you, this made the proud man commit murder.

824. Wo de anyɛ yiye a, wonkɔfa obi de nyɛ wo de.
When what you have is not good you do not go and take what belongs to someone else.

825. Ɔde a ɛbɛhyew, wototo a, ɛhyew, wonoa a, ɛhyew.
The yam which if you roast will get burnt, will also get burnt when you boil it.

826. Ɔde ammɔ a, ne ti nyera.
When a yam does not grow (ripe) it's head it never lost.

827. Ɔde ammɔ kɛse a, wɔmpan no kɛse.
If the yam has not grown big, you don't make a big hole around it when digging it up.

828. Ɔdeɛ kokorɔw nti na Asafo man bɔe.(Afi Akokoro) Cf.1068.
It is because of a piece of the inner part of the roasted yam that ruined the town of Asafo.

829. Ɔde-pa nti na wotɔ afasew a, wotua kaw.
It is under the lure of the good yam that when you buy a water yam you pay for it.

830. Ɔde-pa nyɛ noa-na.
A good yam is not difficult to cook.

831. Ɔde, ose: ne ho adɔ, na wakyene sɛ akyekyere ɔda bonam'.
Dea...s. Nea...2113-2283.
The yam says it is fat, for it becomes hard like the
tortoise in his hole.

832. Ɔdɛfoɔ a ɔso ne botɔ (:n'atwa), wokyi.
The rich man who holds his pocket tightly is hated.

833. Ɔdɛfoɔ, yegyam no, na yenni ne to.
A rich man, we bewail him, but we don't pay him tribute.

834. Ɔdehye bɔ dam a, wɔfrɛ no asabow. Cf.2954.
When a man of noble family is mad, people say he is only
drunk.

835. Ɔdehye din nyera da.
A royal's name is never lost.

836. Ɔdehye, wodi no apata, na wonni no sono.
Nobility should be born as one eats fish (humbly) and not
as one eats elephant meat (proudly boasting about it).

837. Ɔdehye, wonni no yafunum'.
A free man, you are not free in your mother's womb.

838. Ɔdehye nhyehye, na sika na ɛhyehye. Cf.841.
Royalty is not valued, it is money that is valued.

839. Ɔdehye anko a, akoa guan.
If the chief does not (stay to) fight, the slave runs away.

840. Ɔdehye mu nni abofra.
Among royalty no one is a child.

841. Ɔdehye, wonnoa wonni (:Ɔdehye nyɛ biribi): (na) sika
ne asɛm. Cf.838.
Even if you belong to the royal family, if you don't
cook your own food you don't get anything to eat;
money is all that matters.

842. Ɔdehye, wɔmpae.

A man of the royal family does not need to have his name proclaimed.

843. Ɔdehye nsɔre, wosi no mfensa. Cf.847.

A member of the royal family does not rise up for the dead, but we hold funeral rites for him many times.

844. Ɔdehye te (hɔ) a, akoa nni ade.

When a free man is there the slave does not take command or inherit.

845. Ɔdehye wu a, akoa di ade.

When a free man dies, a slave inherits.

846. Ɔdehye nyɛ abofra na wɔabɔ ne din abɔ owu din.

A member of the royal family is not a child that his name can be mentioned in association with death.

847. Ɔdehye ayi, wɔkɔ no (:wɔyɛ no) mfensa. Cf.843.

The funeral rites of a chief or a member of the royal family is celebrated several times.

848. Ɔdehyewa wu ne menewa (:Adehyewa wu n'ano).

A young royal person dies in his throat (mouth).

849. Adehyesɛm, wonni no koko ahaban so.

Nobility is not shown off on a cocoyam leaf.

850. Ɔdekuro ba pɛ n'aho(ro)hora, a onya.

If the son of the chief wants abuse, he'll get it.

851. Ɔdekuro ba mpɛ ntɛm nkofwɛ twi. Cf.1321.

The chief's son doesn't run to look at a leopard.

852. Adekyɛ akatua (:n'ayeyi) ne aseda. Cf.3658

The reward of benevolence is gratitude.

853. Ɔdemanni biara nyɛ abofra.

No person responsible for the affairs of the state is a child.

854. Ɔde-ne-man nsɛe no.

The head of a country does not destroy his own country.

855. Ɔdemerefua kɔda ara ne ahema yi.

It is only at dawn that the (wild) bush-dog goes to sleep.

856. Odemerefua, gyae foɔ haw.
Wild dog, stop your plundering.

857. Odemerefua ho wɔ biribi (:od. wɔ anohyirade) a, anka
ɔnnam nsu ho (:asu mu) mmɔ akɔtɔ. Z.105.
If the bush dog were rich he would not have gone along the
river banks digging for crabs?

858. Dɛn na ekum de-pa na wɔde afasew (:wode nkani) kɔhyɛɛ
nkɔmoa mu yi?
What has killed the yam that you are putting the water
yam in the yam hole.

859. Odenkyɛm da nsu mu, nso ɔnom mframa.
The crocodile lies in the water but it breathes the air.

860. Odenkyɛm werɛɛ sene were-pa dɛ.
The crocodile's skin is more precious than any other
animal's skin.

861. Odesani pɛ: mmoa nni nkɔ.
Man likes animals not to go away.

862. "Di bi, na minni bi" nyɛ aboadi.
"Eat some and let me eat some", is not deception.

863. "Madi bi" nyɛ ɔme.
"I have eaten some", doesn't bring full satisfaction.

864. "Medi, minni", wokyi.
I eat, I don't eat, is taboo.

865. "Medi mprempren" yɛ amono.
I will eat it just now gives you uncooked food.

866. Wudi bi ade a, na wofɛre no. Gr.#276,2.R.263.
If you are supported by someone, you respect him.

867. Wudi bi ade-kan a, wunni ne fwe.
On the day you inherit someone, you don't spend any of
his wealth.

868. Wudi bi de na obi di wo de a, ɛnyɛ yaw.
If you eat someone's food and he eats yours, it isn't
painful.

869. Wudi bi asɛm ma no a, woma ne ntama ka ne 'mati.
If you take care of someone's case for him, you make it
unnecessary for him to remove his cloth from his shoulder.

-73-

870. Wobedi biribi a, wudi no preko.
   If you are going to eat something, you eat it at once.

871. Wobedi biribi a, wo ho tan.
   If you are going to inherit something, you become hated.

872. Wudi ɔbɔ(mɔ)fo ade (:biribi) a, na wofrɛ no Asiemiri.
   If you enjoy the benefits of the hunter's efforts you call
   him Asiemiri.

873. Wudi bone akyir' a, woyɛ bone.
   If you try to get revenge, you commit a crime.

874. Wudi aboro na wobewu a, fwɛ wo yafunu.
   When you thwart the success of someone, look at your
   stomach when you are dying.

875. Wudi brɔfere awia o, anɔpa o, ne nwini mpa mu da.
   Whether you eat pawpaw in the morning or in the afternoon,
   its coolness never goes away.

876. Wudi Buroni ade a, woko aprɛm ano.
   If you are supported by a white man, you will be fighting
   at the mouth of the canon.

877. Wudi ade a, woyɛ kɛse.
   If you come upon inheritance, you become a big man.

878. Wudi fwimfwim-ade a, basabasa bisa wo. Cf. 1204.
   If you receive what is gotten quickly, you are questioned
   in a rough manner.

879. Wudi gua na ɛbɔ wo tɛkrɛma so a, ɛnyɛ yaw.
   If your trading comes to a stand still because of what you
   eat, it is not painful.

880. Wudi hia na wobɔ akora a, wonhu.
   If you are poor and you grow old, it isn't noticed.

881. Wudi woho wɔ woho a, wokyi.
   It is a taboo to masturbate.

882. Wobedi nkesua a, wɔnsew asekan.
   If you are going to eat eggs, you don't sharpen your knife.

883. Wɔbedi koko amono a, anka wodi no afuw so. R.128. Z.180.

If cocoyam was eaten raw then they would have eaten it quickly on the farm.

884. Wudi managua a, wompɔw.

If you trade by sending for articles instead of going yourself, you don't get rich.

885. Wudi mmerehua a, gom', na ɛpɔ wɔ akyiri.

If you inherit the finest part of gold-dust, go slowly for gold nuggets are far away.

886. Wudi nokware da na wudi atoro a, wonhu.

If you always are trustworthy and you tell a lie, it isn't noticed.

887. Wodi panyin anom' asɛm, na wonni ne tirim de.

We say what the elder has said, not what he is thinking.

888. Wudi asɛm na wobu wo bem da a, wɔfrɛ wo hufo.

If you have a case and you are always justified (innocent) you are called a coward.

889. Wudi asɛm na woanhu ano a, na woahu ano ara nen.

If you are solving a problem and don't know how to solve it then that is the solution.

890. Wudi asɛm na wokyea wo aso bu ntɛn, na wudi mu abaguade a, wofe.

If you deliver a false judgement, you have to refund the court fees.

891. Wudi nsew na woanwu a, ɛma kaw.

When you yourself swear by an oath and then don't die, you put yourself in debt.

892. Wudi Asiemiri ade a, woyɛ Asiemiri ayi.

If you inherit Asiemiri (a famous hunter) you perform the funeral customs for Asiemiri.

893. Wudi sono akyi a, wontoa. Cf.256

If you follow the elephant, you never get tangled (in the forest).

894. Wudi sua nsa a, fwɛ wo nsa!

If you are eating a monkey's hand, look carefully at your own hand.

895. Wudi Tanyase kokoram akyir' a, ankra ɔdanya bɛda wiram'.
If you always pursue the goitres in tanyase, the "ɔdonya" plant would get finished.

896. Wudi toro a, woberɛ.
If you tell a lie you become tired.

897. Wudi wo fi asɛm na wunhu di a, efi gua.
When the settlement of any friction in the family becomes difficult, it is because of the arbitrators.

898. Wudi wo agya akyi a, wusua ne nantew.
When you walk behind your father, you learn to walk like him.

899. Wudi wo koma akyi a, woyera.
If you allow your emotions to rule you, you are lost.

900. Wodi wo ni a, di woho ni.
If you are honored, honor yourself.

901. Wudi wo to aboro a, wota wo yam'.
If you injure your buttocks, you fart in your belly.

902. Wodi wo yɔnko ho asɛm a, dakye wodi wo de bi.
If you help your neighbor with his problems, in the future he will help you with yours.

903. Yedi afompata, na yenni afom-akum.
If one injures us, we ask for compensation; we do not ask for a bloody vengeance.

904. 'Yeredi adi bio' na ɛma ɔhɔho serewe.
Eating again and again makes the stranger smile.

905. Yebedi ampesi a, yennyam yɛn anim.   Enni...s. 2305-2308.
If we will eat boiled yams we don't squeeze our face.

906. Wonni a, wɔnnoa.=1029.Gr. # 202,2.
Food which you don't eat, you don't cook.

907. Wunni abɛn (:abentia) na wokɔko a, obi nte. (:wo din nhye.)
If you don't have a horn and you go to war, nobody hears (about you).

908. Wunni biribi a, wonhoahoa woho.
If you don't have anything, you don't boast.

909. Wunni biribi fwɛ mu a, wofwɛ wo nsam'.
If you don't have anything to look into, look into your hands.

910. Wunni adagyew a, wontow ware.
If you don't have time, you don't play "oware."

911. Wunni kasakyerɛfo na obi kasa kyerɛ ne ba a, wofa yɛ wo de.
If you have no adviser and someone is advising his child you take it for yourself.

912. Wunni na na wokɔ obi fi agoru na otu ne mma fo a, wode tu woho bi. Gr.p.176
When you have no mother and go to someone's house to play and the mother is advising her children, you take her advice for yourself..

913. Wunni anɔpa-seawa a, wunnye atweawa ayɛn.
      (:-sɛn)   (:ɔtwea)

If you don't have a small pot, you don't get a small dog to rear.

914. Wunni saman aduan a, womfa wo nsa nto mu.
If you don't eat food given to the dead spirits, you don't put your hand in it.

915. Wunni asia da ho a, wuntia kankan tuo. (Wonni... wontia...)
If you don't have six dollars, you can't even cock the gun.

916. Wunni sika a, wunnye anini ayɛn.
If you don't have money, you don't get male animals to raise.

917. Wonni sika a, anka ɛyɛ nhwea (:wofrɛ no nhwea kwa).
If gold dust were not used in trading it would just be called sand.

918. Wonni sika (ade) a, wɔnyɛ sɛn.
If you have no money you can't become a hearld in the chief's house.

919. Wunni ntrama a,na wuse: nsa nyɛ dɛ.

When you don't have a single cowry shell (for buying palm wine) you say the wine is not good.

920. Wunni tuo a, wonsere ntoa.

If you don't have a gun, you don't ask for the leather belt containing bullets.

921. Wunni wura a, obi kyere wo tɔn di. (Mp.)

If you have no master, anyone at all can catch you and sell you into slavery.

922. Wunni yanom a, womfrɛ yanom. R.140.

If you have no comrades, you do not call out "comrades".

923. "Didi ma yɛnkɔ. (:Woadidi a, soa!)"na ɛmma (:amma) ɔbatani akoa (a)nyɛ kɛse.

Eat and lets go (If you have eaten, take up your load) is why the trader's slave never grows big.

924. Didi-anka-woho ne apiapɔ.

A person who is slow in eating can be seen by his protruding hip bones.

925. Didi-anto-woho ne pim' apɔw.

A person who eats and does not let it settle in his stomach can be seen by his protruding hip bones.

926. Wudidi a, gyae, na wunnim adekyee mu asɛm.

When you eat, reserve some for you don't know what will happen tomorrow.

927. Wudidi bata anim a, gua bɔ wo.

If you spend your profits before they come, you don't flourish.

928. Wodidi bata anim, na wonnidi n'akyi.

If you spend your profits before they come, then you don't have anything to spend when you're finished trading.

929. Wudidi afanu a, na wome. (Akwam' Dako.)

If you eat on both sides of your mouth, you become fully satisfied.

930. Wudidi afanu a, wuwu awusin.

If you eat on both sides of your mouth (seek double advantage), you die a sudden death.

931. Wudidi wo fi na woamme a, na woreko ahua (:afwa).

If you eat at your home and you are not satisfied, you go begging for food.

932. Wudidi me a, na wuregyaw nnuanfin. (Wonnidi mme a, wogyaw nnuanfin?)

If you have eaten your fill, you leave stale food. (If you haven't eaten your fill, do you leave stale food?)

933. Wudidi na woamme a, na woanu woho.

If you eat and are not satisfied, you change your mind.

934. Didi me na eyi brɛbo nansin adi. R.13.

Eating your fill is what causes Brɛbo to reveal his leg that has been cut off (his secrets).

935. Didime nyɛ adepɛ. (Adidi yɛ adepɛ?)

Eating your fill does not make a person rich.

936. Adiama ne adiama ne agoru.

Good fellowship is sharing food with your friends.

937. Adi-amma-me (:Wadi-wamma-me) nti na Adammoro-bɛfo nhina yɛɛ (:ayɛ) abɔ(mɔ)fo.

It is because "he ate and did not give me some" that all the people of Adammorobɛfo became hunters.

938. Adipuw awupuw.

Excessive eating causes a speedy and painful death.

939. Adiasie nyɛ di-na.

A matter settled before-hand is not difficult to be adjusted.

940. Wodɔ adɔde a, wokɔ Mrafi.

If you love oysters, you go to Mrafi.

941. Wodɔ wo yafunu a, wosom srafo.

If you love your belly, you serve warriors.

942. Odɔ sene, biribiara ansen bio. Cf.2945.

Love is the greatest of all virtues.

943. Odɔ nti na nwara fam bo ho.

It is because of love that the sea shell is attached to the rock.

944. Ɔdɔ, wonni no sika.
    Adoa, Ɔdoa...s. Adowa, Ɔdowa.. 984-986.
    Love is not based on wealth.

945. Adobɛ-ɔnwam ne ɔnwam-pa nsɛ.
    The "adobɛ" toucan and the real toucan are not the same.

946. Ɔdodobɛn na egyigye ma ɛbom.
    The reed, (through which the palm-wine drops into the pot)
    catches the palm wine for the pot.

947. Ɔdodobɛn pae mmofra nsam', na ɛmpae mpanyin nsam'.
    The reed breaks in a child's hand but not in an adult's
    hand.

948. Dodow kyɛ sakora-ma.
    A great number of people divide a full calabash of palm
    wine.

949. Dodow kyiri bako asɛm.
    Many people fear the problem one person has.

950. Dodow wu sen asawa dɛ.
    The death of a great number of people at one time is even
    more amazing than the sweetness of the "asawa" berry.

951. Dodow yɛ ade.
    Numbers can achieve anything.

952. Wo dɔfo kyɛ wo yere a, na wakyɛ wo akasakasa.
    If your good friend gives you a wife, he gives you a
    quarrel.

953. Ɔdɔkono bɔ dam a, ɛnennam sɛn mu. R.255.
    If kenkey goes mad, it dances about in the cooking pot.

954. Ɔdɔkono (a) ofura tam, na wɔyɛ no dɛn? (:wɔmfa nyɛ fwe;)
    na(anka) abodo a ɔda adagyaw! (Ɔhenewa).
    Even the kenkey that wears a native cloth is not noticed,
    so how much more the bread that is lying there naked!

955. Dɔkonkankyeɛ, wode dɛ yɔ a, mede wo bu mewes.
    "Dɔkonkankyeɛ" (bread made of plantain) if it is made
    delicious, I break and eat it.

-80-

956. Dɔm gu a, wɔnhyɛn no abɛn.
When an army suffers defeat a horn is not blown.

957. Dɔm nnui a, wɔnkan atɔfo.
Those killed in war are not counted before the army has been defeated.

958. Dɔm, wɔko no abooduru, na wɔnko no ahi-dodow.
Any army is driven back by courage and not by many insults.

959. Dɔm kum ano-sese-ade, na dɔm nkum dɔmmarima.
The army kills those who shout out challenges and insults, but it spares the brave men.

960. Dɔm nnim dɔm akyi.
The army does not know what is at it's rear.

961. Wodom aberewa a, ohuro wo.
If you do a favor to an old woman she mocks you.

962. Ɔdomfo nan, wɔtwe no nya.   Cf.719.
A gracious person's leg is pulled gently.

963. Ɔdomankama bɔɔ adefoɔ na ɔbɔɔ ahiafoɔ.
God created the rich and the poor.

964. Ɔdomankama bɔɔ owuo na owuo kum no.
God created death but death killed him.

965. Ɔdomankama bɔɔ owu ansa-na ɔbɔɔ akom.
God created death before he created the fetish dance.

966. Ɔdomankama na ɔma owuo di akane.
It is God who made death come first.

967. Ɔdomankama kowui no, ɔde n'akyi gyaw agyina.
When the creator went to his death he left the world to the care of man.

968. Ɔdomankama owuo suro tutu a, ankra ɔbɛfa onipa?
If Creator Death were afraid of pulling up, would he be taking man?

969. Ɔdɔmpiafo na ɔma ɛdɔm gu.
The commander of an army causes the enemy to be defeated.

970. Odompo, wunim asu-nu a, konu po!
Bush dog, if you know how to fish go and fish from the sea.

971. Odompo se: wɔbɛrɛ ansa-na wodidi. Cf.1870.
The bush dog says: "you have to be tired before you eat."

972. Odompo-tiri yɛ nam: yentwa were nto so.
The bush dog's head is meat: "we don't eat it's skin in addition."

973. Odondonwa ne yɔnko ne kwadu?
Is the "odondonwa" plant really the friend of the banana?

974. Ɔdɔnkɔ de aguan na ɛbɔ neho asu.
The slave in running away holds a feast.

975. Ɔdɔnkɔ nya ade a, ɔbɔ dam. R.125 (Akokɔba Toku Asiare.)
If a slave become rich, he goes crazy.

976. Nnɔnkɔfo banu fwɛ nantwi a, ɔkɔm kum no.
If two slaves look after a cow, it dies of starvation.

977. Donkore hene pɛ neho ano; onnya a, obisa ne man?
If the chief of Donkore can not afford something for himself does he beg from the ordinary people.

978. Odonno: menyɛ dɛn? wɔayere me to, wɔayere m'ano.
Ɔdorobɛn...s. Ɔdodobɛn...

The odonno (small drum) says: "What will I do? You stretch my bottom, you stretch my mouth."

979. Dɔteɛ ka wo nantin a, ɛka wo to.
If mud clings to your heels, it sticks to your buttocks.

980. Dote a wompɛ sɛ ɛka to no, ɛka wo nantin a, na adu to.
The mud which you don't want to touch your buttocks clings to your heels and thus touches your buttocks.

981. Ɔdotɔ, hama-koro mmua.

One creeper does not make a thicket.

982. Oduro (Kɔkɔ) se (=agya) Korantene se: Aboadeɛ, na ɔte sɛ Ofosu Apea?

Oduru's father Korantene says: "A thank-offering, is it like Ofosu Apea?"

983. Dow bi di (nko) a, asamampɔw hu! (:as. kora ana?)

Clear any land for your farm use does not bother the cemetery.

984. Adowa, ɔde ne man te-ase, na kurotwiamansa(:ɔsebɔ) abɔ ntoa rekɔko.

If even the antelope who rules the state is resting peacefully, why should the leopard take up arms to go to war in defense of the state?

985. Adowa nya owu a, bisa nsɛmma.

If the antelope has died ask the dry fibres of the "adobɛ" plant.

986. Ɔdowa nsen, nwansana nsen, na sakwarama resa.

Neither the bee nor the fly goes away, but the calabash full of palm wine is getting finished.

987. Adu nea wode koko bɛkɔ atwe (:akyɛ?) a, anka nkamfo bedi mu bi.

If you are going to let the plantain ripen, the "nkamfo" yam is included.

988. Wudu ntɛm a, wogu wo so abɛ.

If you arrive on time, they give you palm nut soup.

989. Wonnuu ko so a, wɔntran.

If you haven't reached the battlefield, you don't discharge many guns at once.

990. Wunnuu nea wuguare awowa mu na wuguare mu a, wuyi ton.

If you have not come to the stage of taking your bath in a well-designed bucket and you attempt to, you hit the bucket and hear it's clanging sound.

991. Dua (a ɛ)bata bo yɛ twa-na. R.69.Gɯ.p.154. Z.34.

The tree which is near a stone is difficult to cut down.

992. Dua a ɛbɛn (ne yɔnko) na etwiw. Cf.1015.
If a tree is near another tree, they rub against each other.

993. Dua a ɛbɛpo (:d. bɛpo a, e)nnim asusow.
A tree which drops it's leaves does not know the first
great rainy season (April to July).

994. Dua a ɛbɛwɔ wo ani no,wobu so, na wonsen ano. R.224.
The branch of the tree which will pierce your eye is
broken off, it is not sharpened.

995. Dua a aboa (no) pɛ na owu da ase.
The animal dies under the tree it likes best.

996. Dua a ananse adi awu, ntikuma nkɔtra ase ntɔ nkom. R.118.
Ananse's son, Ntikuma, does not go and sleep under the
tree which his father was killed.

997. Dua a esi nsu so (na ɛ)mpo ntɛm..
The tree which grows near a river does not readily lose
it's leaves.

998. Dua a ɛtеɛ gyina dua kontonkye so.
A tree which is straight supports the crooked tree.

999. Dua a ɛto nam na ano hyew. Gr. #165,5 Z.96.
It is the stick that the meat is roasted on that gets
its end burned.

1000. Dua a awu na aporɔw no, yentwitwa mfa mma ofie mmɛsɔ.
A tree which has died and is rotten is not cut up and
brought home for firewood.

1001. Dua a ɛyɛ den nkyɛ afuw so.=1246.
The tree which is hard does not remain for a long time
on the farm.

1002. Dua a ɛyɛ den na ebu.
A tree which is hard is cut down.

1003. Dua a ɛyɛ den na womantam mu aboa no. (:nantwi.)
An animal is always tied to a strong tree.

1004. Dua biara nsow nnya nfwiren da. Gr.#237c.
No tree ever bears fruit without first having flowers.

1005. Dua biako (:koro) gye mframa a, ebu. R.88.
If one tree faces the storm alone it gets knocked down.

1006. Dua biako nyɛ kwae.
One tree does not make a forest.

1007. Dua (bu) bɔ dua so a, na edu nkwa-ase.
One tree is next to the other til the end of the forest.

1008. Dua bɔ dua so ansa-na ɛpae du nkoa.
A tree always hits another tree before it splits into pieces.

1009. Dua bu bɔ ɔkwaku a, (ɛnyɛ ɔno(ankasa) na ohum', na) obi na ohuw ma no. (Aduobe.)
If a tree hits the monkey it is not he who groans, but someone else groans for him.

1010. Dua da bon mu a, ɛbra wo, na wo nsa da mu a, ɛmmra wo.
If a stick lies in a hole, it hinders you, but if your hand lies in the hole, it does not hinder you.

1011. Dua mfa mfe adusa nkyea, na wɔmfa afe koro ntee no.
A tree that has grown bent for thirty years cannot be straightened in one year.

1012. Dua kɛse bu a, brofere na esi ananmu.
When any great tree falls down, the pawpaw tree grows in it's place.

1013. Dua kɛse bu a, ne mma (:n'aba) bubu wɔ ne ho kwa.
When a big tree is cut down its branches are shaking for nothing.

1014. Dua kontonkye na ɛma yehu dwumfo. R.159.
The crooked board lets us see who is the real carpenter.

1015. Dua ne dua mmɛn a, entwiw. Cf.992.
If two trees stand apart they do not rub against each other.

1016. Dua si akura a, ne ntini wɔ fie. (Ɔhene.)
If a tree stands in a village it's roots are in the house.

1017. Dua si pampa so a, ɛnkyɛ tenten-yɛ.
If a tree grows on a hill, it soon becomes tall.

1018. Dua-so wɔkɔ no tipɛn (so).
People go to the toilet with others their same age.

1019. Dua osupono nyɛ biribi a, ɛyɛ agyensuo.
If a gutter made from the bark of a tree is nothing, at
least it is a gutter for catching water.

1020. Dua tan wo a, na ebu bɔ wo.
When a tree hates you, it falls on you.

1021. Nnua nhina yɛ aduru; na wunnim a, na wuse: ɛyɛ bone.
All plants are medicinal, but if you don't know you say
some are useless.

1022. Adua bere gow ansa-na ɛtɔ.
Ripe fruit becomes soft before it falls.

1023. Wudua aburo na woamma epo a, ɔsa.
If you plant corn and don't give some to the lizard, he
digs some up.

1024. Wudua aburow ne abra a, abra na efi (kan).
If you plant corn and falsehood, falsehood comes up
first.

1025. Wudua nkontompo a, wutu abra.
If you sow falsehood, you reap deceit.

1026. Oduahyɛn se: nea ɛwɔ m'afonom' nyɛ me dea; nea akɔ
me yam' na ɛyɛ me dea.
The white tailed monkey says: "what is in my cheeks
is not mine, but what has gone into my belly is my own."

1027. Aduam-mone nkwati kɔm nkum nipa.
Poor food does not kill as many people as starvation.

1028. Aduan ba na wotɛw brɔde a, tɛw kwadu bi: na wunnim
nea, ɔkɔm ba a, ebegye wo.
If there are plants and you plant some plantain, plant
some bananas also for you don't know which one will
save you in times of famine.

1029. Aduan bi a wonni no, wɔnnoa. R.170. Cf.906 Z.212.
Food which you don't eat, you don't cook.

1030. Aduan bi a wunhuu bi da wɔ wo na ne wo agya muka so no,
na nea wukyi nen. (... da a wo na... anka so da no...).
Some food, the like of which you have never seen on your
mother's or your father's fire place, you don't like.

1031. Aduan bi a ɛkwati ɔwaduru nyɛ ɔdɛ.
(Aduan biara kwati w. a, ɛnyɛ dɛ).
Whatever food that is made without the use of the mortar
is not sweet.

1032. Aduan bi nye a, wodi yi-fi-hɔ.
If a certain food is not good you say, "take it away."

1033. Aduan tra tɛkrɛma a, na enni bo.
If the food passes by the tongue without touching it,
it has no value.

1034. Aduan yɛ dɛ a, tɛkrɛma na ehu.
If the food is delicious the tongue knows.

1035. Aduane panyin ne aburo.
The chief among foods is corn.

1036. Aduanfwɛm' nti na Oburoni tu kɔ Aburokyiri. R.244.
Because of obtrusive curiousity of Africans the white man
went back to Europe.

1037. Due due mu wɔ due.
Among many sympathizers only a few are sincere.

1038. Due (due) nkum (:nsa) kuru.
Sympathy doesn't cure a sore.

1039. Dufɔkye berɛfo, wotra a, wo to afɔw; wokwati a, woayera.
The poor old rotten leg, if you sit on it, your seat
gets wet, if you refuse to sit on it, you are lost.

1040. Dufɔkye da nsu ase mfrihyia apem a, ɛnnan dɛnkyɛm da.
If a log lies on the bottom of the river for a thousand years
it never changes into a crocodile.

1041. Dufɔkye rebɛdan dɛnkyɛm, na yɛaye no dɛn?
If a log would change into a crocodile, what would we do?

1042. Odum nnya ntɔe no, na wonɔw wɔ ne dabere.
If the Odum tree has not been felled you don't weed in
it's resting place.

1043. Dunsin Kwati: me-ne biribi te.
Tree stump Kwati: "I and something are still alive."

1044. Aduru a efi kɔmfo nsam' nhina yɛ aduru-pa.
All the medicines that come from the fetish priest are
good ones.

1045. Oduruyɛfo nnom aduru mma ɔyarefo. Cf.286.Z.6.
The doctor can't drink the medicine for the patient.

1046. Adusɛe Akyakyawa se: obi ntumi nsere m'akya-kyawa sɛ
Ɔsɛe.
Adusɛe Akyakyawa says: No nne can laugh at my hunchback
as Ɔsɛe does.

1047. Dutan tutu a, ne ho nhama twetwe.
When a large tree is uprooted the vines growing on it
get stretched.

1048. Adutwes nim twe a, ɔtwe kwaem'na ɔntwe ssrɛso.
Odwane...s.1227-1233.
If the teeter totter knows how to teeter, it teeters in
the bush not in the grassland.

1049. Odwantene wɔ nsa a, anka odidi nnipa nsam'?
If the sheep had hands, would he eat from the hands of
people?

1050. Adwe, wɔwe no nkoro-nkoro.
You eat palm kernel nuts one at a time.

1051. Odwen, wɔfa no anoɔhare.
A lost article which is found is taken by him who claims
it first.

1052. Adwene da nsum, nso odidi kokoso.
The mudfish lives in the river but it eats on the river
bank.

1053. Adwene dabere bɛn ne ogya-so (:muka-so)?
       Which mudfish's sleeping place is on the fire?

1054. Adwene nko nnɔ.
       The mudfish alone does not get fat.

1055. Adwene ntɔ nsum' (:asuom') Kwasida, na wɔnfwew nyi no
       Dwoda (:na Dweada wɔafwe ayi no).
       The mudfish doesn't jump into the water on Sunday, then
       on Monday is looked for in order to be caught.

1056. Adwene te sɛ mmasu.
       An idea is like running water.

1057. Odwene redwene na odwenwenawa redwene.
       The wise man is planning and the thoughtful man is also
       planning.

1058. Odwendwenekoma a ɔnam na n'ano regu nsuo; afei wokose
       no sɛ: hyira wo ano?
       There is always sap dripping from the "Odwendwenekoma"
       tree and then do you go and tell it to bless you?

1059. Odwennini kɔ n'akyi ansa-na wayɛ tɔ.
       The ram goes backwards before it butts something.

1060. Odwennini yɛ asisi a, efi ne koma. (:efiri ne konona,
       emfiri ne mmɛn; ɔde firi ne konona na ɔnne mfiri ne
       tirim.)
       If a ram is brave, its courage comes from its heart,
       (its courage is from its heart not from its horns; its
       courage is from its heart and not from its head).

1061. Wodwensɔ fako a, na efi ahuru.
       If you urinate in one place, it produces foam.

1062. Dwetiri a afwete yɛ fwefwɛ-na.
       Capital for trading which is squandered is hard to find again

1063. Wudwo wo ani kum tɛtea a, wuhu ne nsono.
       If you skin the tiny ant slowly you can see its intestines.

1064. "Ennwo, ennwo!" dwo obi anom'. Cf.2513.
       "It is not cool! it is not cool!" then it cools down in
       someone else's mouth.

1065. Wunnwo a, wudwo obi san mu.

If it has not cooled off, it cools off in someone else's pot.

1066. Woannwo annwo a, wodwo wo.

If it has not been tamed, you keep yourself calm.

1067. Wodwow bayerɛ na ammo a, nnunu no.=57.1290.

If you are taking out the yam with a digging iron and it is not fully grown don't blame it.

1068. Dwokorɔw nti na (ɛmaa) Abotakyi kurow bɔe (:Adome kurow hyewe). Cf.828.

It was a piece of roasted yam that ruined the town of Abotakyi.

1069. Edwom nkɔree a, wonsua ne nne.

If the song doesn't sound well, you don't imitate its tune.

1070. Adwumfo di ahomasin.

The craftsman is entitled to a piece of leather.

1071. "Fa ha hyia me!" (:Fa ha na memfa ha na yenkohyia ha nkɔ") nyɛ akwankɔ.

Pass here and let me pass there and let us go and meet there does not go is not a journey . (Go and meet me there is not a good way to travel with a friend.)

1072. Fa asɛm kyɛ!

Forgive the offense!

1073. "Fa tom'! fa tom'" na ɛyɛ (:nhina yɛ) adesoa. R.176.

Add it! add it! this makes a heavy load.

1074. "Fa twa wo ani so" ne "fa to wo ani so" nhina yɛ biako.

"Turn your eyes on it," and "put your eyes on it" are both the same.

1075. "Fa woho kodi" nyɛ yaw.

"Become self-dependent" is not an insult.

1076. Mfa abɔnten, mfa mfikyiri, nso yɛ-ne wo rensen kurom' ha, ase ne dɛn? Cf.2110.

Don't pass through the main streets and don't pass through the back streets, and we shall not stay in this town with you, what does this mean?

1077. Wofa abarima kwanmu (:abarimakwan mu) a, wo sekan yera.
If you take a dangerous course you may lose your knife..

1078. Wofa aboa no (:ɔsebɔ) yɔnko (:adamfo) a, wunsuro ham'
(bio).
If you befriend an animal (leopard), you don't fear
anything in the forest.

1079. Wofa nwansana ho abufuw a, wobore wo kurum'. Z.147.
If you get impatient with the housefly you hurt your sore.

1080. Wofa tope na woanwe a, efi nea wofaa no.
If you take a large snail and don't eat it, it is because
of where you have taken it from. (latrine).

1081. Wokɔfa obi atopɛ kɔyɛ adwuma a, wohohoro so (:ho)
koto no ho (:nea ɛda). R.193.
If you take someone's hoe (with a large blade) to do
some weeding you wash it off and put it in its place.

1082. Womfa obi asɛm ho biribi a, wofa ntɔdii.
If you don't help another person with his problems, you
create trouble for yourself.

1083. Womfa ade anum nto aduonum ho.
You can't compare five things with fifty.

1084. Womfa akara ntow sono.
A wax bullet is not used to shoot an elephant.

1085. Womfa ano-kurokuro nkɔ Apɛsɛ.
You don't take an empty boast to Apɛsɛ.

1086. Womfa ɔnopɔn-hunu na ɛkɔ Pɛsɛ.
We don't take and empty boast to Pɛse.

1087. Womfa "woanya me nyɛɛ!" nyɛ ɔman.
We don't build a nation with an "I don't care" person.

1088. Woamfa Memereda ansra ɔkwan a, wode Kwasida guan.
If you don't use Saturday to keep watch on the road, you
will use Sunday to run away.

1089. Afammoa, wompon no (:wompam no).
The "afammoa" animal (that clings to you), you really
pull him off by force.

1090. Afana, ɔkɔɔ anyan, wannya bi amma a, wɔfrɛ no huhuni.
The female slave goes for fire wood, and if she doesn't
bring some back, she is called worthless.

1091. Ɛfanim Botwe Nyamma a ne ba ye na osua (na ɛmfanim
Botwe kora).
Botwe Nyamma whose child is good but is small is greater
than Botwe's fellow-wife.

1092. Fante ayɛ Akamfoɔ a, ɛnyɛ 'yɛnne Akompifoɔ.
If a Fante is an Akan, it is not that we are Afutus.

1093. Ɔfarebae (:Ɔfrabae), wonyi no agoru mu.
Someone who brought the dance can not be excluded.

1094. Wo afase ammɔ a, na efi wo asase.
If your yam doesn't grow big, it is due to the soil.

1095. Mfaso nti na wɔyam awi (:wɔtɔ ako).
It is because of profit that we grind corn.

1096. Mfatoho na ɛde mpoatwa ba.
Comparison brings about challenges.

1097. Ɔfatwafo, ɛbɛka wo nko! R.253.
Betrayer, you will be left all alone.

1098. Ɛfe akyi nni abofono.
After vomiting there is no nausea.

1099. Fe fe (fee) wɔ atwewa yam' a, abofono mpa ne mu.
If the desire to vomit is in the stomach of a young
antelope, the nausea doesn't go away.

1100. Ɔfeam de berɛberɛ na otwa ɔkwan mu.
The shrew (stinking mouse) crosses the road quietly
and with caution.

1101. Wofefe purow a, wudi apetebi. .
If you try to examine the meat of a squirrel you may find
out that it is an "apetebi".

1102. Wofefe asɛm mu a, wuhu fefe.
If you look deeply into a case, you discover partiality.

1103. Mfɛfɛwade, wode skia na ɛyɛ.
Pomp and luxury are gotten with money.

1104. Wo mfɛfo som asra na woansom bi a, ɛte sɛ so awerɛw awu.
When your neighbours take snuff and you don't take some it means your finger nails are dead.

1105. Wo mfɛfo tan wo a, wofrɛ wo saara bi.
If your mates hate you, they call you any kind of name.

1106. Afei ne ampa! (See 1718.)
What is present is sure!

1107. Fɛn fɛn ne pen pen nhina wie mpoano.
Leaps and bounds and measured paces all end at the seashore.

1108. Ɔfene hyia a, wonni bio.
When a joke is understood, it isn't told again anymore.

1109. Fenni da me so, Aberekwasi da me so, ade bɛkye Kwasida a, na matwa ntama mama me kora ba. R. 214.
If I have to get a loan to pay for the expensive cere-monial rites at the annual festival and than when Sunday comes should I buy a cloth for the child of my fellow wife?

1110. Ɔfere da fako a, ɛbere.
If cucumber or pumpkin lie in one place for a long time they ripen.

1111. Ɔfere nti na odammanin (:ahenkwa) ti bɔ akyene ho.
It is because of shyness that the skull of a great warrior is fastened to the drum.

1112. Ɔfɛre nti na agya Ananse de otwe-kyɛw hyɛ adow.
It is because of shyness that father Ananse wears an antelope's skin hat when he goes to ask people to help him in weeding his farm.

1113. Wofɛre a, wofɔn.
If you are shy, you become thin.

1114. Wofɛre nipa bi a, ɛte sɛ wusuro no.
If you are shy of someone, it is like you fear him.

1115. Wofɛre wo afana a, wudi nnuanfin.

If you are shy to correct your slave girl, you will
eat stale food.

1116. Wofɛre wo ase a, wo yere nhu wo aware (:ɔkɔm de wo).

If you are too shy of your mother-in-law, your wife does
not treat you well.

1117. Wofɛre wo yɔnko ba a, ɔtetew wo kyɛw.

If you are shy to correct your neighbor's child, he will
tear your hat to pieces.

1118. Wo fɛrefo fɛre a, woafɛre. Cf. 2159.

If the person you respect, respects, you also respect.

1119. Wo fɛrefo hu wo ntɛbɔe mu a, ogyae wo fɛre.

If the person you respect sees your behaviour, he stops
respecting you.

1120. Ofi kata asɛm so. Cf. 40. 1136. Ofie... s. 1128-1132.

The home covers over domestic problems.

1121. Wo fi ne wo fi.

Your house is your own house.

1122. Wufi fie bobɔ nkuku na wode fi adi a, wonkyi.

If one begins breaking the pots at home, he should not
be blamed them when he goes elswhere.

1123. Wofi ahamano na ɛsan.

The knot is untied from the end of the rope.

1124. Wufi Nsaba gua so a, wuse: wotɔɔ onipa taku, nso
wo nko na wonam.

If you are coming from Nsaba Market and you say: "they
sold a slave for 5 pesewas, but you alone are coming."

1125. Afiafi-anoma (atrannɔ) na ogyigye samankrofi na ɔteasefo
nyaa aguantware.

The "afiafi" bird provokes ghost of a person dead for a
long time and the person living has to do the killing of
a sheep for a sacrifice.

1126. Afiase yɛ fɛ sɛ dɛn ara a, ɛnyɛ ahotɔ na wode tra hɔ.

No matter how beautiful a prison is, you are not at
peace staying there.

1127. Fida anto Ata a, onnuare abam.

Since Ata did not live til Friday, his birthday, he could
not celebrate the washing ceremony for twins.

1128. Ofie mmosea, woka woho a, na emia wo.

If you step on the gravels around your home, they
hurt you.

1129. Ofie dwo a, na ha mu dwo.

If the town is at peace then it is also peace in the
forest.

1130. Ofie yɛ yiye a, na ahamu reyɛ yiye.
Ofie yɛ yiye ansa-na wuram' (:ham') yɛ yiye.

If things are well at home, then all is well in the
forest.

1131. Ofiedentuo (:Ofi a ada ntuw), ɛfanim-nipa bone. Z. 89.

A house containing a bad man is better than an empty house.

1132. Ofiepanyin ne wekɔ.

The old pot containing red clay and chaff to rub the
floor of native houses is the servant.

1133. Afikyi-borɔde, wonte no mmɔtɔ.

The plantain planted behind the house is not cut down
when it is still green.

1134. Yefiri tete na yɛfrɛ Twumasi Ankra.

The name Twumasi Ankra was handed down by our ancestors.

1135. Afiri huan a, ɛkɔ n'akyi.

If the trap is set off, it springs back.

1136. Afisɛm nyɛ atamagow na woasi ahata gua so. Gr. p. 160.

A family matter is not like a dirty rag which is washed
and spread out to dry in a public place.

1137. Wufiti kurotia a wodɔ wo; di nnansa fwɛ!

When you arrive in a village they love you, but after
three days watch how they treat you!

1138. Ɔfom ba a, na mpata reba.

If an offence comes, the pacification also comes.

1139. Wofom dako a, wonnu agoru.

If you make a mistake in the beginning, you can't lead
the dance.

1140. Aforeɛ nyɛ biribi a, ɛyɛ asafohenneɛ.

If a sash with a bell in the middle of it is nothing, it
is the decoration of a war chief.

1141. Ofori nkoa Akuapem: wɔnsom bi, wɔnnan bi, nanso wɔnne
wɔnho.

The subjects of Ofori of Akuapem: they are subject to
no one, they depend on no one, but they are not independent.

1142. Woforo a, na wopia wo to.

If you climb they give you a push from behind.

1143. Maforo dotɔ minsuro akrokraw.

I climb the vines on trees and I don't fear the water
dripping from the trees.

1144. Wo (bɛ) foro dua na wunya obi pia wo to a, wuse: mempɛ!
ana?

If you climb a tree and you get someone to push you from
behind, do you say, "I don't want any help?"

1145. Wɔbɛforo dua a, wofi n'ase na womfi soro.

If anyone is going to climb a tree he starts from the
bottom, not from the top.

1146. Mfɔte pam ansa-na wɔayɛ ya.

The termites unite in great numbers in time of danger
before they make a noise and scatter.

1147. Mfɔte te sɛ dwie, nanso ɔ-ne no nsɛ.

The termites are like lice, but they are not really the
same.

1148. Mfɔte we ade nhina, na wɔnwe tumpan.

The termites eat everything but they can't eat a bottle.

1149. Mfɔte a wuwu a wobedi wo nam no, na wote ho a, wɔwe
wo tam.

Mfɔte, wuwu a, wɔbɛwe wo; na wote-ase a, wɔwe wo dan.

The termites that will eat your flesh when you die, eat
your native cloth (house) when you are alive.

1150. Foto mu ne anim nsɛ.
Ɔfrabae s. Ɔfarebae. 1093.

The inside of a bag is not the same as the outside.

1151. Mframa fa ɔbo na apakyi-ti, da woho so!

The wind can blow a stone away, so, cover of a broad
calabash, take care!

1152. Mframa mmae a, na fwereɛ mu yɛ krana. .

It is before the wind comes that the elephant grass is
motionless.

1153. Frampon se: ɔmfa atoro ho biribi; nanso wobɔ atumpan
so a, wose Frampon dammirifa.

Frampong says he doesn't tell lies about anything, but
if you blow on a bottle, you say,"Frampong, have my
sympathy."

1154. Wofrɛ ɔba-bone a, na onim nea n'ani da.

If you call a bad child, he knows what he has set his
eyes on.

1155. Wofrɛ obi na wannye so a, na ɛwɔ nea wahu.

If you call someone and he doesn't respond, it is because
of what he has seen.

1156. Afɛɛduan na ɛyɛ dɛ.

A meal to which one is invited is a delicious meal.

1157. Afu si wo akyi a, na wohu wo 'mobɔ; na esi wo koko a, na
woara na woyeree wo bo gyei..

If there is a hump on your back, we pity you; and if it
is on your chest, you are happy to have it.

1158. Wufua bebrebe ne bobo a, wuse: mirehu biribi (:amanne)?

If you hold bustle and noisy crying you say, "am I suffering?"

1159. Wufua Yane heneba a, wuse: mepɛ Kramo-hene madi?

If you carry the son of the chief of Yane do you say: "I
want to be the chief of the Mohammedans?"

1160. Wofua wo a, wo wer' afi nkeka.'

When someone grabs a hold of you, you even forget to bite.

1161. Fufu nni ho nti na yedi asɛ ada.

Because there is no fufu we eat beans.

1162. Fufu tum tum kɔ akyiri.

The sound of pounding "fufu", tum-tum, carries far.

1163. Efunu a ebesi nnim sudɛw.

The corpse which is coming to knock against his murderer
isn't concerned about cries of sorrow.

1164. Efunu nya ɔsoafo a, osi.

If the corpse has carriers, it points out the murderer.

1165. Efunu nya ɔsoafo a, (na) ɔfwefwɛ n'agya kurom' (kwan).

If the coffin has carriers it looks for its father's village.

1166. Furefure fi ɛsɔ yam'.

The baby of a shark comes from belly of the shark.

1167. Ofuruntum nya owu a, efi matatwene Cf. 2022.

If the large rubber tree dies it is because of the strong vines growing on it.

1168. Mfutumakokonini ne kotɔ anom nsa aboro safo.

The small insect that always goes backwards and the crab drink wine beating the palm wine seller.

1169. Mfutumakokonini ne kotɔ nserew afe-koro (so).

The small insect that always goes backwards and the crab are not happy in the same year. (depending on the type of weather).

1170. Mfutumakokonini pɛ dabere nti na ɔkɔfaa ɔsebɔ agoru.

Because the small insect that always go backwards wants a place to sleep he even goes to play with the leopard.

1171. Afutu-afutu Dɛnkyɛmmerefunu: yɛn nhina afuru biako, nso yekita aboa a, yɛperepere no.

The two headed crocodiles, they have one stomach, but if they catch an animal each one is struggling to get it for himself.

1172.. Futumerefu (:Afuntumereku, Pentemerefu) ne Dɛnkyɛmmerefu (ti yɛ abien na wɔn yafunu yɛ biako) se: ma kakra ntwiw (mfa) wo menewam' na kakra ntwiw (:ebi mfa) me de mu, na ne nhina nkohyia yafun-korom'.

The two headed crocodiles-they have two heads and one belly-say to one another: "let a piece of meat go down your throat, and a piece of meat go down my throat, and they will both meet in one stomach."

1173. Ofuturufuturu dɔm osua, na osua dɔm no.

The "ofuturufuturu" animal makes an alliance with the monkey and the monkey makes an alliance with it.

1174. Afuw mu nni biribi a, ɛwɔ kranana.

If a farm has nothing else in it, at least it has quietness.

1175. Afuw mu panyin ne ahyeɛ.

The elder of the farm are the boundaries.

-98-

1176. Afuw te sɛ adesoa: wɔn(fwe)fwɛ mu nhu no (:mu) dakoro.
       Cf. 2001.
       A farm is like a head load; you don't look into it and
       see all its contents immediately.

1177. Mfuwa nyɛ ba, kwae na ɔyɛ ba.
       If an old farm doesn't come the bush comes.

1178. "Fwɛ ɔbere! fwɛ ɔbere!" a, wɔfwɛ nanka?
       If they are shouting, "look at the female! look at the
       female!" do you look whether they mean a female viper?

1179. "Fwɛ di ma me" nti na ani sɔ panyin.
       "Look after this for me", is why one respects an elder.

1180. "Fwɛ wo ha! fwɛ wo ha!" nyɛ agoru.
       "Look at this part of your body", is not good fellowship.

1181. "Fwɛ woho! fwɛ woho"nyɛ amanyɔ (:amammu).
       Looking for your own interest is not helpful to the
       nation.

1182. Nfwɛ me sɛ karawa refwɛ asibe.
       Don't look at me as the "karawa" monkey is looking at
       the "asibe" monkey.

1183. Wɔfwɛ Obiri (:obi) anim na wɔnom nsasin. Cf..262. 696.
       To please Obiri, one drink a little palm wine from the
       bottom of the calabash.

1184. Wofwɛ onipa anim na esen dua-onipa.
       You look at a man's face, but it hangs on his body.

1185. Wofwɛ onipa anim na wosoa no akyene.
       If you respect someone, you let him carry the drum at
       a festival.

1186. Wofwɛ wo samarafo sɛn mu a, wubua da.
       If you look into the pot of one who sells palm wine,
       you will fast.

1187. Monfwɛ Saw, na monnfwɛ kyɛm.
       You look for Saw, but you don't look for a leopard.

1188. Afwɛ-wo-da(bi)-ba na wɔfwɛ no.
       The one who always looks after you is your real benefactor.

1189. Wofwe apapafwekwa (:aberante) yere a, woko tɔ'ɔwa perennu.

If you beat the wife of a young man you will fight twice.

1190. Wɔfwe wo atɔkwa ase na obi amfi wo akyi a, wokyi (:na woafɛre).

If you are going to beat your slave's father-in-law and no one comes to help you, you fear doing it.

1191. Ɔfweam na ɛma asu ho yɛ hu.

It is the current that makes the river dangerous.

1192. Mefwefwɛ Ɔsaben makra no, na ɛnte sɛ nankasa nam.

I am looking for Ɔsaben to say good bye to him, it is not good that he alone should walk.

1193. Wofwefwɛ (:Wopɛ) abɔfo adi a, na wokeka.

If you are looking for the carcass to eat then you cut it up and boil it with salt, pepper and tomatoes.

1194. Wɔfwefwɛ mma akyekye kurow na wonnya a, wonkum apemfo.

If you are looking for people to build a town and don't get enough, you don't kill the pregnant women.

1195. Wɔnfwefwɛ nea wɔ-ne sɛ ansa-na wɔne no agoru.

They don't look for that which they and he are similar in, before they and he play.

1196. Wofwefwɛ asɛm mu a, wuhu fwefwɛ.

If you examine a case carefully you will see differences.

1197. Wofwefwe asɛm ani mma na wudi mu ade a, wɔberɛ.

If you beat your children for something and you yourself do it, you become tired.

1198. Ɛfwene nya a, na aniwa anya. = 2448. R. 134. Afwenhema s. Anwhenhema 2576.

If the nose finds something, the eye also finds it.

1199. Fwennɔre yɛ aduan a, anka abofra rempene kɔm da.

If snot (mucus) were food, a child would never be hungry.

1200. Fwento mmɔ kyim mu kwa. Afwentu yɛ ahohora.

A noseless person is a disgrace. To cut off someone's nose is a great disgrace.

1201. Ofwerem de bɛrɛbɛrɛbɛrɛ (:bɛtɛ) na ɛde twa kwan mu.
The creeper with large thorns slowly crosses the path.

1202. Ofweremu yɛ bi ma 'yɛsere, ɔyɛ bi ma 'yesu.
The creeper with large thorns does something to make us
laugh and it also does something to make us cry.

1203. Fwie gum' ne dan gum' nhina yɛ bako.
Pouring out and drawing out all amount to the same.

1204. Fwimfwim ade kɔ sorɔwsorɔw.
What you gain quickly goes quickly.

1205. Ofwini Agyawa nim sɛ ɔbɛwo ba a, ankrana wansɛe n'adeɛ.
If Ofwini Agyawa knew she would give birth to a child,
she would not have allowed the ants to spoil her wealth.

1206. Ofwirema na ɛde dwom ba.
Whistling causes people to sing.

1207. Agohia sen hia pa.
Having no one to play with is worse than poverty.

1208. Agohina nsen bɛsan.
A pot of palm oil is not greater than a plantation of
palm trees.

1209. Ogohyɛease nyɛ ɔto.
A warning of one's intentions by means of a play does
not cause dissension.

1210. Ogom wɔ hɔ, ɛsen ntɛm.
Slowness is sometimes more advantageous than speed.

1211. Agoru a ɛreba wo na ne wo agya abobow-ano no, wompɛ
ntɛm nkɔfwɛ.
You do not hurriedly go to see the play which is coming
to your mother's and father's house.

1212. Agoru-fɛw nko, na ntam nko. (Oheneba Bampo).
A beautiful play and an oath are not the same.

1213. Agoru-fɛw nti na wotɔ abamma, na ɛnyɛ asefwe ntia.
It is because of the beautiful dancing that they put their
hands on each other's necks, it isn't because they are
afraid of falling down.

1214. Agoru, wogoru no tipɛn.

When you play, you play with some one you own size and age.

1215. Agoru nnu mpanyin anim.

One does not cease playing as long as the elders are present.

1216. Agoru bɛsɔ a, efi anɔpa.

If the singing and dancing will be good, it will be so from the morning.

1217. Agoru ansɔ a, egu.

If the dance is not good it stops.

1218. Agoru yɛ fɛ a, na 'yɛwea kɔfwɛ (:ɛnna ɛwea kɔ ase).

If the singing and dance is good we will even crawl to see it.

1219. Wugoru doko ho a, ɛdan wo dɔ.

If you neglect a simple stomach trouble, it develops into a more serious disease.

1220. Ogosoafo nni aguamsɛm.

The palm oil carrier doesn't make a public palaver.

1221. Gua bɔ bum a, ohiani ade na ɛyera.

If the whole assembly rises at once the poor person's things get lost.

1222. Gua so hantan, ofie awerɛho, wokyi.

We shouldn't be proud in public and sad at home.

1223. Oguabon mma na egua wɔn abon.

The children of the one who skins and guts animals stink.

1224. Aguadi mu wɔ amanne.

There are difficulties in trading.

1225. Guaman-so wommara.

It is not forbidden to do things openly.

1226. Aguaman kotokuwa de, ɔbiako nse (:ɛnyɛ obiako na ɔbɔ).

The small bag of the prostitute is not carried by only one person.

1227. Oguan bewu: na onnya nwui a, wɔmfrɛ no guanfunu.

When a sheep is going to die, but it is not yet dead,
it is not called a dead sheep.

1228. Oguan-funu mpaw ɔsekan. Cf. Z.43.

A dead sheep does not choose the knife it is to be cut
up with.

1229. Oguan ho babi de bersbo (:bers-wo-bo-ase).

There is an organ of the sheep called the liver, meaning,
"bring your chest down".

1230. Oguan ano ka nkyene a, onnyae we.

Once a sheep tastes salt it can't stop eating it.

1231. Oguan wuda yɛ ɔdasani wuda.

The day on which a sheep dies, a man also dies.

1232. Oguanten se: mefwɛ ɔsebɔ na mawo no so.

The sheep says: "I am looking at a leopard that I may
give birth to one like it."

1233. Oguanten nwo aberekyi.

A sheep does not give birth to a goat.

1234. Aguaree fowe ansa-na osu retɔ.

The bath house is wet before it rains.

1235. Aguare na ɔkeyerɛ ne ntoaso.

Bathing is something that always continues to be done.

1236. Miguare na me ho amfi a, misusuw sɛ meboro asu.

If I bathe and I don't become clean, I think I have beat
the water with my hands and feet.

1237. Mireguare suɔhyew na ananse reguare ne mma, na meguare
suonwini ɛ?

I am bathing in hot water, and the spider keeps washing
his children in it, so shall I wash in cold water?

1238. "Agya, gyae na menka! wokyi.

"Father, stop and let me tell you" is objectionable conduct.

1239. Agya mma nya a, mepɛ; ɛna mma nya, mepɛ papapa.

When my father's children get anything, I like it; when
my mother's children get anything, I like it even
better.

1240. Agya Ananse adi asɛmmɔne na 'yɛpam no, na wannya baabi
      ankorɔ na ɔsɛn padeɛ ani.

      Father Ananse committed crimes and we drove him away,
      and as he had no place to go he hangs from the cross-
      beams of the roof.

1241. Agya Ananse nwoo ne ba Ntikuma na owɔ nea ɔso ne botɔ.

      Before Father Ananse begot his son Ntikuma he had someone
      to carry his money bag.

1242. Agya, wɔnyɛ no abien.

      Nobody has two fathers.

1243. "M'agya dea, memfa! me na dea, memfa!" na ɛberɛ awi. =2058.

      It is my father's so let me take it, it is my mother's so
      let me take it, this brings a child to stealing.

1244. Wo agya akoa twa dua a, wuse, ɛyɛ merɛw. R. 70.

      When your father's slave cuts down tree, you say it is
      easy to do.

1245. Ogya a ɛbɛdɛw ne ne wisie nko.

      The fire which is going to blaze up is not the same as
      its smoke.

1246. Oyga a ɛyɛ nnam nkyɛ afuw so. =1001.

      The firewood which is good for fuel does not remain long
      on the farm.

1247. Ogya dedaw ano nyɛ sɔ-na.

      Wood already touched by fire is not hard to start burning
      again.

1248. Ogya-fwirenfwiren akyene, wonto no yampaeaw. B.

      One should not toy with the drum of an asafo band.

1249. Ogya hye wo a, wɔperɛw to wo ba so ansa-na woayi afi no so.

      When a spark from the fire burns you, you shake it off onto
      your child before you finally shake it off completely.

1250. Ogya hye wo a, ɛnyɛ wo dɛ, na woretafo.

      When fire burns you, you do not find it sweet, but you
      keep licking the place nevertheless.

1251. Ogya perɛw a, ɛhye nea ɔda ano.

      When a firebrand rolls out from the fire, it burns the one
      sleeping nearest to it.

1252. Ogya ne atuduru nna (:ntra). R. 47. Z. 7.
Fire and gunpowder do not sleep together.

1253. Ogya, wɔtu no ahuhua. (Dwaben Boatene.)
Firewood, you buy it in times of famine.

1254. "Gya apini-si!" Ose: minhu biribi a, ankra misi apini?
"Stop sighing!" He says: "If I didn't see anything
would I have groaned?"

1255. Ennyae wo hia a, wunnyaw mmɔbɔ-yɛ. Cf. 2334.
If you are still in poverty, you are still to be pitied.

1256. Gyagyafo se 'n'ano yɛ nnam' a, ɔde kum Aburifo na ɔmfa nkum
Adukurofo.
If Gyagyafo says his mouth is sharp, he can kill the people
of Aburi with it, and not the people from Adukuro.

1257. Gyahene ho nyɛ den a, ɔnne kankan.
Even if the leopard is not strong is not called a civet cat.

1258. Agyanka dan akrommɔ.
An orphan becomes a thief.

1259. Ogyapam ne ne ntɔtea firi tete.
The "Ogyapam" tree and its small black ants were always
here.

1260. Gyata dɔso wiram'a, anka nnipa nnya baabi ntra.
If lions were numerous in the forest, then man would have
no place to stay.

1261. Woannyaw no fam' a, wugyaw no putu ho.
If you don't leave it on the ground, you leave it remain
by the hut for storing yams.

1262. "Gye akyekyere koma agya" nso yɛ ahayɔ?
"Take the tortoise and give it to father," would you call
this hunting?

1263. Gye otam koma me yere, na woterɛ mu wo kurotia fwɛ, sɛ
tenten a, wuretwa so, anasɛ tia a, na woretoa so.
Take this piece of cloth to my wife, you stretch it out
at the town's entrance to see if it is too long, if so
will you cut off a piece, or if it is too short, will
you make it longer?

1264. Begye-a-egye, wɔde biribi na ese! =71.

"I will fetch it because I can," one says with a reason.

1265. Migye wo ban abia, wuyi hama hintaw me (:wuyi, fra sie)?
Z. 120.

I am helping you make a fence, and are you going to hide the
string from me?

1266. Wugye obi na wode no si wo anim a, na woagye no; na
wode no si wo akyi de a, na wunnyee no ɛ.

If you capture someone and set him in front of you, then
you have him, but if you put him behind you, you don't
have him.

1267. Wogye nea ɔbɛkɔ kyena ade ma nea ɔbekɔ 'nɛ.

You take away the thing from the one who will go tomorrow
and give it to the one who will go today.

1268. Wogye wo sɔba a, na wokyerɛ wo ahuruhuruw.

If you are tossed to and fro you are being taught jumping.

1269. Muregye me aku me, anasɛ muregye me ama madidi?

Do you want to get me to kill me or do you want to get me
so that I can eat?

1270. Nnyedua si afikyiri, nanso ne nhin wɔ fie.

The umbrella trees stand behind the house but their roots
are in the house.

1271. Agyekum wu na ehia, na ɛnyɛ nea obedi n'ade.

Agyekum's death was necessary, but not he who inherits
him.

1272. Agyenannyenen-nsu na ose: okogyen nsu, ansa-na ɔkɔfonoo no.

The dragon-fly says he looks closely at the water before
he makes it muddy.

1273. Agyenimma se 'ɔpɛ osu'a, na enti ɔnam bisa nea onipa awu?

If Agyenimma says he likes to cry and therefore does he
walk about asking which person has died?

1274. Gyentia katakyi, ebehi ato wo!

Bold fire-brand, you will be burned out and thrown away!

1275. (Nea) ogyigye (nsa) ammow a, (nea) ɔhyɛ mmow.

If he who received wine does not get drunk, neither does
he who serves it.

1276. Agyimako anuonyam ne Apea.
The glory of Agyimako is Apea.

1277. Ogyimi na mfasoɔ wɔ so.
There is gain even in stupidity.

1278. Wugyimi a, na wokum wo.
If you are stupid, you will be killed.

1279. Wugyina obi 'mati na ehu guam'.
You stand on someone's shoulder's to see into the assembly.

1280. Wugyina dua kontonkye so na etwa dua-pa.
We stand on a crooked tree to cut down a good tree.

1281. Wugyina sasin akyi na ɛbɔ kaseɛ.
Once you have drunk the dregs of palm wine, it delivers
a message.

1282. Wugyina ntenten bɔ atuo a, wonse sɛ: ma yɛnna (ansa).
If you are standing in front of a gun being fired, you don't
say: "let's sleep before shooting it."

1283. Agyinamoa nam fie se ne kotuku a, anadwoboa mfa ne nsa
ntom'.
When the cat walks about the house carrying his bag, the
mouse does not put his hand inside.

1284. Agyinamoa akoa ne botokura.
The cat's slave is the mouse.

1285. Agyinamoa wɔ piafo a, anka ɔyɛ nnam kyɛn kraman.
If the cat only had someone to help it, it would be more
bold than the dog.

1286. Agyinamoa wu a, nkura yam!
When the cat dies, the mice rejoice.

1287. Oha tu a, ɔfam, ɔda hɔ a, ɔfam.
If a bat flies, it encircles with its arms and if it is
lying there, it also encircles with it arms.

1288. Oha na onim ha tokuru mu.
The bat knows the inside of the bat hole.

1289. Haban dwannwan sɛn hɔ na momono retew.

The dry leaves are on the tree while the green ones are
falling off.

1290. Ahabayerɛ ammɔ a, obi nnunu no, =57. 1067.

If the wild yam is not fully grown you should not blame it.

1291. Ahabammema pae a, ɛpae gu kwaem' na ɛmpae nnu mpoano.

If the "ahabammema" tree splits, it splits and lies in
the forest, and not on the seashore.

1292. Hae, hae! na amma akroma anyɛ kɛse. R. 58.

Shouting "hai ha :" has prevented the hawk from becoming
big.

1293. Hama, hama kyere ketebɔ. R. 40.

Many ropes (tied together) catch the leopard.

1294. Hama ware a, ɛtoa.

If a rope is long it gets entangled.

1295. Ɔhantanni na okyi nnipa. R. 252.

A proud person dislikes people.

1296. Aharamata abien ka bom' a, ɛyɛ pepe.

If two harmattans come together, the haze is dense.

1297. Wo hare fako a, wubutuw. Cf. 1731.

If you paddle a canoe on one side you crouch.

1298. Ahataw dan pam. (Agyakwa)

The bush and weed shooting up afresh on an early weeded
farm change to a place needed to cleared.

1299. Hena na ogyina siw so a, anka ɔnyɛ tenten?

Who is there who wouldn't be tall when he is standing on
an ant hill?

1300. Ɔhem-mone nni babi, na ɔsafohene-bone na ɔwɔ babi.
R. 186.

There is no where a bad chief, but there may be a bad
sub-chief.

1301. Ɔhene a obekum wo mmae a, na wokan ahene dodow a woasom.

When the chief who will kill you has not yet come to reign,
you tell how many chiefs you have served under.

1302.   Ohene a obekum wo mmae a, wunse se:mpanyin(na: wuse:
        manyin makye.)

        When the chief who will kill you has not yet come to
        reign don't say, "I'm old" (but you say: "I'm old,
        I've lived a long time".)

1303.   Ohene bi bere so wohu, na obi bere so woayere.

        During one chief's reign animal skins are treated by
        having the hairs burned off, during that of another chief
        skins are spread in the sun to dry.

1304.   Ohene bedi wo kasa a, efi mamfo.

        When a chief is going to fine you for something, he does
        so by the authority of the people.

1305.   Ohene bekum wo a, ennim ahamatwe.

        When a chief is going to kill you, you don't cast lots to
        decide (whether you will be killed.)

1306.   Ohene na oyi dansefo adi.

        The chief reveals the false witnesses.

1307.   Ohene ne wo ka a, na okum wo.

        If you are friendly with the chief, he kills you.

1308.   Ohene anim na wonka, na n'akyi de, wose.

        One does not speak out one's mind in the presence of a
        chief, but behind his back one does.

1309.   Ohene nufu doso a, amansan na enum.

        If a chief has many breasts then all the people can be
        fed by him.

1310.   Ohene nya ahotrafo pa a, na ne bere so dwo.

        When a chief has good advisors then his reign is peaceful.

1311.   Ohene nnya wo a, na wuse: one me ka.

        As long as the chief has not got a hold of you, you say:
        "he and I are good friends."

1312.   Ohene aso te se sono aso. Gr. # 269.

        The ears of a chief are as big as those of an elephant.

1313. Ɔhene aso te sɛ sɔne: emu akwan boro apem.

The ears of a chief are like a seive; there are more than a
thousand ways to them.

1314. Ɔhene ntam te sɛ bayerɛ amoa: obi ntɔ mu mfa neho tɔtrɔtɔ
mfi adi da.

A chief's oath is like the hole a yam is planted in,
no one falls into it and gets out again unhurt.

1315. Ɔhene tamfo ne nea ɔne no fi mmofraase.

The enemy of a chief is the one who has grown up with him.

1316. Ɔhene tan wo a, na ogye wo ba aware. Cf. 2054.

If the chief hates you he marries your daughter.

1317. Ɔhene tesɛ odum: onni anim nni akyiri.

A chief is like an odum tree, he has no front and no back.

1318. Ɔhene nyɛ dɛ a, fwɛ nea ɔsafohene rekyerɛ. R. 201.

If the chief is not pleasant, look at how the sub-chief
is boasting.

1319. Ahene tew mpanyin anim a, ɛnyera. R. 148.

If a string of beads break in the presence of elders, they
are not lost.

1320. Ahene-pa nkasa.

Good beads don't make any noise.

1321. Ɔheneba ntutu 'mirika nkɔfwɛ tiri. Cf. 851, Z. 47.

A chief's child does not run to look at a head that has
been cut off.

1322. Ahenkwa di adwene na wadwen asɛm.

A chief's servant eats fish(adwene) and gets ideas (adwene).

1323. Ahenkwa di atanyi na onni ntanto guan.

It is the chief's servant who gets the money forfeited by not
keeping an oath, but he doesn't get the sheep paid for
the transgression.

1324. Ahenkwa na ɔma ɔhene ho yɛ hu.

It is the chief's servant that causes people to fear the
chief.

1325. Ahennua nyɛ babayɛnten (bobayemfi) na woatra so banu.
Z. 92.
Chiefs' stools are not like a bundle of dry sticks so
that you would sit on two of them at the same time.

1326. Ahensia (kwaku) se: nea (onipa a) obedi me nam soa
berefi (:so aberefi.)
Ahensia (kind of mouse or rat) kwaku says: "the person
who comes to eat my meat carries a bundle of palm branches."

1327. Ahentam nti na aberewa di nya.
It is because of the chief's oath that the old lady
possesses a slave.

1328. Ahi nti na wukum mpaboa a, wuhua tie.
It is because of dislike that if you kill a bed bug you
smell it.

1329. Ahia nte baako anom'.
Poverty doesn't live in one person's mouth.

1330. Ehia batani hia pani. Gr. p. 154.
When the hirer is in want the hireling is also in want.

1331. Ehia onipa a, ɔda wuram'.
When a man is poor, he sleeps in the forest.

1332. Ehia onipa a, ma womfa no nkɔ! R. 258.
If a man is in distress, let them take him away.

1333. Ehia wo a, na worewe sumana-dwe.
If you are poor, you eat the palm nuts left on the
garbage heap.

1334. Ehia wo a, nwu.
When you are poor, don't die.

1335. "Ahia me na fwɛ ma me" nti na obi yɛɛ akoa.
"I am in want, so look after me," that is why someone
became a slave.

1336. Ohia de wo na ennuu nea edu a, ennyae.
If poverty has overtaken you and if it has not reached
where it will reach, it doesn't stop.

1337. Ohia, wodi no fie, na wonni no gua so.

When you are a poor man, you remain at home and do not
mix in public affairs.

1338. Ohia wo a, wodɔw Akuropɔn abɔnten so. (Mpere.)

If you are really poor you weed in the main streets of
Akuropɔn.

1339. Ohia hia wo a, wowe aberekyi were.

If you are really in poverty you eat goat's skin.

1340. Ohia hia wo na wuti abete a, ɛdan' fan. R. 173.

If you are poor, and you pick out the maize from the pot,
it turns out to be only vegetables.

1341. Ohia hia wo na wotɔ nsu-onwinim' a, ɛhye wo.

When you are suffering from poverty and happen to fall in
cold water, it scalds you.

1342. Ohia nhyɛ da.

Poverty does not have set times to come upon anyone.

1343. Ohia na ahia Opekyini na ɔne Ɔkwamni nam. =1350.

Because of poverty a man from Pekyi is related to a man
from Akwam.

1344. Ohia na ɛma ɔdehye yɛ akoa. R. 31. Gr. p. 157.

Poverty causes the free man to become a slave.

1345. Ohia na ɛma ɔtwea kɔ anɔpa-bɛ soɔ.

It is poverty that causes the dog to go and tap palm trees
early in the morning.

1346. Ohia ne gyimi. = 1354. 2224.

Poverty is stupidity.

1347. Ohia nni Aburokyiri a, anka Oburoni ammɛhata ne ntama
Abibirim'.

If there had been no poverty in Europe, then the white
man would not have come and spread his cloths to sell in
Africa.

1348. Ohia te sɛ 'wo:ɛnnɔ faako. Cf. 1813.

Poverty is like honey, it is not peculiar to one place
alone.

1349. Ohia nti na ɛma yɛn akotodwe ntama afura.

It is because of poverty that we cover our knees with a cloth.

1350. Ohia nti na Pekyini ne Kwamni nam. = 1343. 801.

It is because of poverty that a man from Pekyi is related to a man from Akwam.

1351. Ohia nti na aseredowa sisi aburobia so.

It is want that causes the little aseredowa bird to alight on the burobia plant.

1352. Ohia nti na yɛde bowereɛ twa brodeɛ.

It is because of poverty that we cut open plantain with our fingernails.

1353. Ohia tumi nyɛ tumi-pa.

The display of power exhibited by a poor person is not real power.

1354. Ohia yɛ adammɔ. =1346.

Poverty is stupidity.

1355. Ohia bɛyɛ ya. (Akwam hene Dako Yaw safohene Kwame Boo).

Poverty will be painful.

1356. Ohia yɛ yea a,yɛde firi fie, na emfiri abɔntene so.

If poverty is painful, it comes from one's house not from outside.

1357. Ohia-da na wohu nipa.

It is on the day of want that you see who are your true friends.

1358. Wuhiahia aboa no (:ɔwɔ) ho a, ɔka wo. Cf. 1399.

If you disturb the bush near an animal, it will bite you.

1359. Ohiani abawa koro nkyɛ berɛ, nso wankɔ a, yennidi.

The poor man's only slave girl soon gets tired, but if she does not go (and work) we do not eat.

1360. Ohiani bo mfuw. Cf. Z. 196.

The poor man can not become angry (with those on whom he depends).

1361. Ohiani bu bɛ a, ɛnhye. R. 136.
If a poor man makes a proverb it does not spread.

1362. Ohiani di pɔwade a, ɛyɛ sɛ odi dwane.
When a poor man eats something of the value of half penny,
it is as if he eats a sheep.

1363. Ohiani didi abraw-abraw. Cf. 2929.
The poor man eats scantily.

1364. Ohiani funu yɛ dada a, emuni.
If a poor man's corpse is old, it rolls about.

1365. Ohiani fura kyeme a, ɛyɛ sɛ efura dunsin.
If a poor man wears an expensive silk cloth, it is like
cloth on a tree stump.

1366. Ohiani hyɛ sika a, wobu no awowa.
If the poor man wears gold, people say it is brass.

1367. Ohiani ne ɔdefo nnoru.
A poor man and a rich man do not play together.

1368. Ohiani nni biribi a, ɔwɔ tɛkrɛma a ɔde tutu ka.
If a poor man has nothing else, at least he has a tongue
with which to defer the payment of his debts.

1369. Ohiani nni yɔnko. R. 18.
The poor person has no friend.

1370. Ohiani nom tawa-pa, ɛyɛ sɛ tasɛnfi.
When a poor man smokes good tobacco, it is as if he were
smoking the remains of some old tobacco.

1371. Ohiani nya ade a, ɔman bɔ. R. 120.
If the poor man gets rich, the town goes to ruin.

1372. Ohiani pam akorogow a, na ɛyɛ no sɛ odidi sanyam'.
When the poor man mends his broken wooden bowl, he thinks
he is eating off a pewter dish.

1373. Ohiani mpaw dabere.
A poor man does not choose his sleeping place.

1374. Ohiani asɛm, 'yedi no nitantiam'.
The complaint of a poor man is investigated very briefly.

1375. Ohiani asommɛn ne batafose, R. 147. Gr. p. 111.
A poor man's ivory is the wild-boar's tusk.

1376. Ohiani tam ara ne aboka.
A poor man's cloth is his favorite delight.

1377. Ohiani nton na ohiani ntɔ. =637.
The poor man can not sell and can not also buy.

1378. Ohiani yane gorow a, 'yɛse: ɔyane nnwahama.
When the poor man wears a necklace of the soft silky
'gorow' leaves, it is said he is wearing a cord with which
sheep are tied.

1379. Ahina reserew ahaha.
One speaking with a hoarse trembling voice laughs at one
speaking through the nose.

1380. Ahina a esi kukukon so besi fam' a, epirew.
If the water pot which is on top of the earthen ware
vessel falls down, it rolls about.

1381. Ahini bɔ a, na kora ata ho.
When the water pot breaks, the calabash in it remains
unharmed beside it.

1382. Ahina ammo a, anka n'abomana mu ntere. B.
If the pot doesn't break, the pit where the clay is dug
will never become wide.

1383. Ahina ho hyɛhyɛ no (:yɛ hyɛhyɛ a,) na nsu na ɛwom'.
Cf. 332.
When the surface of the pot glistens that is because
there is water in it.

1384. Wuhintaw yɛ a, wohintaw hu wo.
What you do secretly, others see secretly.

1385. Ohintimpraku agoru, wokɔfwɛ a, worewu, woankɔfwɛ a, wo
yere ne wo mma gu so.
(Oh. ag., wonkɔfwɛ a, wo ani nsɔ (:nnye), woakɔfwɛ a, wo
ani rebɔ (:wo yere ne wo mma da so a.s. atotɔ wo so).

There is a game in which a piece of wood is contrived so
that it flies back upon whatever touches it: if you go to
watch it, you die, if you don't go to watch it, your wife
and your children continue to watch it.("Ohintimpraku
agoru", if you don't see it, it isn't pleasant, and if you
go to see it you go blind, (your wife and your children
continue looking at it.)

1386. Hinti-praku, wo na wotew abun na wotew akɔkɔ.

Piece of wood contrived so that it falls back upon whatever
touches it, you pluck green fruit and ripe fruit.

1387. Wohintiw prɛko mmɔ ahina.

You don't knock your foot against something and at the
same time break the pot.

1388. Wo ho bɔn a, wɔteta gu wo mu.

If you stink, you fart on yourself.

1389. Wo ho yɛ den a, wose bo.

If you are strong, you carry a value.

1390. Wo ho yɛ den a, wonyɛ banu adwuma. R. 103.

However strong you are, you don't do the work of two men.

1391. Wo ho nyɛ den a, na wuse: kahiri nyɛ. Z. 198.

When you are not strong, then you say, the head pad is
no good.

1392. Wo ho yɛ a, wonsen (:wonte sɛ) me tɛkrɛma.

If you are handsome, you are not greater than my tongue.

1393. Ahodaso nyɛ hu.

Readiness has no fears.

1394. Ahooden bebre yɛ mmusu.

Too much strength brings trouble.

1395. Ɔhoɔdenfo soa (:so) bew-nam a, ɛporɔw.

If a strong man carries the meat of the 'bew' animal, it
means it is spoiled.

1396. Ɔhoɔdenfo soa ta a, ewu.

If a strong man carries tobacco, it dies.

1397. Ahoɔfɛ ntua kaw.
       Physical beauty does not pay debts.

1398. Ohofwini, wowoo no.
       A squanderer (sensual person) is born that way.

1399. Ahohiahia na ɔwɔ de ka. Cf. 1358. 3446.
       A snake bites when it is troubled.

1400. Ɔhoho a ɔbae se 'wanto bi'a, nkurofo a ɔbɛtoo won ka se:
       yeanhu bi a ɔbae.
       If a stranger comes and says he didn't meet anyone, those
       whom he met also say they didn't see anyone come there.

1401. Ɔhoho nko kyɛn nkurofo-mma dodo.
       A stranger is respected more than many people from one's
       own town.

1402. Ɔhoho nkyere hoho.
       A stranger doesn't capture a stranger.

1403. Ɔhoho akyi mpa asɛm.
       Once a stranger has gone there is always something to be
       said about him.

1404. Ɔhoho ama woanya sika ama woanya kaw.
       A stranger is the cause of one getting money, but he is
       also the cause of one going into debt.

1405. "Ɔhoho-nni-nko" yɛ ɔmanni-fone.
       A stranger eats the good things and goes, and causes the
       relatives to starve.

1406. Ɔhoho ani akɛsɛ-akɛsɛ, nanso enhu man mu asɛm (:ɔmfa
       nhu kurow mu asɛm; na nea ɔde kurow aniwa nkete-nkete
       na ohu mu asɛm). Z.72.
       A stranger may have very big eyes, but he doesn't see
       what is going on among the people he is living with.
       Whereas the native with very little eyes knows all the
       town's affairs.

1407. Ɔhoho nnim a, ɔmanni kyerɛ. Cf. 245. 532.
       If the stranger doesn't know, the townsman shows him.

1408. Ɔhɔho nsoa funu ti. R. 171.

A stranger does not carry the head of the casket.

1409. Ɔhɔho sɔɛ wo fi na wannyaw wo biribi a, ogyaw wo kaw.

When a stranger lodges at your house and doesn't leave
you anything, at least he leaves you debts.

1410. Ɔhɔho te sɛ abofra.

A stranger is like a child.

1411. Ɔhɔho te sɛ sunsuansu.

A stranger is like water running over the ground after
a rainstorm (which soon dries up and leaves little
trace behind).

1412. Ɔhɔho nto mmara. (Krɔbofo, Huafo: Ɔhɔho na ɔto mmara).

A stranger doesn't break the law. (The Krobos, The Ewes,
:the stranger breaks the law).

1413. Ahɔhoduan yɛ wo dɛ a, wo anuonyam yɛ ketewa.

If you are too fond of food obtained through the hospitality
of others, you will not be praised.

1414. Ɔhohorafo de n'ahohora fi ne kurom'.

The despised person brings his infamy from his own town.

1415. Wohohoro nammɔn mu sɛ dɛn ara a, ɛnyɛ sɛ nsam' da..

No matter how well you wash the soles of your feet, they
never become clean like the palms of your hands.

1416. Ahohuru na wɔde hyew tana.

A person who burns a pile of wood suffers from the heat.

1417. Ɔhoankani fi gye ntuw.

A selfish person's house becomes moldy.

1418. Nhoma hunu nkɔ Aburokyiri.

Book learning doesn't take one to Europe.

1419. Nhoma suane nea ɛyɛ hare. = 3413.

An animal hide tears where it is thinnest.

1420. Ɔhonam mu nni nhanoa.

There are no boundaries in the body.

1421. Ohonam panyin ne ti(ri).
The head is the leader of the body.

1422. Ohonam, wonto.
You don't buy the flesh of man.

1423. Honankuru, wode atirmoden na ctoto.
You dress a wound in a rough manner.

1424. Honankuru woantoto a, cporow; wototo nso a, eye wo yaw.
If you don't dress a flesh wound, it gets infected, but
if you dress it, it hurts.

1425. Ahonu ntu kuru.
Repentance does not cause an open sore.

1426. Wohoro wo asuwa mu na amfi a, wode ko asuten mu.
If you wash clothes in a small stream and they don't get
clean you go and wash them in a river.

1427. "Huw m'ani so ma me" nti na atwe abien nam.   R.63.
"Blow the dust from my eyes," is why antelopes always go
about in pairs.

1428. Wuhu (:Wuhyia) a, woto, wuhu a, woto; na dakoro wuhu a,
na woguan (:wuhuro).
If you buy what you see, one day you will see something you
really want to buy and will be put shame because you have
no money.

1429. Wuhu obi a oye kitikiti wo abonten so a, fwe no komm, na
se oye obarima a, edom beba na woahu no.
If you see someone who is stamping and trampling the ground
roughly in the street, look at him quietly, for if he is
a strong man, an army will come and you will get to see it.

1430. Wuhu obi ade so fwe a, eka wo nsam'.
If you know how to look after someone's property it becomes
your property.

1431. Wuhu koto ani a, wuse: eye dua.
If you see the eye of the crab you say it is a stick.

1432. Wuhu kraman wɔ pata so a, na obi na ɔmaa no so sii hɔ. Cf. 1772.

If you see a dog on the roof, someone has lifted it up and put it there.

1433. Wuhu na woanka a, ɛfa wo so.

If you see wrong doing and say nothing about it, it may come to you later.

1434. Wuhu nea wabɔ (:wayare) waw awu na n'anim da hɔ a, ma no due, na wahu amanne (:nea wahu dɔso).

If you see someone who has died from coughing (chest troubles) and he is lying there show him sympathy, for he has suffered.

1435. Wuhu nea wudi na wo ano yɛ pɔw a, ɛnyɛ yaw.

If you see what you are eating and your mouth becomes puffed up it is not painful.

1436. Wuhu anoma wɔ ne berebuw ano na sɛ ɛnyɛ ɔno na ɔnwenee a, na wɔnwenee gyaw no.

If you see a bird at the opening of a nest and if it is not that bird that has made the nest, it means those who made it have left it behind for it.

1437. Wuhu ɔtwe (:atwewa) mmɔbɔ a, woda ɔkom (:wudi aduane huno).

If you are merciful to the antelope, you go to bed hungry.

1438. Wuhu wo kaw tutu a, wonyi wo adwow.

If you know how to put off the payment of your debt, your creditor does not seize your property. (doesn't kidnap you as a pawn).

1439. Wuhu wo wura som a, wofa woho di. Cf. 1620.

If you know how to serve your master, you become free.

1440. Wuhu awiri koro a, ntow (:mmɔ) no bo, na ebia ofi dodow mu.

If you see a single parrot, don't throw a stone at it, perhaps there are many more from where he came.

1441. Wohu (:yehu) adidi ansa-na wohu (:yehu) ade-pɛ. Gr#165,3.

We know how to eat before we know how to get rich.

1442. Wohu asu ansa-na wɔanom sam.

You know how to drink water before you drink palm wine.

1443. Yehuu bofu ansa na yehuu nsa.

We saw the bark of a tree that can be used as a cloth before we saw the blanket.

1444. Mahu okisi a ɔsen sono kɛse pɛn. (Mp.)

I once saw a rat which was bigger than an elephant.

1445. Mahu kontromfi a ne yere awu na wasiw atimum; na wo wansan de, ɛfa wo ho dɛn? R. 61.

I have seen a monkey who let his hair grow long (did not shave off his hair) when his wife died and you, antelope, what is that to you?

1446. Mahu apopokyikyi a wakum dɛnkyɛm pɛn.

I once saw a certain river fish (apopokyikyi) which killed a crocodile.

1447. Woahu dokono a amia akɔtoa ɔtwea da?

Have you seen kenkey which has ever squeezed a sack of a dog?

1448. Woahu no si a, hu no sonn.

If you see him stand, (you) see him safe and sound.

1449. Woahu sɛ nsoroma fi soro abebisa po sɛ "da bɛn na osu bɛtɔ" da?

Have you ever seen the stars coming down to the sea to ask when it will rain?

1450. Wonhu ɔwɔ ti a, wommɔ no aba.

Unless you see a snake's head you don't hit it with a stick.

1451. Wonhuu nea nkramfoa rehu wɔ po mu.

You did not see what sea fish "nkramfoa" see everyday in the ocean.

1452. Woanhu wo fi asɛm di a, na e(re)fi gua so (:efi adi, ɛkɔ abɔnten so).

If you don't take care of your family affairs, they become known to the public.

1453. Mihunu sɛ na bewu a, ankra mekɔ Nkrane meba ntɛm.

If I know my mother would die, I would have gone to Accra and returned quickly.

1454. Ohunu wom' a, wɔnkobisa.

If the one who has seen is present, you wouldn't go and ask.

1455. Ahu(nu) wonhu(nu) mperennu.

A calamity should not befall the same person twice.

1456. Hunuamanne bra, wɔmmmɔ.

You don't call something that causes suffering to come.

1457. Hua abete, wodi no abusuam!. R. 243.

A life of suffering gibe roasted maize-flour boiled in
water, is eaten only by members of the family.

1458. Ohuammɔ sen merenkɔ koraa (:somanka).

To be disappointed is worse than not going at all.

1459. Ahuboa ɔbako nhu.

A dead animal whose hair is being burned is not seen by
only one person.

1460. Ohufo suro dɔm nti na otwa abrodɔ. Gr. p. 157.

A coward deserts because he fears the enemy.

1461. Ahuhubo fra abrammo-pa (:bram' abo) a, woyi no kyene
(:'yeyi no).

If false weights get mixed in with true weights, you
throw them away.

1462. Wohuhuw abofra nnwomma so na wɔkaw so.

If you blow on a childs' cooked yam to cool it off you
bite upon it.

1463. Ohurii di bem; nwansana na ɔyɛ me sɛ.

The tsetse fly is innocent (in biting me) and yet the
common house fly is doing the same thing to me.

1464. **Ohurii ni gyamfo.** Cf. 1480.

The dead tsetse fly has no one to mourn him.

1465. Ohurii si akyekyere akyi kwa. (Ohurie di aky. akyiri hunu).

The tsetse fly gets nothing from alighting on the back
of the tortoise.

1466. Nhurubia: yenim ko na yesua. Ɛhwene, Awhenhema, s. Ɛfwene
1198. Anwenh. 2579.

A certain small bird "nhurubua", we know that particular
one, but we study it.

1467. Nhwi nyɛ na a, anka akyekyere nni bi? (:wɔ bi.)

If hair was not difficult to grow, would not the tortoise have some?

1468. Wohyɛ abofra asoɛ na woansoɛ no a, ne kɔn bu.

If you force a child to put down a heavy head load but you don't help him, his neck breaks.

1469. Wohyɛ afiri a, wunwu agyan.

If you set a trap, you don't die from an arrow wound.

1470. Wɔhyɛ wɔ nim a, wonhyɛ woho ntwo.

If they ascribe victory to you, don't ascribe defeat to yourself.

1471. Woanhyɛ woho (nsa) a, wonhyɛ wo.

If you don't serve yourself wine, you have not been served.

1472. Ɔhyɛ-bone nti na ɔpete di bi bin.

It is because of a bad command that the vulture eats others' excreetment.

1473. Nhyehye wo akyi nti na wɔsa ɔketew bɛn a, ɔnka neho.

It is because of boasting that if you shoot the lizard with an arrow, it doesn't hurt him.

1474. Hyɛn kɛse si hɔ a, abonto fam ho.

When a big ship is standing near the shore, there are canoes clinging to it.

1475. Ahyiae wonhyia nea ɔda nsow.

A meeting place, you come together where it is marked out.

1476. (ɛ)ka me nko a, anka asɛ sow sɛ ntɛw.

If it concerned only me, beans would bear fruit like the seeds of a climbing plant.

1477. (ɛ)ka nea ɔkɔ Aburokyiri nko a, anka Abibiman abɔ.
Gr. p. 171.

If it only depended on those who went to Europe, Africa would have been destroyed long ago.

1478. (ɛ)ka nea onni tam nko a, anka woguru asafo da. =3284.

If only the man who has no cover cloth was concerned then they would always dance warrior dances.

1479. (Ɛ)ka nwaw ne akyekyere nko a, otuo rentow wuram' da.
R. 26. Gr. p. 171. Z. 149. 181.

If the snail and the tortoise were the only animals in the
forest, no gun would have ever been fired.

1480. "Mɛka nnipa nhina" nti na ohurii annya ogyamfo. Cf. 1464.

"I shall bite all men", because of this the tsetse fly has
no one to mourn him.

1481. Woka nna-akyiri a, wote mmoadoma nhina osu. =1524.

If you go to sleep very late at night you will hear the
sounds of all the animals.

1482. Ɛnka, ɛnka,-ɛka mmofra.

It is not missing, it is not missing, only the children
are missing.

1483. Wɔnka nto a, anka wonyi hadu. B.

If you don't feel your hens to know whether they will lay
eggs, you don't get ten eggs.

1484. Ɛka wo nsa a, egyae fɛ-yɛ.

As soon as you obtain it (something precious), it looses
its beauty.

1485. Ɛka efunu a, nsono ka no.

If only the dead body remains, the worms eat it up.

1486. Wɔka afoatunu ansa-na wɔtwe.

You touch the handle of the sword before you pull it out.

1487. Wɔka ɔhene anom' asɛm na wɔnka ne tirim asɛm.

One says what the chief says, not what he thinks.

1488. Woka asɛm bi na woto tafarakyɛ a, wonkyi.

If you say something objectionable but you make an excuse
for it, it is not objected to.

1489. Woka wo agya a, woka wo na bi.

If you swear the oath of your father you should also
swear that of your mother.

1490. Woka wo kurom' asɛm na ennim a, (na) wo (ankasa) na
wo ani awu.

If you talk about your town and it is not true, you have
disgraced yourself.

1491. Woka wo asɛm na woante a, wokɔ ante-ade.

If they tell you something and you don't do it you are
going to the dogs. (ante-ade; place in Akan folk lore.)

1492. "Maka, maka (:mase, mase a)" na ɛyɛ ahi; na 'menkae'
nyɛ ahi.

If you say "I have spoken, I have spoken" it is intolerable
but "may I speak", is tolerable.

1493. "Woaka na ka bio" nyɛ yaw; na "woakari na kari bio" na
ɛyɛ yaw.

"You have spoken and speak again" is not insulting but
"I have weighed and weigh again" is insulting.

1494. Worobɛka asɛm akyerɛ nea ote, na nea ote nso akɔka akyerɛ
nea onte, na menne sɛ nea waforo te te so! (Dako).

You will be telling something to someone who listens, and
he who listens goes and tells it to him who didn't hear it,
like the one who climbs a "te" tree and sits on it.

1495. Wonka nkyerɛ nea onte mma onte, na onka nkyerɛ nea ote
na onte!

You didn't tell him who doesn't listen that he shouldn't
listen, and you don't tell him who is listening that he
should listen!

1496. Nka, nka! wote no amannone.

Don't touch, don't touch! you hear it in a foreign country.

1497. Ɛkaw kyɛ a, ɛkyɛ mpemanim.

If a debt is not paid on time, it continues to double in
amount.

1498. Ɛka kyen, na ɛmporow.

If the debt becomes hard it doesn't spoil.

1499. Ɛka nni ago (:agoru). (Gyamfua.)

Debts are nothing to play with.

1500. Kaw nni "ka wo nsa pɛ!"

Incuring debts doesn't follow: "make haste accurately!"

1501. Ɛkaw te sɛ asuohyew (:yɛ ns.) ɛnkyɛ dwo.

A debt is like hot water, it cools down quickly.

1502. Ɛkaw yɛ ade a, anka aka nna nsu mu.

If debts brought wealth, then there would be no "aka"
fish in the river.

1503. Ɛkaw nyɛ srade na woati (ti) asra.

A debt is not grease which you smear on your body.

1504. Anka bere kɔ nyɛ dɛ. R. 230.

A lemon that is over-ripe is not sweet.

1505. Anka-dwena,n'ayeyi ne mma. Cf. 1514.

Women are the best promoters of the young fruit of the
lemon tree.

1506. Ɔkabɔfo nni man mu a, anka yerenhu sikafo da.

If there is no contractor of debts in the town, we would
never see rich people.

1507. Ka-dedaw dom wura.

The unexpected payment of an old debt is a real blessing
for the creditor.

1508. "Kae da-bi!" wode se bonniayɛ.

It is to the ungrateful we say, "remember the past!".

1509. Wokae Akosua ne Amma wu a, anka nusu begu.

If you would remember how Akosua and Amma died, then you
would shed tears.

1510. Ɔkafo nni hom.

A debtor has no strength.

1511. Ɔkafoni te hɔ. wo ntama tetew (wo) wo ho a, wunnya obi
ntɔ bi mfura wo.

If your debtor is present and your cloth is all torn you
don't get any one to buy a new one for you.

1512. Kaguam nyɛ awerɛho.

Part payment should not make the creditor sad.

1513. Kahi na ɛde adwo-yi ba.

It is constant refusing to pay a debt that causes the
kidnapping of someone from the debtor's town.

1514. Ankahono: m'ayeyi ne mma! Cf.1505.

The lemon peel says: "My praise comes from women!"

1515. Okaɛa bu sono se.

Toothache breaks the elephant's tusk.

1516. Okaakyiri soa akuma (:nk.).

The one who remains behind carries the axe home.

1517. "Ankama, kotua ka!" Fa ka bera?"(wokyi.).

Ankama, "go and pay the debt!" Do you like, "Go and bring a debt?"

1518. Ankamabrafoɔ nunum, obi anka no a, ɔmmon.
Ankamawaframoa onunum: obi anka me a, memmon.

If no one touches the "ankamabrafoɔ nunum" plant, it doesn't stink.

1519. Kamese-kwakye se: ote sɛ ɔkropon a, anka ɔde abogye bɛnwene berebuw adam'.

Kamese-Kwakye says that if he lived like the large eagle "ɔkropon" he would weave a bird's nest with jaw bones to sleep in.

1520. Nkamfo: mempere owaduru da.

The yellow yam says: "I never cause the wooden mortar to move around."

1521. Wokamfo wo atutow a, wokamfo wo basin.

If they praise your shooting, they praise the shortness of your arm.

1522. Wokan nantwi a, wokan ne dua.

If you count a herd of cattle, you count them by their tails.

1523. Kankan-hyɛn butuw a, obako nni mmusu.

If a Dutch ship capsizes, no one suffers any misfortune.

1524. Aka-nna-akyirie na ɔte (:onim) mmoadoma nhina su (:mate mm. su).=1419.

The one who goes to sleep very late at night hears the cries of all the animals in the forest.

1525. Okanni ba nnantew nkowu.

An Akan does not willingly walk to his death.

1526. Akantannwa nyɛ biribi a, ɛyɛ amutenetene.
Kara...s. kra... 1758-1783.

If the chair does nothing at all, at least it keeps
ones' back straight.

1527. Woankari damma a, taku yera.

If you don't value two pesewas, you will loose five
pesewas.

1528. Ɔkasa esu aduasa wɔ hɔ, ɛfana me (ɛfanim?) mmiako-
mmiako. S.

There are 30 different languages which trouble me one
by one.

1529. Kasabɔdin nti na (ɛmaa) ɛko yam' bɔe (:tui).
Ɔkasakye ...s Kokosakyi.

It is because of the repeated mentioning of a matter with
indignation that the buffalo's stomach burst.

1530. Ɔkasame yɛ ɔkarabiri. Cf. 2453.

Talkativeness is a misfortune.

1531. Wokasakasa a, wo ano pa.

A slip of the tongue is the outcome of talkativeness.

1532. Ɔkasa-pa pam abufuw. Z. 10.

Peaceful talking drives away anger.

1533. Ɔkasasie sen Brɔfo.

A previously arranged agreement is better than what the
Europeans would say.

1534. Kataman kura ade a, obi nnye.

If the Creator holds something in his hand, no one can
take it away from him.

1535. Akatanini-agyabena, onni mfuwa mu na onni kwae mu.

The mighty "agyabena" tree can not be found in the farm
nor in the forest.

1536. Wɔkeka funu a, wɔkeka (no akɔ) ma ɔdampan.

If you dress a corpse by washing, anointing and putting
on clean clothes, you do it for an empty house.

1537. "Ɔkese, fwe o!" na "mede wo ka?"

"Hey, big man," "do I owe you anything?"

-128-

1538. Kesrekesre do krobene, odwene do ne de.

The "kesrekesre" tree has a red dyeing substance in its pith, and the "odwene" tree has its own.

1539. Nkesua to nkran mu a, ma snna mu, na wonam ho kwa.

If an egg falls among soldier ants, let it lie there for they walk over it without doing any harm.

1540. Aketekyere bo fa a, ebi ka n'ani.

If a cricket digs out the earth some gets into its eyes.

1541. Oketesoafo nni aguamsem.

The carrier of the chief's mat does not make a public palaver.

1542. Oketew a otare poodo ho bo ye tow-na.

It is difficult to throw a stone at a lizard clinging to an earthen water pot.

1543. Okete-hunui nti na obi anni ne nam (:na amma woanni ketew nam).

It is because the lizard is worthless that no one eats its meat.

1544. Oketew na obu ne be se: Odesani didi me a, ooo dam.

The lizard gives his proverb: "If man is fully satisfied in eating, then he becomes crazy."

1545. Oketew ne ketebo se din na wonse honam.

The lizard and the leopard have names which are similar, but they are not similar in bodily appearance.

1546. Oketew nim se ayamkaw beba nti na obutuw (ho) siei. Z. 61.

Because the lizard knows it will get a belly-ache, it is crouched in preparation.

1547. Oketew wo yam aduru a, anka yam ansi no adurade.

If the lizard had medicine against skin disease, then its body would not be covered with eczema.

1548. Oketew nwe mako na fifiri mfi atweroro.
Oketew nkowe mako na fifiri afi atwerede.
(Ok, kodi m. na fifiri fi atwere?)

The lizard does not eat pepper and make the frog sweat because of it.

1549. Ɔketere di hia 'ti na ɔkeyere ananse.
      Because the lizard is poor it catches spiders.

1550. Wukisa ɔde bebrebe a epirim. R. 246. Gr. 165,3.
      When you roast the yam too much, it will get burned.

1551. Okisi bankam ne adwe.
      The rat's amber bead is the palm kernel.

1552. Okisi bon mu (nni biribi a, ε) wɔ dwewa-mu.
      If there is nothing in the rat's hole, there are at least
      palm nuts.

1553. Okisi kɔfa adwe na Onyame bɔ ayeremu a, ɔdan atwene.
      S. Cf. 510.
      When the rat goes to take palm nuts and God flashes the
      lightening he drops them.

1554. Okisi-aku, wogye no Aku; Akrante-aku, wogye no Aku;
      Abotokura-aku wogye no Aku, nanso wɔn nhina san kɔsom
      Akrante-aku.
      The rat-"aku" and the grass-cutter "aku", the "abotokura"
      mouse "aku", are all entitled to Aku in the response for
      greetings, but they all enter into the service of the
      grass-cutter "aku".

1555. Okisi apo adwe.
      The rat has rejected palm nuts.

1556. Okisi pε fufu adi a, wɔmfa nsi ne bɔn mu.
      Even if the rat likes to eat fufu, it is not put into
      his hole.

1557. Okisinini anhu adwe-bɔ;na ɔbere bɔ a, ɔwe bi.
      If the male rat does not know how to crack palm kernels,
      but when the female rat does, he eats some of hers.

1558. Mikita n'ankana migya n'ankana. Cf. 203. 220.
      I seize fortune and I let go of fortune.

1559. Akitereku amoaduodu, wo akyi wɔ bi a, na wodi wo ni.
      "Akitereku amoaduodu" if you are from a rich family, you
      are respected.

1560. "Kɔ ahua turu ba!" wokyi.
      It is forbidden to go begging with a child on your back.

1561. "Kɔ wo kurom" nyɛ ɔyaw. Gr. p. 156.

It is not an insult to be asked to go to your home town.

1562. "Mekɔ a memma ha bio," wose no kurotia.

"When I go I'm not coming back here again", is said at the outskirts of the town.

1563. Mekɔ sa na mamfa biribi a, mɛfa nonontututuo.S.

If I'm going to war and I didn't bring anything, at least I bring rags.

1564. Ɛkɔ a, na, akohu. F. (Wokɔ a, ansa-na woakohu.)
Merekɔ, merekɔ...... s. Sa tow, sa tow!......2729.

Traveling gives one experience.

1565. Wokɔ obi abɛ so na ɔbɛma wo nsa anom a, na otwa abɛ a, ɔma wo asahuru hua tie.

If you go where someone is tapping a palm tree he will give you some palm wine to drink, and if he is felling a palm tree, he gives you the foam of the palm wine to swell.

1566. Wokɔ obi (:aponkyerɛn) fi na ɔkotow hɔ a, wummisa no agua.

When you go to someone's house and he is squatting, you don't ask him for a chair..

1567. Wokɔ obi kurom na woanko wo kurom' bi a, wobu wo abɔa.

If you go to someone's town and he doesn't go to your town, he doesn't respect you.

1568. Wokɔ obi kurom na okum akokɔ ma wo di a, ɛnyɛ ne de no na woadi na wo de a ɔwɔ fie no na woadi (:wuredi).

When you go to someone's town and he kills a chicken for you to eat, it is not his fowl you have eaten, but your own which is at home.

1569. Wokɔ afunsie na woamma ntɛm a, na abo na ɛwom'.

If you go to dig a grave and you don't return quickly, it is because there are stones in the ground.

1570. Wokɔ gua so na atweserɛ abien sɛn hɔ na wotɔ biako a, nea aka no, wonni ano bio.

If you go to the market and there are two antelope thighs hanging there and you buy one, you don't bargain for the one left.

1571. Wokɔ Kankan gua so kɔtɔ ade na woannya a, wɔpata wo kaw.

If you go to Kankan market to buy something and cannot
get it, then you are kept from debt.

1572. Wokɔ okisi kurom' na ɔwe nnwea a, wowe bi.

If you go to rat's village and he is eating palm nuts,
you eat some too.

1573. Wokɔ Krɔbɔ na wuse womforo bo a, na wokɔ a, wo nso woforo
bo no.

If you go to Krobo and say you won't climb the mountain,
but if you go you will climb the mountain.

1574. Wokɔ Kumase na woannu na wudu Asene nkwanta a, na woawie
odu.

If you are going to Kumasi and you haven't reached there
but you have come to Assin junction, it means you have
reached there.

1575. Wokɔ kurom' a, wofa yonko a, fa ɔbarima; na wofa ɔba a,
ehia wo.

If you go to a town and you make a friend, take a man
for your friend, for if you take a girl friend, you will
become poor.

1576. Wokɔ kurom' na wuhu ntakara fufu siaw onipa tirim' a,
wummisa ne nipasu.

If you go to a town and see white feathers sticking out of
a man's head, you don't ask about his human nature.

1577. Wokɔ kurow bi mu, na dwom a mmofra to no (na) mpanyimfo
na ɛto gyaw wɔn. (...na asɛm a mmofra ka no, nea mp.
ka ara nen.)

If you visit a place and hear children singing songs,
these songs are the very ones sung by their ancestors
and handed down to the children.

1578. Wokɔ kurow bi mu na wuse: "mammɛto nnipa bi wɔ ha" a,
wose wo sɛ "yɛanhu onipa a waba."

If you go to any town and say I have not met anyone here
of importance, they say we have not been aware that
anyone of importance has come.

1579. Wokɔ Akwam sa na sɛ woannya biribi a, wotew ɔsapow.

If you go to Akwam to fight and you don't get anything,
at least you can pick up a sponge.

1580. Wokɔ na obi ne ne yere reko a, mpɛ ntɛm mmua, na ɛwɔ nea wayɛ no. Wokɔ aponkyerɛn fi...s. 1566.

When you go to someone's house and find him fighting with his wife, don't be in a hurry to give an answer for there is a reason why they are fighting.

1581. Wokɔ tɛkrɛma-sa a, wunyi dɔm.

If you fight with your tongue only, you don't win a war.

1582. Wokɔ ntɛmntɛm a, wogu wo so abɛ.

If you walk too fast, you spill palm oil on yourself.

1583. Wokɔ wo yonko nkyɛn aguru na ne na pam no a, na ɔde wo.

If you go to your friend's house to play, and his mother chases him out of the house, it is really you she wants to chase away.

1584. Wokɔ awuru kurom' na odi dote a, wudi bi.

If you go to the village of the tortoise and it is eating dirt, you eat some too.

1585. Woankɔ babi amma a, wɔmma wo akwaba.

If you haven't gone to anywhere and returned, you are not given a welcome.

1586. Wonkɔɔ obi abɛ so a, wunyi (:wunnye) no sakane.

If you never go with someone when he taps palm trees, you can't say he is stingy with his palm wine.

1587. Wonkɔɔ obi afum' da a, wuse wo nko ne kuafo. R. 12.

If you have never gone to another person's farm, you say, "I am the best farmer."

1588. Wonkɔ ɔyarefo ho a, wɔnne nea ɔma no aduru.

The one who never goes near a sick person, is not the one who gives him medicine.

1589. Woko, kɔ wo anim a, na wuyi dɔm.

If you fight, go forward, and you will win the battle.

1590. Wokɔ nkran na ɛnkɔ (:wonkɔe) a, wontwerɛ abɛ nnu mu. R. 154.

When you are driving off the black ants and they don't go away, you do not peel palm nuts to throw among them.

1591. Woko na wunyi dɔm a, womfa nnommum.

When you fight and do not win, you don't lead away any captives.

-133-

1592. Wòko ani-ani a, wofwere tiri.

If you have to fight with opponents on more than one side, you lose your life.

1593. Wòko yere, na wɔnko ba.

One fights with his wife but not with his child.

1594. Ɔkɔ ɛne ba nsɛ.

Coming and going are not the same.

1595. Akɔ-ne-aba na eye.

Going and coming are good.

1596. Akɔ-ne-aba ɲyɛ biribi a, epiw dote.

If going and coming doesn't accomplish anything, at least it makes the ground hard.

1597. Ɛko de anibere na ɛkyere bofoɔ.

The buffalo catches the hunter when it has been annoyed.

1598. Ɛko kum Kranni a, menkɔ no ayi, na Ɔkranni kum ko a, minni ne nam.

When a bush-cow kills a person, I do not go to his funeral, and when a person kills bush-cow I do not eat its flesh.

1599. Ɛko pusupusu onunum a, matie sɛ ɛbɔn. S.

If the bush-cow rubs against the "nunum" plant, I smell it.

1600. Ɔko aba a, na nsise aba.

When there is a war, there are many rumors.

1601. Ɔko ba a, na nsise bɔ kurow.

When there is a war it is rumors that cause the fall of the town.

1602. Ɔko na ɛkyerɛ nsise.

War teaches rumors.

1603. Ɔko-bone yɛ aniwu.

A bad war is a disgrace.

1604. Ɔko wɔko no agya mma.

War is fought by the father's children.

-134-

1605. Oko (:ɔko) anim minsuro, na menne asɛm anim.

I don't fear the face of the bush-cow, but the face of
trouble.

1606. Oko nyɛ aduan na woadi.

War is not food to be eaten.

1607. Ako ano yɛ den a, obi nkyere no nni.

As long as the parrot can cry aloud, no one catches hold
of it to eat it.

1608. Ako mpɛ sɛ obi hu ne nkesua nti na ɔtow gu duam' (:wuram',
onya nkonmu).

A parrot lays its eggs in the hollow of a tree because it
doesn't want anyone to see them.

1609. Ako se: 'nnɛ ni, na menne kyena'.

The parrot says: "it is today," but he means tomorrow.

1610. Ako ntakra, sɛ wuhu ne nko a, ntow no bo na ofi dodow mu.
Cf. 1440.

If you see a single parrot feather, don't throw a stone
at it, for it comes from where there are many more.

1611. Akoa di fɔ. (Kɔ-manu se: ...)

The slave is always guilty.

1612. Akoa di guan a, ne ho guan no.

If a slave eats a sheep he is really in trouble.

1613. Akoa didi owira ho.

The slave feeds on his master.

1614. Akoa ɔhantanni, wode no sie funu.

A proud slave is taken and buried with the corpse (of
a chief).

1615. Akoa nhyɛ neho ntu sa.

The slave does not decide for himself to go to war.

1616. Akoa koro Kwagyei!

The single slave Kwagyei!

1617. Akoa nkyerɛ mmannua. R. 215.

The slave does not show where sticks for building a house
grow in the bush.

1618.   Akoa nni mpow kwa.

The slave does not eat the second yam crop without a good reason.

1619.   Akoa nni awu na wonkum owura (:wiri). Gr. p. 154.

If a slave did not commit a murder, his master is not killed for it.

1620.   Akoa nim (:hu) som a, ɔfa ne ti ade di. Cf. 1439.

When a slave knows how to serve, he becomes a free man.

1621.   Akoa a onim som di ne wura ade.

A slave who knows how to serve inherits his master's wealth.

1622.   Akoa nim wura.

A slave knows his master.

1623.   Akoa nya neho, ɔfrɛ neho Sonani. R. 249.

When a slave becomes a free man, he calls himself a member of the Asona clan.

1624.   Akoa nyansa wɔ (:da) ne wura tirim.

A slave's wisdom is in his master's head.

1625.   Akoa mpaw wura. R. 216.

The slave does not choose his master.

1626.   Akoa ampɔw a, na efiri wira.

When a slave is not well behaved, it is because of his master.

1627.   Akoa sare asukɔ na woma ɔkɔ a, oguan.

When a slave has ceased to go for water and is again made to go, he runs away.

1628.   Akoa te sɛ kyekyere: wode nsu kakra gu no so a, na ahono.

A slave is like roasted corn that is ground into flour, when a little water is sprinkled on it, it becomes soft.

1629.   Akoa te sɛ twɛrebo: enni otuo ano a, ɛnyɛ 'ye.

A slave is like the flint on the striker of the gun, if it were missing, the gun wouldn't work well at all.

1630. Wo nkoa suro wo anim asɛm a, wonni nim mma wo.

If your slaves are afraid of you, they do not win
victories for you.

1631. Ɔkɔɔ-afow na ohuu afow-antwi.

He went and searched for food, and he returned with nothing.

1632. Ɔkɔ asu ama a, wommisa ahina.   R. 95.

If someone goes for water and doesn't return, you don't
ask for the water pot.

1633. Kobere mfamfa: aban nhyewe a, menhyewe (na ɛnhyewe).

Copper pans used in weighing gold; if the government
did not burn them, I can not burn them.

1634. Kɔdomasiamoa (:Kwasi amoa) di awu a, (:na) obi ankum no
na efi kakyerɛ.

If Kɔdomasiamoa (Kwasi amoa) was murdered, no one has
killed him, but the cause is from the information he was
given.

1635. Koekoe kɔ aburow, ɔkɔ nkuruma, na ɔnkɔ bo.

The bettle bores into corn and into okro, it can't bore
into stones.

1636. "Kɔfwɛ sɛn mu" nyɛ awerɛhow.

"Look into the pot" does not make you sad.

1637. Akogyinamoa da mfofom' a, ɛyɛ sɛ(nea) wawu.

If a bush cat is sprawled out on the ground it looks
like it is dead.

1638. Wo koko yɛ duru a, na wotow sono tuo.

When you have courage, you shoot an elephant.

1639. Kooko kyɛ pata so a, na egyae hene-yɛ.

If cocoyam stays on the roof for a long time, it ceases
to be itchy.

1640. Kooko nyɛ aduan bi na woabɔ no din akɔ afow.

Cocoyam is not a special food, but you mention its name
in going out in search of food.

1641. Akokɔ a wo ne no da no, wompɛ no ntɛm.

You are not in a hurry to search for the chicken which
sleeps with you.

-157-

1642. Akɔkɔ da ntɛm a, onyi kaw (mma ne wura.)

When a chicken goes to roost early, it does not get its master into debt.

1643. Akɔkɔ de fwete de fwete a, ohu gyansakyi bopea (gyane apeapeawa). S.

If the chicken scratches and scratches, it see "gyansakyi bopea" a mythical animal.

1644. Akɔkɔ di wo yɔnko awi a, pam no, na dabi obedi wo de. R. 34.

When a chicken is eating your neighbour's grain, drive it away, for one day it will eat yours.

1645. Akɔkɔ fwɛ (:yɛn) aberewa, na aberewa fwɛ (:nso ayɛn) akɔkɔ. Gr. p. 150.

The old woman cares for the hen, and the hen cares for the old woman.

1646. Akɔkɔ-hyɛn kyɛ ofie a, ɔbere.

If a white hen stays in the chicken house for a long time, it turns red.

1647. Akɔkɔ na ɔyɛ aboa, na odidi a, ɔde n'ano twitwi (:twutwu) fam'.

The chicken is an animal for when it eats, it rubs its beak back and forth on the ground.

1648. Akɔkɔ nan (:nantam) nkum (ne) ba. Z. 86.

The foot of the hen does not kill its chick.

1649. Akɔkɔ ne honam ntakara aduasa, ne nhina tuatua werɛm'. S. Cf. 1659.

There are all kinds of feathers on the body of a chicken (thirty) and they all stick to its skin.

1650. Akɔkɔ ne krakum ko.

The chicken sometimes fights with the turkey.

1651. Akɔkɔ nni aso nanso onnya ne sotɔre a, wode bɔ no ara.

The chicken has no ears but if it doesn't get them boxed, it still gets its beating.

1652. Akɔkɔ ani sa burofua. R. 104.

The chicken has its eye set on the grain of corn.

1653. Akokɔ nom nsu a, ɔde kyerɛ Onyankopɔn.

When a chicken drinks water it shows it to God (when it lifts up its head to swallow).

1654. Akokɔ-pa na ɔwo asensɛ: asensɛ: me nko mifi he?

An ordinary chicken hatches out a chicken with curled muffled feathers, and the chicken with curled muffled feathers says: "I alone where did I come from?"

1655. Akokɔ se: ade ansa a, anka memee?

The chicken says, "If it had not got dark, would I have had my fill?"

1656. Akokɔ se: kyere akyekyere tutu no! na ɔno akyekyere se: na wo de, woaberɛ.

The chicken says, "catch the tortoise and pluck it," but the tortoise says, "as for you, you will get tired of trying to do that!"

1657. Akokɔ se: asɛmpa nti na mayɛ m'ano feafea.

The chicken says: "it is because of good news that I have made my mouth pointed."

1658. Akokɔ ntakra na ɛma akokɔ yɛ kɛse.

It is the feathers of a chicken that make it big.

1659. Akokɔ ntakara nyin a, etuatua ne honam nu.

When the feathers of a chicken grow, they still remain attached to its body.

1660. Akokɔ ti si ahe na worebɔ mu fɛ?

How many chicken heads are there that people always keep wounding them in the head.

1661. Akokɔ wɔ nkwa aduru a, anka 'yɛde no twa abosom soo?

If the chicken possessed life-giving medicine, would it be taken and sacrified over fetishes?

1662. Akokoa: ɔbɔmene atwɛre; ma ɔmmene, na obehu akyiri.

The infant: he tries to swallow a frog; let him swallow it, for he'll see what will happen.

1663. Kokobe aduru ne ten. (Ofɛe Kwasi.)

The medicine for leprosy is the "ten" amulet.

1664. Akokɔbere nim adekyee (:nim se ade bɛkye) na (nso)
       ɔfwɛ onini ano.

       The hen knows when dawn is coming but she nevertheless
       leaves the crowing to the cock.

1665. Kokobo se: akokɔ nkogya no anadwo-su mu; na awia te
       dɛn?

       The weasel says: "the chicken doesn't go and see it off
       at the night, what about in the afternoon?"

1666. Akokoduadua se: ohiani tra fwerem so a, ɛyɛ sɛ ɔte
       akentennua so.

       The yellow wagtail says: "when a poor man sits on the
       creepers with large throwns, it is like he is sitting
       on a chair."

1667. Akokoduadua ayefasan, wokyi.

       The yellow wagtail, you hate the one who denies the
       charge of adultery.

1668. "Akokɔfwereɛ, gyae pini!" ose: "ohia ntira!"

       If you tell a wood-hen to stop groaning it says "it is
       all due to poverty."

1669. Akokonini bow nsa na ne werɛ afi akoroma.

       When a cock gets drunk it forgets about the hawk.

1670. Akokonini, gyae akuntun-akuntun, na yɛn nhina yɛ kesua
       (:kerefua) mma.

       Cock, stop your boasting for we all came out of an
       egg-shell.

1671. Akokonini, gyae woho kyerɛ, na wo na ne kesua-hono.

       O cock, stop being puffed up with pride, after all, your
       mother was only an egg-shell.

1672. Akokonimpa fi kesuam'.

       A large cock also comes from an egg.

1673. Akokonini se: tɔ tamfo nko a, anka mabɔn anadwo na
       wɔakum me. R.162.

       The cock says: "the enemy would like me to crow at
       midnight and be killed."

1674. Akokono de bɛtɛbɛtɛ na awe adwe.

       The palm tree grub slowly eats away the palm tree.

-140-

1675. Akɔkono nua ne samanaiwo.

The big grub found in felled palm trees is the brother
of the beetle.

1676. Kokɔra firi bamfoɔ yam'.

The "kokora" comes from the thorny plant's stomach.

1677. Kokora nnim bamfoɔ.

The "kokota" doesn't know "bamfo".

1678. Kokosakyi a okotwa (n')akyene (ne) ti bɔ ho a, wommisa
nea ɔso (:ɔka).

The vulture who goes and cuts his drum and hits his head,
you don't ask what he hit.

1679. Kokosakyi akrampa, ne din anyɛ dɛ, na ne ho anyɛ huam.

The vulture doesn't have a good name and its body
doesn't have a good scent.

1680. Kokosakyi mpɛ ofie aba a, anka onsisi sumana so.R.247.

If the vulture did not wish to come into the house, it
wouldn't stand about on the garbage dump.

1681. Kokosakyi se: odompo ho bɔn.

The vulture says the civet cat stinks.

1682. Kokurobeti nnye asra kwa.

The thumb doesn't receive snuff on it without a good
reason.

1683. Okokuroko da akoe mu no, na biribi hyɛ n'afonom. Cf. 2813.

If a big man is lying down in the field of battle, it
means there is something sticking in his cheeks.

1684. Ɔkɔm bere ɔkasamu (perh.-mo?).

Hunger gets tired in speaking.

1685. Ɔkɔm de aberewa a, na ose: toto (:mompɛ) biribi ma
(:mma) mmofra na wonni!

When the old woman is hungry she says; "roast something
for the children that they may eat."

1686. Ɔkɔm de hoho a, ɔda; na odidi me a, obisabisa nkurofo
yerenom.

When a stranger is hungry, he sleeps; but when he has
eaten his fill he goes about making inquiries about
peoples' wives.

1687. Okom de hoho a, ɔde fi ne kurom'. Z.36.

When a stranger is hungry, he brought it with him from his town.

1688. Okom de akoa, na ɔkɔm de hene.'

Hunger is felt by a slave, and hunger is felt by a chief.

1689. Okom de wo a, bisa m'akoa; m'akoa nim ɔkɔm aduru.

When you are hungry, ask my slave; my slave knows the medicine for hunger.

1690. Okom de wo a, ɛde wo nko.

When you feel hungry, you feel your own hunger.

1691. Okom de wo a, womfa wo nsa abien nnidi. R. 56. Gr. p. 172

Though you are hungry, you don't eat with both hands.

1692. Okom ne ka, na ɔfanim ka.

Of the two, hunger and debt, debt is preferable.

1693. Okɔm-pa nko, sukɔm nko.

Hunger and thirst are not the same.

1694. Koma bone kum owura.

A bad temper kills its owner.

1695. Akomboafo yɛ na.

It is difficult to get a good helper for the fetish priest.

1696. Okɔmfo a osei sɛ osu bɛtɔ ne ɔkɔmfo a ose osu rentɔ
nhina yɛ akɔmfo-trofo. Cf. 3056. 3285.

The fetish priest who says it will rain and the fetish priest who says it will not rain, they are all lying fetish priests.

1697. Okɔmfo nni nkɔntoro na wontwa ɔbosonsoafo ti.

When the fetish priest has given a false prophecy, the fetish carrier's head is not cut off.

1698. Okomfo annya asapate a, ɔnkom.

If the fetish priest doesn't get an assistant, he doesn't perform the practices of the fetish priest.

1699. Akɔmfo aduasa fwɛ ɔyarefo a, wodi atoro.

When thirty fetish priests are looking after a sick man, they all tell lies.

1700. Wo nkɔmmɔ yɛ den a, wofwere debisafo. Cf. 3569.

If you have a strong complaint, you expose the life of the inquirer.

1701. Okompi-were ne ne mersbo: wowe a wurewu; woanwe a, wo
yere ne wo mma da so. (Ete se a.s. akoyɛ ok....)
The "okompi" skin and his liver, if you eat it, you will
die; if you don't eat it, your wife and children continue
to get it.

1702. Wo kon tiatia a, wokofa saworowa ato mu ana?
If you have a short neck, do you wear a string of
cowries around it?

1703. Akɔnhyɛase ne wuo. (Akyemfo).
The prediction given in sooth saying is death.

1704. Konkon ankɔ agyina a, na oburoni Ampomma (de) ɔkɔm de no.
If the "konkon" bird doesn't go for consultation, then
the European Ampomma is hungry.

1705. Okonkonsafo antɔ a, ɔdommarima ntɔ da.
If the double tongued person is not killed then the
powerful warrior never dies.

1706. Ankonam di toro. (Onam me asɛm. 2086.)Cf. 450..
The person who travels without a companion tells lies.

1707. Ankonam kohuu peduasa, na ɔdansefo ne hena?
The lone traveller went and saw 30,000 people, but who
is his witness?

1708. Ankonam mmɔ hu.
The lone traveller doesn't make a loud noise.

1709. Ankonam yɛ odwen (:mmusu). Cf. 451.
The person who travels alone is seized and made a slave.

1710. Wo ankonnua to wo so a, wosan ana?
If your chair is lying on you, do you take it off?

1711. Kontiwa mpɛ ahohora nti na ɔsɛn dɔtɔ mu.
Because the "kontiwa" gourd doesn't like disgrace, it
hangs in a thicket.

1712. Okotonkurowi, ɛda amansan nhina kɔn mu. Cf. 2844.
The luminous circle around the sun lies around all peoples
necks.

1713. Nkontomere nyɛ nam bi; na wuyi no nkwan mu a, na ɛnyɛ dɛ.
Kontommire is not some kind of meat; for if you pick
it out of the soup, it is not delicious.

1714. Okontomponi dan. wopa, na wonnyew.

The deceitful man's house is pulled down, it is not burned down.

1715. Kontromfi akwakora na oware kontromfi aberewa.

The old male monkey marries the old female monkey.

1716. Kontromfi kyea senea akyeafo kyea, nso ne to ko.

The monkey struts about just as a conceited person does, but its buttocks are red nevertheless.

1717. Kontromfi se: oberan wu ne koko. R. 89.

The monkey says: "the brave man dies only from his chest being hurt."

1718. Kontromfi se: afei ne ampa.

The monkey says: "Now I shall really speak the truth."

1719. Kontromfi se: ohia ayi akyeafo adi.

The monkey says that poverty shows up the conceited person.

1720. Kontromfi se: wohye m'afonom' a, na meyi asempa maka makyere mo. R. 223.

The monkey says: "If you fill up my cheeks, then I bring forth good things to tell you."

1721. Kontromfi se: me suman ne m'ani(wa) R. 90. Z. 218.

The monkey says: "My talisman is my little eyes."

1722. Akora a wanyin dan ne mma.

An old man is dependent on his children.

1723. Akora nua ne duwui.

The old man's brother is the rotten tree.

1724. Korabo nnim manni.

A musket ball does not know the native.

1725. Korakitafo nfwere nsa.

The one who holds the calabash doesn't spill the wine.

1726. Kor'-a-nkye nte se wo ankasa wonam.

"Come back quickly" is not as good as going and getting it yourself.

1727. Korankye a odi aketehene na oda fam!

Korankye who is the chief of the mat weavers lies on the ground.

1728. Korankyewa abɛ, wɔnara nu na wɔnara yɛ.

Korankyewa palm tree, they pick palm nuts from the tree and they also make palm oil.

1729. Ɔkɔrefa bamkyininii ne sie (=siw).

The ɔkɔrefa animal's umbrella is the ant hill.

1730. Kɔre-kyerekyere ne kɔre-dada ne kɔre-a-na-obi-aba, hena ne panyin. (Ɔpanyin ne hena? ɔpanyin ne kɔre-dada.)

The one who went in the beginning and the one who has gone before, and he who will come in the future. Who is the eldest? The eldest is he who has gone before.

1731. Ɔkorow, wɔhare no afanu. R. 165. Cf. 1297

A boat is paddled on both sides.

1732. Ɔkoro(-kɛse) yɛ ma a, tantia (:dwenti) ka.

If the big boat is full, the vessel to cover it remains.

1733. Korodo-korodo nhina wie asɛmti (:sempim).

All prattling ends in a big case.

1734. Akoroma fa me fa na odi a, minni bi.

If the hawk takes my part and eats, I have none to eat.

1735. Ɔkoropatu sisi ne ti ase, ɔkoropɔn agye ne nsam hene.

If the owl bows (nods his head), the eagle takes the chieftancy.

1736. Kose: "wonnya agoru" a, - wokoso mma mu!

Kose, if you aren't allowed to play, you continue playing with women.

1737. "Kosi" a, "nkosi"; " ɔda" a, "nkɔda!"

If you tell him to stand up he doesn't, and if you tell him to lie down, he doesn't.

1738. Akosua mmɔ mmusu na Akua mfa. R. 55.

Akosua doesn't cause trouble and Akua takes the punishment.

1739. Ɔkɔtɔ a ɔda sika ho po twɛre abɛ.

The crab that lies by the gold in the river peels the palm nut with his teeth.

1740. Ɔkɔtɔ (ba) nwo anoma. R. 127. Z. 2.

The crab doesn't give birth to a bird.

1741. Ɔkɔtɔ bɛne asuo 'ti na onim asuo kasa.

When the crab comes near to the source of the river he hears the sound of the water.

1742. Ɔkoto bo pemmo a, ɔsan n'akyi.
When the crab falls on its back it goes backwards.

1743. Ɔkoto-foforo aperɛw mu nni nam.
Inside the young "aperɛw" crab there is no meat.

1744. Ɔkoto guan a, oguan kɔ pom'.
When the crab flees, he runs into the ocean.

1745. Ɔkoto na onim sika dabere.
The crab knows where the gold is lying.

1746. Ɔkoto annya adaye nti na ɔda amoa mu.
Because the crab didn't get a good place to sleep, he sleeps in a hole.

1747. Ɔkoto po di sukɔm, na menne okwaku a ɔda ɔsoro.
Even a crab gets thirsty, and what about the monkey who sleeps in trees.

1748. Kɔtɔbankye se: ɔbɛkyene abo, na ɔhyɛ fam' hyɛ fam' no, ɔporɔwe.
Cassava says he will become hard like a rock but if he stays in the ground for a long time, he becomes rotten.

1749. Kɔtɔkɔ ne gyahene nni ato-nhyia (:atunhyia).
The porcupine and the leopard do not render anyone tribute.

1750. Kɔtɔkɔ rekɔ Kɔtɔkɔ a, ɔmfa adidie.
If the porcupine is going to the land of the porcupines, he does not take anything to eat.

1751. Kotoku-saabobe, onni ano na ɔhome. =3580.
The flower of the "kotoku-saabobe" vine has no mouth, and yet it breathes.

1752. Kotoku tew a, na 'mati adwo.
If the bag tears, then the shoulders get a rest.

1753. Kotokurodu yɛ nnam a, ɔyɛ wɔ ne twawu ho.
If the black wasp acts brave it does so when it is with a swarm of wasps.

1754. Kotɔ-(kɔ)sabire kasa ntɛm, nso pra da gya no. S.
The black singing bird "kotɔkɔ-sabire" speaks quickly, but the armadillo is lying near the fire.

-146-

1755. Akoto-wo-nan-aśe, wompae no atifi!
You don't beat the heads of those who prostrate before
you.

1756. Akotow (mu)-akotow mu wɔ biribi a, anka ɔsebɔ afuw abɛn.
Cf. 1829.
If frequent crouching had any value, then the leopard would
have horns.

1757. "Kotu bɛtɛ" anyɛ ye, ...s. 3367.

1758. Mekra wo asɛm a, menya amanne?
If I give you a message, should I suffer because of it?

1759. Wonkra Kosi a, wonyi wea.
If you don't send a message to Kosi you won't catch a
tree-bear.

1760. Wo⌁kra nye a, na wunya asafo nsam' amanne.
If you are not fortunate, you suffer at the hands of the
soldiers.

1761. Nkra (:ɔkrakose) nyɛ akommu.
Sending word that one shall go does not cause one's
neck to be broken.

1762. Nkrabea nhina nsɛ.
All destinies are not the same.

1763. Krabea wonkwati. Cf. 2538.
Your destiny can not be evaded.

1764. Ɔkrakɔfwɛ na ɛyɛ fɛ, na ɔkrakɔsu nyɛ.   Ɔkrakose ...s. 1761.
Sending word that one shall go and look is nice, but
sending word that one shall go and weep is not nice.

1765. Ɔkraman a ɔkɔ ahayɔ, wanhu, na agyinamoa na ɔbɛyɛ dɛn?
The dog which goes hunting didn't see anything, so what
can the cat hope to do?

1766. Ɔkraman fa kesua a, ɛbɛbɔ wɔ n'anom'.
If the dog steal eggs, they will break in his mouth.

1767. Ɔkraman na obu bɛ se: ade-kɛse nyera.

The dog gives his proverb: "A big thing does not get lost."

1768. Ɔkraman anom yɛ no dɛ a, ɔnew ne kɔnmu nnawa. R.141.
Cf.1774.

If the dog likes sweet things, he doesn't eat the hair
from his neck.

1769. Wo kraman se 'ɔbɛkyere sono ama wo' a, ɔdada wo.

If your dog says he will catch a lion for you, he is
deceiving you.

1770. Ɔkraman se: ɔremfa ɔyere da; na ɔfa ɔyere no, ɔfa
n'agya yere.

The dog says he will never commit adultery but if he does,
he commits adultery with his father's wife.

1771. Ɔkraman se: ɔpɛ 'mirika-hunu atu, na menne sɛ n'ase
guan atew ayera.

The dog who likes to run about aimlessly says his
mother-in-law's sheep has broken loose and is lost.

1772. Ɔkraman si pata so na ɛnyɛ ɔno na ɔforee a, na obi na
ɔmaa no so sii hɔ. Cf.1432.

If there is a dog standing on a roof, he didn't climb
there, someone put him there.

1773. Ɔkramane atirimsɛm da ne bo, na ɛnna ne tirim.

A dog's thought lies in his chest, but not in his head.

1774. Ɔkraman bɛwe ade nhina a, (:we adeɛ nh., na) ɔnwe ne kɔnmu
(:kɔnom') dawa. Cf.1768.

A dog will chew everything, he can't chew the bells hung
around his neck.

1775. Nkramfana nyɛ atom'deɛ pa a 'yɛde no frafra nam (mu).

If the "nkramfana" small sea fishes are not sufficient for
the soup, we mix them with other fish.

1776. Nkramfoa nyɛ nam bi na apofofo (:wɔ)abɔ (ne) din aforo
(po). Gr.p.160.

"Nkramfoa" is not just any kind of fish that the fisher-
men go to the sea for.

1777. Nkran nam a, atibiri wom'.

If the black ants travel, the soldiers ants are with them.

1778. Nkranfo rebedi toa a, na wofrɛ no konyo.

If the black ants are eating a bottle, it is called a watermelon.

1779. Wokrankran wo ani sɛ worepɛ ɔbo abɔ anoma no, na ɔno nso krankran n'ani fwefwɛ dua a obetu asi so.

When you are eagerly looking for a stone to throw at a bird, the bird is eagerly looking for a tree to fly to and perch in.

1780. Nkrante nkɔ babi nnyaw ne nnaw.

The cutlass doesn't go anywhere without losing its sharpness.

1781. Karanini te-ase a, karabere mmɔ adwe.

If the male "kra" monkey is alive, the female "kra" monkey doesn't crush palm nuts with her teeth.

1782. Ɔkarawa, ma oguannam nyɛ wo dɛ; da bi wɔde mmoroba bɛboro wo.

The female slave (that is destined to be sacrificed upon the death of her master), make the sheep meat tasteless to you; someday you will beat her with clubs.

1783. Ankra-wo-sa-gua, wonni.

You don't say good-bye to someone at a palm wine drinking place.

1784. Ɔkroboni ba nnuan kokotem' kwa. R.164.

A Krobo child does not run through the cornfield without a good reason.

1785. Nkrokrotibane 'ti na 'yɛrefwe asuo? S.

Is it because of the frogs' heads that we are bailing water out?

1786. Ɔkromfo nsen kwa wura.

A thief is not greater than a farm owner.

1787. "Eku, gye!" (a), eku gye; "eku, ma me!" a, eku "kye!" (Owusu Akyem.) Cf.1977.

If you give it to the monkey the monkey accepts it; if you ask the monkey to give it to you the monkey says no (kye!).

1788. Eku ankɔ a, n'atwea kɔ.

If the monkey doesn't go, his slave goes.

1789. Akua nhintiw na wɔmma Kwasi due.

If Akua stubs her toe we don't sympathize with Kwasi.

1790. Okuafo afɛre ɔbankye, na kotɔkɔ nso afɛre. Cf.38.

The farmer is ashamed to eat cassava and the porcupine is also ashamed to eat it.

1791. Akuama, ɛyɛ aduru a, anka ɔtwe nam ntenten wɔ wuram'?

If the "akuama" plant is medicine, would the antelope that lives in the forest have to travel a long distance?

1792. Akuapem nya okyigyinafo a, na ekum aboa.

If the Danish musket gets a shooter, it kills animals.

1793. Akuapem asɛm te sɛ etiri nkwahama, wɔde kyere wo a, wuntumi nsan.

Problems of the Akuapems are like a knot in a cord that is used to bind trading articles, if you are tied with it, you don't get loose.

1794. Akuapem asɛm yɛ akyekyerekona: wɔde yaw wo a, amanne.

Problems of the Akuapems are like different kinds of beads strung together, if you are troubled by them, it is a real problem.

1795. Akuapem yɛ apagyakwa, wonni agyinanan.

Akuapem makes "apagyakwa," they have no place where they can live undisturbed.

1796. Akuapemfo bibifo, wonim atono; obi nto aprɛm da.

Black Akwapim people, they know blacksmithing but no one has ever discharged a cannon.

1797. Akuapemfo owu akyi asɛm nti na wonya asɛm aka akyerɛ mmofra.

It is because the problems of the Akwapim people that after one dies that they have something to tell their children.

1798. Okuapenni se 'ɔbɛkasa Akyem' a, ma ɔnkasa, na abufuw bɛba dedaw.

If the Akuapem people want to speak the Akyem dialect, let them speak, for anger has already come.

1799. Kube haha huno, ɔbɛten sen no nno.
       Kube wawa hunu, abɛ kyɛn no nsa.

       The coconut boasts in vain, the full grown palm tree with a
       long, slender stem is greater than it in giving oil
       (palm wine).

1800. Okufo mmɔ afɛ (:nni aguma).

       A person full of sores and wounds can not fight and wound
       others.

1801. Akukomfi ani soso kyɛn no a, ɔyɛ (:na wayɛ) omumo.

       If the eyes of the praying mantis are bigger than its body,
       it becomes ugly in appearance.

1802. Okukuban mfa ntɛm nsoa adwerɛwa ne dua a ɛware.

       The "okukuban" squirrel doesn't quickly prove its innocence
       by its long tail.

1803. Okukuban se: me nko, me nko-nko (:menkoko)!

       The squirrel says: "I don't fight, I don't go to fight."

1804. Kukurubinsin se: onim nea, ɔde bin ko a, wɔbɛto nti
       na opirew, na ompirew no kwa.

       The dung bettle says that if he knew where to go to
       toilet he would go there, but if he is afraid it is for
       a good reason.

1805. Okum nkyi "mayɛ dɛn?"

       If someone is going to kill you he doesn't mind, "What
       have I done?"

1806. Wukum aboa bi a, na wode no ayɛ wo de.

       When you kill an animal, you make him your own.

1807. Wukum manni a, wokata n'ani.

       If you kill a friend, you cover his eyes.

1808. Wukum manni na woankata n'ani a, ɔyɛ wo sesa.

       If you kill a friend and don't cover his eyes, his
       spirit will return and trouble you.

1809. Wukum nyansafo a, na woasɛe ade; na woton no a, wonyɛɛ
       fwe ɛ.

       If you kill a wise person you spoiled something valuable,
       but if you sell him you have done nothing wrong.

1810. Wukum wo de a, woto wo yonko de. R.194.
If you kill your own child, you get your neighbor's child (who is as bad as your child).

1811. Wurekum aboa no (:osebɔ) a, womfrɛ no asabontwi.
If you kill a leopard don't call it "asobontwi" (a small species of leopard).

1812. Wokum wo a, na woawu wu-pa, na wuwu wo kra wu a, ɛn'de enye. (Dwabenfo a wɔ-ne Boaten baa Akyem no.)
If they kill you then you die a good death, but if your soul really dies then it is not a good death.

1813. "Wokum wo a, wodi wo aboa" (,ɛ) yɛ ka!
If they kill you, they have treated you as a beast causing debts.

1814. Worekum wo, a, wunse sɛ: wɔbore me kurum'!
If they are killing you, you don't say you are hurting my sore.

1815. Merebekum akoko, makum ɔbrɛko (:obereku) na mafwɛ sɛ adekyee bɛyɛ dɛn?
I am going to kill my chicken, I have already killed "ɔbrɛko" and I will see what the dawn will do?

1816. Yekum bi ansa-na yɛapam bi.
Some are killed before others are put to flight.

1817. Munkum Kutuankama na ne nkapo hyehyɛ hom.
You don't kill Kutuankama, and his bracelets adorn you.

1818. Wonkum aboa a, wonni n'ayam'de.
If you don't kill an animal, you don't eat its entrails.

1819. Wonkum mmarima a, wɔmfa mmea.
If the men are not killed, you can't take their women.

1820. Nkuma-nkuma mma na wonyin.
Small children grow up.

1821. Nkuma-nkuma nyini dodo.
Small children have grown too much.

1822. Kumase aduan biara ne nsu.
The people of Kumase is the drink taken in swearing an oath of mutual fidelity.

1823. Okumfo amfɛre a, osifo amfɛre.

If the killer is not afraid, the spirit of the dead person is also not afraid.

1824. Kunadan mu na wɔfa kunabea.

The things in the widow's room belongs to the widow.

1825. Okunini (=ɔsɛn) fwe ase a, na ne kyɛ ka he?

If a very distinguished person falls down, where does his hat land.

1826. Akuntumma kuntun n'afɛ, na onkuntun mpanyin. R.180.

A bully fights someone his own size, he doesn't fight with grown ups.

1827. Okuntumpa didi sareso.

The hyena eats in the grassland.

1828. Okuntumpa ne n'akoa, ɔte-ase a, ɔyɛ no akoa, owu a, ɔyɛ ne nam.

The hyena and his slave, when he is alive he makes him a slave, when he dies he makes him his meat.

1829. Akuntun-(a)kuntun mu wɔ biribi a, anka ɔsebɔ afuw abɛn. Cf.1756.

If arrogance were something, the leopard would have horns.

1830. Akuntunkuntun, woyɛ no dɔm ano, wonyɛ nkyerɛ mmea.

You do your boasting at the battle front, you don't boast for women to admire you.

1831. Wukura afwetefwete a, wummisa (:wompɛ) dua.

If you hold something that is all scratched up, you don't ask for a stick.

1832. Wokura wo, a, wo werɛ afi nkeka. R.232.

When you are caught, you forget to bite.

1833. Wokura wo ti a, wommisa wo anom asɛm.

When you are holding up your head, we don't ask your mouth anything.

1834. Wokura wo yere a, na wokura wo ba.

If you support your wife, you also support your child.

1835. Minkura ankara minnya ankara na mense sɛ: mihune ankara.
(Wonkura n'ankara nnya n'ankara nse sɛ: mihuni ankara.)
Cf.203.220. 1558.

If I hadn't seized fortune I would not have let it go,
I didn't say, I would have seized fortune if I had seen it.

1836. Akura se: nea okum me nyɛ me yaw sɛ nea ɔde me fwe fam'.

The mouse says "He who kills me does not hurt me as much
as he who throws me on the ground (after I am dead.)

1837. Akura te sɛ nantwi a, na agyinamoa akɔa ara nen. R.110.

Even if the mouse were the size of a cow, he would still be
the cat's slave.

1838. Nkura-dodow bɔre tu a, ɛnnɔ.

Even if many mice dig a hole, it doesn't become deep.

1839. Kuro bi a ɔhene nni mu, wudi asɛm a, entwam' ntɛm.

If you have a case in a village in which there is no
chief, it doesn't get settled quickly.

1840. Kurow gu, na mɛnre abobow.

The town is destroyed, so certainly the gates are destroyed.

1841. Kuro so a, ɔmanni-bere yɛ ɔna.

If the town is large, the guest's stay is difficult.

1842. Akurofo so apakyiwa se: gya me adannan', na nea oduaa
me awu.

On the site of a destroyed town a small calabash with a
cover says; "stop turning me over, for he who planted me
has died."

1843. Kurom'hayifo kyi ɔmanni absn.

The town people here dislike the stranger's horn.

1844. Akuropɔn mmasia, woyɛ aboko, wonfwete fako.

The women from Akuropɔn are wild flowers, they are not
scattered in one place.

1845. Akuropɔn nhyira na ɛte dɛn? na won nnuabɔ!

What is Akuropɔn's blessing? Their cursing!

1846. Akuropɔn nim de ne abɛ noa.
      Akuropɔn is known for the boiling of palm nuts.

1847. Akuropɔn nim wɔn ani ase.
      The people of Akuropɔn know their history.

1848. Akuroponfo nkɔ po, nso wotɔn nsukowa.
      The people of Akuropɔn don't go to sea, but they sell
      small sea-fish.

1849. Akuroponfo tesɛ apakyi: woammɔ wɔn a, wommue.
      The people of Akuropɔn are like a broad calabash with a cover,
      if you don't hit them they don't open up.

1850. Akuroponfo (:mpanyimfo) yɛ wo guannuan, na (sɛ) wuguan
      a, woaserew wo (:na akyiri no wɔserew wo).
      The people of Akuropɔn frighten you and if you flee they
      laugh at you.

1851. Kurotwiamansa fa awuru a, ɔdannan no hunu   (:obua da).
      When a leopard catches a turtle, it turns it over and over
      in vain.

1852. Kurotwiamansa nennam sisia ase ma ɔsisia wosow biribiri.
      The leopard that prowls about under the thicket causes
      the thicket to shake greatly.

1853. Kurotwiamansa se: ɔnam ha mu kwa; akyekyere na ɔde
      ne ha.
      The leopard declares that he prowls around the bush for no
      purpose, for the tortoise really owns the jungle.

1854. Ekuru a atwa ntini mu, wonsa bio.
      A sore which has gone through the vein can not be healed.

1855. Ekuru bu dompem' a, wɔntoto bio.
      If a sore breaks the bone you don't dress it again.

1856. Ekuru hia (wo) a, na wobɔ ne dudo (:wobɔ ho d.).
      If your sore is troubling you, you put "dudo" medicine
      on it.

1857. Ekuru sa (:wu) a, (na) ɔdowa (a)fwete. (Kwab. Panyin.)
      If the sore is healed, the swelling in the loins goes away.

1858. Ekuru tow (wo) fwene mu a, ɛmmɔn bio.
      If a sore dries up inside your nose it does not stink
      anymore.

1859. Ekuru ntutu afanu. R.226.

The sore does not pain on both sides of the body.

1860. Akuru (:Akuro) dɔso a, woyi bi ayɛ.

If you have many sores, you praise one of them.

1861. Sɛ nkuruma sɛn ogya ani a, ɛsɛn hɔ ma ɔwansan.

If the okro is hanging in front of the fire, it hangs there for the flies.

1862. Kurutiayisi, wudi no atɛm a, wodi wo bi.

If you insult the pupil of the eye, you insult yourself.

1863. Kusumdi nti na osunson annya aniwa.

Because of deceptiveness the worm did not get eyes.

1864. Kutruku amma ɔtow na efi adekyee-nim'.

If the clenched fist did not hit anyone, it can be seen in the morning.

1865. Okutu-kwaku sere adadwo a, na wame.

If the "okutu" monkey laughs at night, it means he is satisfied.

1866. Wukuw wo nnunsin (:nnyansin) a, wofwere soafo.

If you cut your trees close to the ground, you exhaust the carrier.

1867. Wonkwa wo dan mu mma no mmere 'ye a, wonkɔkwa wo yɔnko de mu.

If you don't rub the floor of your room with a mixture of red clay and chaff to make it red, you don't rub your neighbour's.

1868. Kwabiri so ne nno; (sɛ) ɔrekɔbɔ o, sɛ ɔrekɔtɔn o, obi nnim'.

Kwabiri carries his palm oil, whether he is going to crack palm nuts or whether he is going to sell his palm oil, no one knows.

1869. Ɔkwadu kɔ Nnyedu a, ɔbɛba abɛto n'afirifo.

If the antelope goes to Nnyedu, he will come to meet his debtors.

1870. Ɔkwadu se: woammerɛ na wudidi a, ɛnyɛ dɛ. R.190. Cf.971.

The antelope says: "if you are not tired and you eat, it doesn't taste good."

1871. Kwadwo Akɔte nnya nkɔdɔw Boaboa no, na ɛhɔ nkɔnsɔn didi.
Cf.1912.
Before Kwadwo Akote made a farm at Boaboa, the chimpanzees
were already eating there.

1872. Ckwae a agye wo, womfrɛ no akwaewa. R.135.
The forest which has given you protection is not called
a little forest.

1873. Kwae mu mmobadua se: ɛnyɛ ne mu apɔw nti a, anka
ɔ-ne sibiri sɛ.
The cane reeds in the forest says that if it were not
because of his joints, he and the "sibiri" reed would be
identical.

1874. Kwae mu nni biribi a, ɛwɔ kanana.
If there is nothing in the forest, there is at least
stillness.

1875. Kwagyadu (=kontromfi) kɔ apam a (:apam-mɔ), otwaa ahe
o, otwaa ahe o, nankasa na onim.
If the monkey goes to clear a place for a farm, how much
he weeds, he alone knows.

1876. Akwagyinamoa nni biribi a, ɔwɔ atotɛm (:nt.).
If the bush cat has nothing, at least it has readiness
for fighting.

1877. Akwakora te hɔ (ansa-) na wowoo panyin.
An old man was in the world before a chief was born.

1878. Akwakora wɔ nkwa a, onni mfensa. =2620.
If an old man has vigour, it is not forever.

1879. Okwaku ba a, yekum aduaben (=aberekyi); ɔkwaku amma a,
yekum aduaben.
If the monkey comes we kill a goat; if the monkey doesn't
come, we still kill a goat.

1880. Kwakwadabi bako ntu ne yonko ani.
One black bird can not pluck another bird's eye.

1881. Kwakwasi anhu asɛn bi ansɛn no, na kokosakyi anhu atono
bi antono.
If Kwakwasi has not seen a cooking pot hanging, the
vulture has not seen a forge forging.

1882. Nkwamanfo na ɛbɔ man.

A people without a king ruin a town.

1883. Kwamena mpɛ ne ho asɛm nti na ɔte adukuro mu.

Because the ant hill of small white ants doesn't like itself, it lives in the buttresses of trees.

1884. Kwamena si adukuro mu a, na ne fi ara ne ho.

If there is an ant hill between the buttresses of a tree, that is its house.

1885. Okwamuni se: wowɔ asawu a, na wohata tabon.

Okwamuni says: "if you have a large fishing net, you hang up your paddle to dry."

1886. Nkwam-pa na ɛtwe (:etwiw, etwu, epini) agua.

Tasty soup pulls the chair (close to the table).

1887. Okwan a akwagyansa (=odompo) awu mu no, womfa mu akwagyansa afo.

The road on which the bush-dog died is not where you go searching for bush-dogs.

1888. Okwan a wunsuro mu na aboa kyere wo mu.

It is on the path you do not fear that the wild beast catches you.

1889. Okwan annu ne koda na woko a, wunnu.

If you haven't reached your destination and go to sleep, you won't reach your destination.

1890. Okwan mu nye a, na onipa na ɔwo hɔ.

If the road is not good there are still people on it.

1891. Okwan ase (:ammɔse) ne dan mu.

The journey begins from inside your house.

1892. Okwan ware a, wode wɔn nan na etwa, na ɛnyɛ abonua.
R.150. Gr. 253,3.

If the road is long, you shorten it with your feet, not with an axe.

1893. Okwan wɔ aso.

The road has ears.

1894. Akwanfanu a ɔde ne kwan te-ase na ofwerom (:afwerew?) agye ɔkwan.

Clover which grows on the path, takes over the path all at once.

-158-

1895. Nkwan bɛyɛ dɛ a, efi fam'.

If the soup is delicious, it is because of the good soil.

1896. Kwankora-kitafo na otwa nkontompo, na ɛnyɛ kwankora.

It is the one holding the laddle that tells the lie, it is not the laddle.

1897. Akwankwa hiani de anibere asoa tasiw.

A poor young man eagerly carries a heavy load of tobacco.

1898. Okwankyɛn mako se: wobebu me a, bu me, na mmeyaw me (:gya me animka). R.256.

Pepper along side the road says, "if you see me, pluck me, don't abuse me."

1899. Akwanmusɛm dɛw nti na wofe ntasu gu (:to) nsu ani a, aka abɛfa kɔ. R.62.

Because of the pleasure of hearing news from abroad, the little "aka" fish pick up the traveller's spittle on the surface of the water.

1900. Okwantempon a esiwi na wɔyi no akwa na wɔfrɛ no mmontonkyɛ (:kwan kontonkye). Gr. #247,5.

The main road on which there is an ant hill, you go around it and call it a crooked path.

1901. Okwantenni nim asɛm-ka, na onnim asekyerɛ.

The traveller can tell all he has been on his journey but he can't explain it all.

1902. Okwantenten akwaba (na eye).

It is good to be welcomed from a long journey.

1903. Nkwantia (=okwan tia), ɔbako nĩwɛ.

It is not only one person who looks for short-cuts.

1904. Okwasea redi ne sika a, ose: ne nsenia yɛ merɛw.

When a fool is squandering his gold dust, he says his scales are worn out.

1905. Okwasea aduan bi ne tweapea.

One of the things a fool eats is the chewing stick.

1906. Okwasea na ne guan tew mpɛn abien. R.156.

The man whose sheep gets loose twice is a fool.

1907. Ɔkwasea na ose:wɔde me yɔnko, na wɔnne me. R.185.

It is the fool who says, "they mean my friend, they don't mean me."

1908. Ɔkwasea na wobu no bɛ a, wɔkyerɛ no ase.

When a fool is told a proverb, it has to be explained to him.

1909. Ɔkwasea na wɔtew ne ntɔrowa tɔn no.

It is the fool whose own garden eggs are plucked and sold to him.

1910. Ɔkwasea ani te a, na agoru agu.

When the fool becomes wise, the joking is ended.

1911. Ɔkwasea nnim biribi a, onim ne fufu tow.

If the fool knows nothing at all, at least he knows all about eating "fufu".

1912. Kwasi Afwefwɛ nnya nkɔdɔw Boaboa no, na ɛhɔ nkɔnsɔn didi. Cf.1871.

Before Kwasi Ahwehwɛ had made his farm at Boaboa, the monkeys were already eating there.

1913. Akwasi Konkoruwa (Kwasi Kurommo a ɔte Asiakwa) na obu bɛ se: Ɛnyɛ obi biribi ne me a, me na ɔdehye ne me.

Kwasi Konkurowa gives the proverb: "I am not related to anyone for I am the chief."

1914. Kwasi Poti nnyaa nkowoo ne ba Kwamme Apeagyei no, na ɔwɔ nea ɔso n'agua. Kwasiamoa...s.1634.

Before Kwasi Poti bore his son Kwame Apeagyei, he had someone who carried his chair.

1915. Ɔkwatani rekɔ kurom' se "ma menkɔ minkyia" a, ɛnyɛ wo na wukyia no; okyia wo a, na wunnye no so.

When a leper is going to town he says, "let me go and greet the people," it is not you who greet him, and if he greets you, you don't reply.

1916. Kwaterekwa se 'ɔbɛma wo ntama' a, tie ne din (F.: 'ɔbɛkyɛ wo tam', fwɛ n'asenmu). R.52.

If a naked man says he will give you a native cloth, listen to his name.

1917. "Ɛnkyɛ, ɛnkyɛ" wɔ n'afe.

The year is far off, the year is far off, but it arrives at last.

1918. Ɛkyɛw butuw dan nkyɛn, ɔnwae n'agya dea. B.

If a hat turns upside down near the house it doesn't pull off its father's hat.

1919. Ɛkyɛw mu nni biribi, na wopa a, na ɛbo dwo.

A hat has no purpose, but if you take it off, you become quiet.

1920. Ɔkyeame a wasiesie ɔman na ayɛ yiye na wɔfrɛ no kontomponi.

The linguist who has built up the state and done well is often called a liar.

1921. Nkyekwakyema, wobɔ no foto mu.

Behaving proudly is done with a money bag.

1922. Ɔkyekyefo ade, nkura na edi. R.241.

The miser's goods are eaten by mice.

1923. Woakyekyere funnu asoa ɔbonsam, na ɔde rekosi hena?

They wrap up the dead body to be carried by the devil and whom will he point out as the murderer?

1924. Akyekyere nni nufu, nso ɔwo a, onim nea ɔyɛ yɛn ne ba.

Although the tortoise has no breasts, when it gives birth, it knows how to rear it's child.

1925. Akyekyere kɔ serew serew na oguan ara nen.

The turtle moves in a droll manner, but it is fleeing all the same.

1926. Akyekyere na ɔkyerɛ ne bobere na wɔbɔ no.

It is the turtle itself that exposes its vulnerable spot (its head) and has it struck.

1927. Akyekyere annyin yiye a, na wɔfrɛ no amankrofi.

If the turtle doesn't grow well he is called an "amankrofi" turtle.

1928. Akyekyere pɛ ne yere amanne, ose: wɔw m'akyi mmɛsa (:wɔw mmɛsa gu m'atiko, na menkɔfwɛ agoru).

If the turtle wants to trouble his wife, he tells her to plait the hair falling down his back (and let him be off in search of some fun).

1929. Akyekyere se: ɔbarima mfɛre aguan. R.121

The turtle says: "a man should not be ashamed to run away" (from danger).

1930. Akyekyere se: nsa kɔ, na nsa ba. R.17.

The turtle says: "the hand goes (gives) and the hand comes (receives).

1931. Akyekyere se: ntɛm ye, na ɔgom ye. Cf.622.

The turtle says: "quickness is a good thing, and slowness is also a good thing."

1932. Ɔkyɛm a wɔatwitwa (mu) no, wɔnwene bio.

A shield woven of twigs which is all cut up, can not be woven again.

1933. Ɔkyɛm tetew a, (na) ɛka ne berɛman.

If the shield woven of twigs falls apart, only the handle of the shield is left.

1934. Akyem kasa-dɛ 'ti ma obi ntama mfura.

It is because of the flattering language of the people of Akim that no one has a native cloth to wear.

1935. Akyem akasadie 'ti (mma) obi nnya ntama mfura.

Because of the debt of the people of Akim, no one has a native cloth to wear.

1936. Ɛno Akyem na ekum Asante, ana Asante na ekum Akyem?

Did mother Akim kill Asante or did Asante kill Akim?

1937. Akyene anim da hɔ a, wonnyae nyan nkyɛn.

When the face of the drum is there, you don't beat the sides.

1938. Akyene nyɛ dɛ a, ɛnfwere putuputu (:po po, pɔ pɔ.)

Even if the drum doesn't have a nice sound, the sound of drumming is not exhausted.

1939. Akyene nyɛ dɛ a, wɔsaw no saara.

Even if the drum does not sound well, you dance to it all the same.

1940. Nkyene fi nsum' na wɔhata (hata), na wɔde gu nsum (hɔ) ara (bio).

Salt is procured from water which evaporates, and yet we put it back in the water again.

1941. Nkyene gu abo mu a, wɔnsesaw (bio).

If the salt is spilled in gravel you can't gather it up again.

-162-

1942. Nkyene nse neho sɛ: meyɛ dɛ. R.131.

The salt does not say of itself, "I'm tasty."

1943. Nkyenesoafo nni aguamsɛm.

The one who carries salt does not cause a public palaver.

1944. Nkyenkyemawe, 'yɛbɔ ne dini fra nkyeweɛ mu, nsoso yɛnkye no nwe.

The fish "nkyenkyemawe" is given a name and mixed with roasted corn, but we don't roast it and eat it.

1945. Akyenkyɛn nya dua a, enyɛ ɔsɛ-na.

If an unripe palm nut has a handle it is not difficult to crack open.

1946. Akyenkyɛn annya dua na wosɛ a, asiw wo nsa.

If an unripe palm nut does not have a handle and you crack it open, it bruises your hand.

1947. Kyenkyɛn-bɛmu fi soro abɛfwe ase a, wahu biribi.

If a whole cluster of palm nuts would fall down from the top of a tree, you would see something wonderful.

1948. Akyenkyena wɔ tonasum' a, (:ntra ɔtonsu mu na) asuakwa nfwere adare.

If the hornbill is in the workshop of a blacksmith the hoopoe doesn't lose his cultlass.

1949. Kyerɛ kum yea (=yaw).

A long duration kills the pain.

1950. "Kyerɛ ase, kyerɛ ase!" yɛ amammɔe.

Explain to me, explain to me, ruins the state.

1951. Wokyerɛ onipa akunse na wokum no a, ɛnyɛ no yaw.

When you have a just reason for seizing a man and killing him, it doesn't pain him.

1952. Wokyerɛ wo ho akwan nhina na ehia wo a, ɛden wo.

If you tell everything about yourself and then get into a difficult situation, it is very difficult for you.

1953. Yɛnkyerɛ ɔyɔnko asɛmpa, yɛnnkyerɛ asɛmmone, asɛmmone kotɔ gyam'. S.

We should teach our neighbor good things, we shouldn't teach bad things, bad things are thrown in the fire.

-163-

1954. Wokɔkyere obirebe ba ofie na wowɔw ɔde-fufu ma no na odi a, ɔne (ne) dwuma-aba ara.

If you go and catch an "obirebe" bird and bring him home and you make yam fufu for him and he eats it, then he shits trumpet-tree seeds.

1955. Wokyere dowa na woma no aduan-pa na wugya no a, ɔsan kɔmene duaba.

If you catch an antelope and you give him good food and see him off, he goes back to swallow the seeds of trees.

1956. Wokyere akokɔtan a, wotase ne mma kwa.

If you have caught the mother hen, you pick up her chicks without difficulty.

1957. Wonkyere aboa no mfensa na da a ade rebɛkye na woasan no no, ɔnse sɛ: nnɛ de, hama mia me.

If an animal is tied up for three years, he does not say on the last day of his captivity, "the string is too tight today."

1958. Akyere mpaw dabere (:mpaw nea ne to kɔ).

A wretch destined to be killed does not choose the place he will be put to rest.

1959. Kyerebenkuku betu ama siw adwiriw.

The queen of the white ants digs out of the hole, and causes the ant hill to break up.

1960. Akyɛrɛkyɛ amma ɔbrode ammere.

The squirrel doesn't let the plantain become ripe.

1961. Ɔkyerɛma Nyannɔ nim ayane a, ɔyane ma Ɔsɛe, na ɔnyane mma ayemfoɔ.

If Nyannɔ the Drummer knew how to drum, he would drum for the Chief of Ashanti, he wouldn't drum for a private person.

1962. Akyi se 'ɔbɛko' a, ɔ-ne n'Akɔmfode. R.146

If Akyi says he will fight, he means he and the "akɔmfode" company.

1963. Wonkyi sɛ asɔw abien gu apampam a, epirim.

If you don't allow two hoes on your head pan, the outside of the yams become black.

1964. Wo akyi dua bu a, wommu wo bi.

If your supporter dies, no one respects you.

-164-

1965. Okyifo kyi ne sɛn mu.
The one who abstains from a certain kind of food, does not put that food in his cooking pot.

1966. Okyinnyegyefo na ɔtɔ asosin (=ɔsoɔdenfo).
A disputer grows disobedient.

1967. Okyinnyegyefo se 'ɔ-ne wo bɛforo dunsin' a, ma onni kan, na di n'akyi.
If a disputer invites you to climb a tree stump with him, let him go first and then you follow him.

1968. Akyiri nyɛ ɔba.
Absence does not raise a child.

1969. Ma ɔdede nwie nkona (:nkoa).
Let the owner not finish the top of the tree.

1970. "Ma me ba nna!" nyɛ afe.
"Let my child sleep!" does not mean for one year.

1971. "Ma me bi minni!" na wɔde betwa Asunempɔn kwan?
"Give me something to eat!" does this shorten the road to Asunempɔn?

1972. "Ma me aduru mprempren!" nyɛ aduru.
"Give me medicine at once!" doesn't make for good medicine.

1973. "Ma yɛnkɔ me na fi" a, dɔkono sebɔw - kora!
If someone says, let's go to my mother's house, ball of dokono hide!

1974. "Ma yɛnkɔfwɛ" nko a, mahu (wo)?
If someone says,"let's go and see," do I say "have I seen it?"

1975. Mma ɔdabɔ nnkɔ ansa-na woafrɛ no agyabonti.
Don't let the antelope go before you call it "agyabonti."

1976. Mma ɛnnyɛ na nan-kontonkye nnkoti dote mmmɛbɔ nam-pa ho.
Don't let the crooked leg scrape the mud and then knock against the good leg.

1977. Mema wo a, wugye; na "ma me" a, wuyi wo nsa guan.
Cf.1787.
If I give you, you take and if I say give me, you take your hand back and run away.

-165-

1978. Mama wo **sika** sɛ fa kɔ aguabire so kɔtɔ nkyene bere me;
na woanya a, afei wuse: mebɛka wo asɛm bi a ɛkyɛn nkyene.

I have given you money saying take and go to the large
market place and buy salt and bring it to me; and if you
get the money then you say: "I will tell you something
that is worth more than salt."

1979. "Memuma wo, meremma womma wo", wokyi.

"I don't give you, I won't allow them to give you,"
this is very disgusting.

1980. Wokɔma odompo akye a, fwɛ dea ɔsam (=onni fwɛ). S.

If you go and say good morning to the bush dog, look where
it is lying.

1981. Womma me a, bɔ me ayamɔnwene.

When you give me something, you are stingy in giving.

1982. Woma atetekwa gyawurusi a, ɔbobɔw hyɛ ne 'mɔtoam'.

If you give an old man a large native cloth, he folds it up
and puts it under his armpit.

1983. Woma wo ba aduan a, woma no nam ka ho.

If you give your child vegetables, you give him meat in
addition.

1984. Woma wo panyin fɛre dakoro a, ɔma wofɛre da.

If you give respect to an elder one time, he will always
respect you.

1985. Woamma wo yonko antwa akron a, wo nso wuntwa du. Cf.2364.

If you don't let your neighbor count nine, you can't
count ten.

1986. 'Yɛmma akye a, 'yɛnna-ase. Mma, Mmea...s. 26-30.
Mmabadua...s. 1873.

If we don't say good morning, we don't thank.

1987. Amma-annwo-kurow biara nyɛɛ kɛse da.

A quarrelsome town has never become large.

1988. Made hyɛɛ ase ansa-na ɔforoe. B.

The "made" yam grew down into the ground before it sent
up its vines.

1989. Ɔmafo anhu ma a, otiefo nhu tie.

If the donor doesn't know how to give, the listener doesn't
know how to listen.

1990. Mmagum' na ekum dom. R.133.
Reinforcements cause the defeat of the enemy.

1991. Mako nnyera se: biribi na aba nti a anka ɔto aniwa a anka biribiara ne no.
The pepper not lost says: "if it is because something has come about, if he looked around everything would belong to him."

1992. "Makye, makye!" kum aberewa.
"Good morning, good morning!" kills the old woman.

1993. "Makye" nko a, "Ya", ɔbayifo ba. ("Makye o" nye, ɔb. ba.)
If you are only greeted "good morning" you respond "Yaa" to the witch's child.

1994. Amaku a ɔte Siade, ɔnwene nkuku ma nnipa nhina, ɔno de, odidi fam'.
Amaku, who lives in Siade, makes pots for everyone, but he himself eats on the ground.

1995. Ɔman rebɛbɔ a, edi akyeame aso.
If the nation is destroyed, the linguists are found guilty.

1996. Ɔman rebɛbɔ a, efi afi mu. (Ɔman bɔ afi mu.)
When a nation is declining, it begins in its homes.

1997. Ɔman rebɛbɔ a, ɔmampam na okura poma.
When a nation is about to come to ruin, then the "ɔmampam" lizard holds the chief's staff.

1998. Ɔman bɔ, na menne abobow (:sika). Cf.727.3319.
A nation can be destroyed, how much more so our homes.

1999. Ɔman Akuapem, wokonya ade a, wɔse: obusufo! nso woannya a, wɔse: ɔkarabiri!
When you get wealthy the Akuapem people say: "you wicked person!" and when you have nothing they say "you unlucky person!"

2000. Ɔman kum wo a, ɔhene kum wo.
When the people want to kill you, then the chief kills you.

2001. Ɔman te sɛ adesoa: wonhu mu ade dakoro. Cf.1176.3261
A nation is like a head-load, you can not see everything in it at one glance.

2002. Ɔman twa wo sama a, wompopa. R.188
When the whole town put figures on your head by unequal
cutting of your hair, you do not cut them off.

2003. Amamfo so mmosea: sɛ ɛnyɛ owu nti a, anka yen nhina ka
boa ano.
The people carry gravel: if it were not because of death
we would all collect gravel.

2004. Ɔmamfrani nnyin kronkron. R.172. Gr. #199,6.
The foreigner never grows perfect (as perfect as a native.)

2005. Amamfrafo na ɛsɛe man (:wɔsɛe kurow).
It is strangers who cause the decline of a country.

2006. Mamponten nni biribi a, ɔwɔ pamafuo.
If a large town has nothing, it has a white cane.

2007. Amanne hyɛ ase ansa-na ɔforo. Cf.1988.
The "amanne" tree grows down in the ground before it
grows tall.

2008. Amanne na ɛyɛ onya-na, na ɛnyɛ ne fakɔbew. B.
It is easy to get troubles, but not easy to find a helper.

2009. Amanne nyɛ onya-na, na ne fakɔbew.
Troubles come quickly to everyone, but it is not always
easy to find a helper.

2010. Ɔmanni ba mmua nna.
The native's child doesn't go to sleep without food.

2011. Ɔmanni, wokum no sum mu.
One's townsman is killed in the dark.

2012. Ɔmanni yera a, wɔde ɔmanni abɛn na ɛfwefwɛ ɔmanni.
If a member of the family is lost, he is called back by the
horn of the family.

2013. Amanniko, wɔko a, wɔkekaw nhwi so, (na) wontutu ase.
If members of a family fight with each other, they only
bite off the hair, they don't pull it out.

2014. Amankuo nim huri a, ohuri ntom, na ontwa adabane mu.
If the large beetle knew how to jump, he would jump
over and not pass around the iron bar.

2015. Manso nyɛ aduan na wɔadi ame.
Litigation is not food which satisfies.

2016. Mansoboafo yɛ na.
The promoter of a rebellion is disliked.

2017. Ɔmansofo tam nhyia no da. Cf.2313.
A litigant's cloth is always small.

2018. Mansotwe te sɛ bayerɛ amoa: obi ntɔɔ mu mfaa neho sonn mfii da.
Litigation is like a yam hole, no one falls into it and gets out safe and sound.

2019. Mansotwefo aduan, wodi no anadwo.
A quarrelsome person eats his food late at night.

2020. Ɔmanyɛfo nyɛ anem.
A good citizen should be industrious.

2021. Mmapɛ mu wɔ ade a, anka ɔpapo da apakan mu.
If there was profit in going after women, then the male goat would always sleep in the palanquin.

2022. Matatwene nya amanne a, ofruntum fa mu asia. Cf.1167.
If the creeper has any misfortunes, the large rubber tree takes six of them.

2023. Me a meda ayannya minhu Nyankopɔn, na wo a wubutuw ho! R.53.
I am lying on my belly and I don't see God; how would you see Him, lying on your back?

2024. Me a mede me Kyebi, wuhyia me Pannɔ.
As for me I have (seized) Kibi, you attack me at Pannɔ.

2025. Me de, mise onya bɛsow kwadu a, sɛ tentrehu!
As for me, I say if the silk cotton tree would produce bananas, it would resemble silk cottom!

2026. Me na mepɛ. (Agya Aboagye a ɔte Anyinasin.)
I like my mother best of all.

2027. Me-ne wo banu kɔ anadwosu a, woka m'ani ase fwɛ?
If we are both keeping watch at night, do you touch my eyes to see if I am sleeping?

2028. Me-ne wo bɛkɔ, wɔde dada funu.
"I will go with you" is said to comfort the dead.

2029. Me-nko-medi (ne) nua(bea) ne nea ɔne ha, ma onwu!
I alone inherit my sister and he who shits here, let him die!

2030. Ɔme nyɛ afu (:twa).
Fullness does not cause a humpback.

2031. Memene-ahene nantwi, waka wo se aka wo ni sɛ: wo-ne no nnna ɔman mu ha nnɛ; wɔmmfa no mmfa abɔnten, wɔmmfa no mmfa mfikyiri. Cf.617.2110.
As for the cow of a powerful chief, you tell your father and your mother: you won't sleep in town tonight with the cow, and you won't take the cow through the main street nor the back streets.

2032. Wo manewa mu wɔ pɔw na wɔbɔ fwerema a, emfi.
If there is a lump in your throat and you whistle, the sound doesn't come out.

2033. 'Mɛnsa bɔ mpɔw fi ne mmofraase.
The "mensa" yam grows new heads of yam from the very beginning.

2034. Mmerɛ bɔ otufo din ansa-na afi.
Mushrooms call out name of the plucker of mushrooms before they come out of the ground.

2035. Amere kum kuru, na ekuru kum no.
The "amere" tree (which is used as a medicine for sores) heals (kills) the sore, and the sore kills it.

2036. Ammere, wonni nka so.
A luxurious life does not last forever.

2037. Wumia na amfata wo a, na wɔfrɛ wo(: wuse mesɛ) ɔbrafo.
If you try to wear beautiful clothes and they don't suit you, you are called a woman in menstruation.

2038. Wumia wo ani a, wufi fufu mu.
If you try your best, you come out victorious.

2039. "Mmo, mmo!" kum aberewa. Cf.1992.
"Mmoadoma...s. s.540-544.
"Well done, well done!" kills the old lady.

2040. Amoakua nim sɛ osu bɛtɔ nti na ɔkɔda fam'.

Because the squirrel knows it will rain, he goes and sleeps in the ground.

2041. Amoakua se: me dua nti m'afɛ kyi me.

The squirrel says: "it is because of my tail that my friends hate me."

2042. Amoakua te ho yi, ɔda fam', nso osu tɔ a, ɛnka no.

If the squirrel is alive, he sleeps in the ground and if it rains, it doesn't affect him.

2043. Mmoborɔ wɔ nammɔn mu.
Mmofra ...s.591.592.
Mogya...s.596.

Compassion is in the sole of the foot.

2044. Momono tew, na guannuan tew. Gr.p.154.

The green leaf falls and the withered one falls too.

2045. Mmɔre mmɔn fa nnyaw fa.

Dough does not penetrate one part and leave another part.

2046. Mmosea kokwaw ntɛm a, wɔde no ko anwam. R.207.

If pebbles become smooth quickly, they could be used for shooting the toucan.

2047. Emum dae aka ne tirim'.

A deaf and dumb person's dream remains in his head.

2048. Omumo mfa ade abien.

A bodily misformed person doesn't take two things.

2049. Omumo se: obenyin ahoɔfe; na Ya de, onyɛ dɛn?

The bodily misformed person says,"he will grow up to be handsome; and as for Yaa, what will she do?"

2050. Mumokyiri na ɛhye, na mumokan na ɛnhye.

The last offence spreads, the first offence does not spread.

2051. Wumuna tra sum mu a, na ɛte sɛ woannuare na woasra.

If you are gloomy and sit in the darkness, you look like someone who has not bathed but has put on pomade.

2052. Omununkum sakyi, onni ani na ɔforo nyame.

The cloud "sakyi" has no eye but it ascends in the sky.

2053. Mmusuo di adwini.
Misfortune does its work skillfully.

2054. Mmusu di wo akyi a, ɛde wo ne ahenware. Cf.1316.
If misfortune follows you, it follows you until you become
the chief's wife.

2055. (Sɛ) Mmusu di wo akyi na ɛda onya so a, wobɔ nname kɔfa.
If misfortune follows you and rests on the firewood, you
hit the wedge and take it.

2056. Mmusu wɔ wo ho a, na nwaw ka wo.
If misfortune comes to you, then even snails bite you.

2057. Na ne agya, gyae ko, na ɛmfanim nea ebi anka.
Mother and father, stop fighting, for in that case it has
no value for either of you.

2058. "Me na dea, memfa! m'agya dea, memfa!" na ɛde awi ba. = 1243.
"This belongs to my mother, I can take it, this belongs to
my father, I can take it," makes the child a thief.

2059. Wo na a onye no na ɛbɛyɛ sɛ obi ne na.
Your mother who is not good, is like someone else's
mother.

2060. Wo na ba ne Kobuobi a, anka wobese sɛ kyene-kɛse fata no
ana?
Even if your mother's son is "kobuobi," would you say
that the big drum was a fit thing for him to carry?

2061. Wo na ɔba ne wo nua.
Your mother's child is your real brother or sister.

2062. Wo na ɔba (:Wo ni mma) wɔ nnwonkorom' a, wo din nyera
(:nharam'.)
If your sister is in the group of singing girls, your
name always comes into the song.

2063. Wo na di hia a, wunnyae no nkɔfa obi nyɛ na.
If your mother is poor, you don't leave her and make
someone else your mother.

2064. Wo na ankɔ gua a, na womana wo na ne kora.
When your own mother does not go to market, then her
co-wife is sent.

2065. Wo na te Abibirim' na wo agya te Aburokyiri na wopɛ ade
a, wonkyɛ nya (:wonkyɛ na wunya woho).

When your mother lives in Africa and your father in
Europe, and when there is something you want, you don't
have to wait long before you get it.

2066. Wo na te hɔ, wo agya te hɔ a, wɔmfrɛ woho ɔdehyewa.

If your mother and father are alive, you do not call
yourself an insignificant person.

2067. Wo na wu na wobɛyɛ ayi a, didi wie ansa, na nkotɔ piti
na wo ani nkowu mpanyimfo anim.

When your mother has died and you are about to celebrate
the funeral customs, finish eating first so that you don't
go and faint and disgrace yourself in the presence of the
elders.

2068. Wo na awu a, wo abusua asa. Cf.2760.

When your mother dies you have no relatives left.

2069. Wo na nye a, na wo na ara nen.

Even if your mother is not a good person, she is still
your mother.

2070. Nabina se: ɔnware ponkɔ, na anka afunum!

Nabina says he won't marry a horse, then what about
a donkey!

2071. Anabo bankye, ɛbɔ o, ammɔ o, ɔde gye ɔban.

Anabo cassava, whether it grows or not, they make a
fence around it.

2072. Anadwoboa nnɔ awonnua. R.182.

An animal caught at night is not fat.

2073. Anadwoboa wiawia ade na ɔde yɛ hɔho.

A night-animal keeps stealing things and this
makes him a stranger.

2074. Anadwoda-gya ho nni biribi a, ɛwɔ "dabi na metee."

If seeing someone off in the evening has no purpose,
at least it has, "one day I heard."

2075. Anafranaku asɔre abrɔde ase na odwennini nwo nta.

If the "anafranaku" (medicininal plant whose flowers are
poisonous to animals) grows at the base of the plantain,
then the ram can't beget twins.

2076. Anakurampon akasagua: wɔsese (:wɔkeka) (na) wɔnne wo
na wokogye so a, woadi fɔ.=2817. 2914.

An angry person's grumbling: If he utters insults and
you think he means you and you reply, then you have
condemned yourself.

2077. Nam nni hɔ nti na wɔde mmerɛ yɛ nkwan.
Because there is no meat around, we use mushrooms to make soup.

2078. Wonam nam a, wuhyia.
If you keep walking you will meet (someone).

2079. Wonam na wuhintiw a, wofwɛ fam'.
If you walk and stub your foot against something, then you look at the ground.

2080. Wonam tempɔn mu na worenoa aduan a, noa no babiara, na ɔtempɔn mu nni asamorofi.
If you are travelling on the highway and want to cook some food, cook it anywhere for there is no fireplace on the highway.

2081. Wonam banu sum afiri a, wɔnam banu (na ɛ) kɔfwɛ.) R. 144.
If two people set a trap together, they also go to check it together.

2082. Wonam dufuaw mu na edi wo ti.
It's in medicine, formed in balls, that one eats the head of a snake.

2083. Wɔnam onipa anom' (:tɛkrɛma so) na ehu ne tirim asɛm.
It is by the words of a man's mouth that you get to know his mind.

2084. Wɔnam sa (:nsa-nsa) kɔ Aburokyiri a, wɔnam sa (:nsa-nsa) ba.
It is through the work of our hands that we go to Europe and it is through the work of our hands that we come back.

2085. Wonnam sɛ menam yi, na wuwia Mampɔn guan.
If you don't walk like I walk, then it means you steal sheep in Mampong.

2086. Ɔnam ne asɛm. (Ɔnan ne asɛm). Cf. 2092.
Walking is what really matters.

2087. Ɔnammɔn ne asɛm.
The sole of the foot is what is important.

2088. Ɔnammɔn fa tiri kwane.
The feet go the way of the head.

2089. Onammon mmutu kwa; ohu dekode a ofwefwɛ nti na obutu.

The feet don't turn over for no reason at all, they turn over because they see what they are looking at.

2090. Onammon ɛyɛ abutukwa.

The foot turns over for a good reason.

2091. Nan bu a, ɛkyerɛ ne tiabea.

If you break your leg, you see the end of the bone.

2092. Onan nni asɛm (;ano na edi asɛm). (Fantefo).

The leg does not cause trouble (it is the mouth that causes trouble.)

2093. Anan ne anan goru a, ɔto mma; (na) ano ne ano goru a, na ɔto ba. = 2456.

If feet play with feet, there is no discord, but if mouth plays with mouth there is discord.

2094. Onana nni nko! omanni fone.=1405.

If the foreigner doesn't eat and go, the real members of the family become thin.

2095. Onanani nkasa.

The foreigner doesn't speak.

2096. Anana-ansafo kurow nyɛ kɛse da.

The town which doesn't permit foreigners to mix with them never becomes a big town.

2097. Onanka da fam' na wanya onwam.

The python lying on the ground caught the toucan which flies in the air.

2098. Ananse a ompɛ anwene bi anwene, na onwene tempon mu.
(An. ampɛ ..., na okonwene kwankyɛn.)

The spider which doesn't like to spin, spins its web on the main road.

2099. Ananse se asantrofi se: sɛ wobɛfwɛ asɛ so a, fwɛ asɛ so; sɛ nso wobedi nkorowa-hene a, fwɛ nkorowa-hene so di.

The spider tells the "asantrofi" bird: "if you are going to look after the beans, look after the beans, but if you are going to be leader in the "nkorowa" dance, then be leader of the "nkorowa" dance.

-175-

2100. Ananse antɔn kasa.
The spider (Creator) did not sell speech.

2101. Ɔnantew na ɛkyerɛ ne dabea.
Walking advises its own position.

2102. Ɔnantefo hu amanne.
Those who travel on foot suffer.

2103. Ɔnantefo na odi ade a ɛyɛ dɛ. R.225.
What a foot-traveller eats, tastes well.

2104. Ɔnantefo nya amanne a, na ɔteasefo bo adwo.
When the traveller suffers, then the one living on
the farm has peace.

2105. Ɔnantefo nya sika a, ɔde brɛ okuafo.
If the traveller gets money, he brings it to the farmer.

2106. Ɔnantefo sen ɔse (:n'agya) asɛm.
The traveller can speak of more things than his father.

2107. Ɔnantefo, yɛ ntɛm, na asuo da ɔkwanem'.
Traveller, go quickly, for there is water on the road.

2108. Nantu sen serɛ kɛse a, na ɔyare wɔ mu (:ɛyɛ amammɔe).
If the calf becomes bigger than the thigh, then it is
infected.

2109. Nantwi mmɛn, ani awo, nso ase yɛ mono.
The surface of the cow dung is dry, but its inside is
still fresh.

2110. Nantwi agya ne ne na awu, na wose: wɔmma ɔmfa abɔnten,
nso wɔmma ɔmfa mfikyiri, nanso wɔmma ɔnna kurom' ho.
Cf. 617. 1076. 2031.
The cow's mother and father have died and you say:"Don't
let it pass in the main street, and don't let it pass in
the back streets, but it can't be allowed to sleep in
the town."

2111. Ɛnnɛ(na e)nye, na ɔkyena ade bɛkye. Cf.2312.
Today is not good, but tomorrow will come.

2112. Ɛne nne wo a, wuse; ɛnnɛ menkɔ dua so.
When you can't have a bowel movement when you want to,
you say, "Today I am not going to toilet."

-176-

2113. Nea ɔbaa da kwan anom' asɛm nsa dakoro.
If a woman lies at the opening of a way, there is always trouble.

2114. Nea waba dakoro, n'anom' asɛm nsa.
He who comes only ocassionally doesn't stop talking.

2115. Nea aba pɛn na ɛba (:ɛsan ba). Gr. p.45. Cf.2805.
What has happened once happens again.

2116. Dea ɛmmae da sua. Gr. p.45.
What has never yet come to pass is not much.

2117. Nea ɔbarima pɛ na ɔyɔ.
What a man likes he does.

2118. Nea aberewa pɛ na ɔpotɔ di.
Whatever the old woman likes, she grinds and eats.

2119. Nea obi abɛyɛ sen nea yɛrebɛye yi.
What someone will do some day is greater than that what we are doing now.

2120. Nea obi de aba no na obi de nam kwan (mu).
When someone's trouble has come, someone else's trouble is on the way.

2121. Nea obiako akohu!
If one man has gone to see,(who was his witness?)

2122. Nea wabɔ di bi.
Whatever animal you have shot, you eat some of it.

2123. Nea wabɔ no fam' na ɔdam butuw n'ano.
Whatever has been knocked down on the ground, lies there turning over on the side of its mouth.

2124. Nea abofra pɛ, ɔtotɔ.
The child buys what he likes.

2125. Nea brɔfere abubu no, wɔnkɔ hɔ anyan. (Ayide Kofinam.)
No one goes for firewood where the pawpaw trees have been blown down.

2126. Nea woda na ɔde ne nsa asi wo so no, wunyan a, n'anim na wofwɛ.
If you are sleeping somewhere and someone puts his hand on you, when you wake up, you look at his face.

2127. Nea wada nananu da nankoro a, εyε yaw.

If he who sleeps on two legs, sleeps on one leg, it is painful.

2128. Nea ɔda ne gya na onim sε ɛhyehye no.

He who is lying by the fire knows how it burns.

2129. Nea ɔda-ase mfa ka. - Nea ɔnna...s.2201.

He who thanks doesn't go into debt.

2130. Nea ade ahia no na otu akwamfo (:ɔboro akw. aba).

He who needs a thing will travel on a bad road to get it.

2131. Nea ade atɔ n'ani so no, ɛnyε nankasa na oyi.

He who has got something in his eyes cannot take it out himself.

2132. Nea ade wɔ hɔ, owu wɔ ho.

Where there is wealth, there is death.

2133. Nea ade wɔ no na odi, ɛnyε nea ɔkɔm de no.

He who owns a thing eats it, not the hungry person.

2134. Nea ɔde n'afwerew na ɔwe n'ase.

The owner of the sugar cane chews the base (the sweetest part).

2135. Nea ɔde n'agosana regye a, wunse sε: me nno wɔ mu. B.

When the owner of the oil pot is taking back his pot do not say: "my oil is in it."

2136. Nea ɔde ne man nsεe no.

The head of the country shouldn't ruin it.

2137. Nea ɔde n'amanne nnyae faba.

The person who keeps getting into trouble doesn't stop stealing.

2138. Nea ɔde n'ani na ofei ase.

The person with good eyes picks at the "itch" disease.

2139. Nea ɔde bedi asεmmone na woatetew sika ama dibem no, fa sa di asεmpa na wo sika ntra hɔ nwεn mmofra.

If you are going to do a wrong thing, and then pacify others with money, do the right thing and save your money to look after your children.

2140. Nea wode begu aboa no kuru mu na ɔbɛtaforo no, fa gu ne tɛkrɛma so prɛko.

That which you are first going to put onto the sore of the animal and he will lick it off, put it on his tongue immediately.

2141. Nea wode bɛka no bone na woasan aka no yiye no, fa sa ka no yiye prɛko.

If you are going to do evil to someone and then later good to him, do him good immediately.

2142. Nea wode betwa no pɛpɛ na wutwa no pɛ a, na woawie.

That which you will go to cut exactly and you have cut it, you have completed your cutting.

2143. Nea wode betwa no kufwekufwe no, na wode atwa no ten.

Instead of cutting it bit by bit, cut it once and for all and finish with it.

2144. Nea ɔdesani pɛ ne nnyam.

Every human being likes the compassion shown him by others.

2145. Nea odi agyirawotwe gua mmisa taku-nam.

He who trades with a two dollars gold weight does not ask for meat that costs five pesewas.

2146. Nea odi nkokɔ no, ɔnam na ɔse pesu.

He who eats chickens, hangs meat on the hen coop.

2147. Nea odi nkokonte se obedi samina a, wonnye no kyim (:akyinnye). R.107.

If he who eats "Kokonte"- dried cassava - says he will eat soap, don't doubt him.

2148. Nea odi wo di wo a, ɛnyɛ yaw.

If he who eats honey eats it, it is not painful.

2149. Nea odi ayiase kan mfa kunabea-bone.

He who arrives first at the funeral place doesn't marry the bad widow.

2150. Nea wadi bem nsoaa oguan da.

He who has won his case has never carried a sheep.

2151. Nea wadi fɔ na ɔkasa. Cf.247.

The one who is guilty talks much.

-179-

2152. Nea wadi kan na wɔfa n'akyi gya.

If one person starts a fire, others take live coals out of it.

2153. Nea wadi ason ason (ahorow) abiɛsa se 'obedi aduonu' a, wonnye no kyim (:akyinnye).

If he who has eaten seven times three says he will eat twenty, he should not be doubted.

2154. Nea wodidi ame se: nea oddidi anadwo yɛ ɔbayifo. R.86.

He who has eaten his fill says,"he who eats at night is a witch."

2155. Nea wadidi ame se: nea oresi pɛ yɛ ayɛn (:ayɔ).

He who has eaten his fill says,"he who keeps wake is a witch."

2156. Nea wodɔ ho na owu dɔ ho.

Whatever you love, Death also loves.

2157. Nea ɛdɔm ako afa no nkyɛ agyapade.

If the army fights and conquers someone, he can't share his wealth (as he wants to).

2158. Nea wɔafa aboa no hɔ ara na wogua no.

An animal is skinned and gutted wherever it is killed.

2159. Nea wofɛre no fɛre a, wofɛre bi. Cf.1118.

If the person you respect, respects you, you respect others.

2160. Nea womfɛre no, ɔkoto nea wofɛre no akyi. R.80.

He whom you don't respect, will seat himself behind him whom you do respect.

2161. Nea ofi kurow bim' na onim mu asɛm (:nsɛm).

If there is someone from the town present, it is he who knows the affairs of the town.

2162. Nea ɔrefwefwɛ yere nto mmea ho mpe.

One who is looking for a wife doesn't speak contemptously of women.

2163. Nea agohina si, wɔntow hɔ abo.

You shouldn't throw rocks around a water pot.

2164. Nea oguan dɔ (:pɛ) na ɔde ne fufu bɔ (sie). R.59.Z.112.

The sheep puts its white wool on what it likes.

2165. Nea oguan gyinae (hɔ) na ne ba gyinae.
Wherever the sheep stands its kid also stands.

2166. Nea oreguan mmɔ wa (:mpo waw).
The person who is looking for a hiding place does not cough.

2167. Nea ogyina ho na ɔde adefom ba.
He who is standing there causes the offence to come.

2168. Nea wogyina we guannam no, ɛhɔ na wogyina gye akorabo.
The place where you stand and eat sheep meat, there you
also stand and receive the bullet taken from the sheep.

2169. Nea ehia Dankyira akoa na ɔde ko abɛyɛ.
What Dankyira's slave needs, he fights to get.

2170. Nea wahintiw awu no, wontutu 'mirika nkɔ n'ayi ase.
If a person has met his death by stumbling, you do
not run to attend the funeral.

2171. Nea ɛhɔ yɛ sum no, wotow sika pete hɔ a, ɛhɔ tew kann. = 33
If you scatter money where there is darkness, it becomes
light there.

2172. Nea ahoɔden kyi ne kɔm.
What strength hates is hunger.

2173. Nea wahu bi pɛn se: wokyi. R.101.
(.... nse sɛ: ɛmmera na yɛnfwɛ!)
They who have seen a thing once say they hate it.

2174. Nea onhuu bi pɛn se: ɛmmera na yɛnfwɛ!
One who has never seen it says: "Let it come and we
will see."

2175. Nea wahu ɔha (:apem) nkamfo aduonu (:ɔha).
One who has seen a hundred does not praise twenty.

2176. Nea ɔkohuu (:wahu) 'wo (no) na ofua (:okura) ɔtɛn
(:ofita gya mu).
He who has gone and seen the honey, holds the house-fly.

2177. Nea ɛhyɛ woamfa anhyɛ a, efi-tɔ. B.
If you do not put it where it ought to be, it will fall
down.

2178. Nea ɔbɛhyɛ nsa no, ɔnka n'ano nsa.
He who pours out the wine doesn't taste it.

2179. Nea woahye akodu no, wotɔ fi a, ɛtra hɔ.
When scandal comes to you, it goes beyond the bounds of your fame.

2180. Nea aka ne ahooyaw.
That which lasts is a grudge.

2181. Nea woboka ntam na woakum wo no, fa phene yere na wonkum wo.
If you swear an oath and they kill you, commit adultery with the chief's wife and they don't kill you.

2182. Nea ɔkasa wɔ no, ade nkye ntɛm.
Wherever there is much talking the dawn doesn't come quickly.

2183. Nea ɔkɔ Dawurampɔn (:Agyinako) kɔfaa ntam bae nfwere "ka-wo-se".
He who went to Dawurampɔn to get and oath does not return and then waste his time saying, "I swear by my father."

2184. Nea wakɔ Koromante akɔko agye ntam aba no nfwere "meka-wo-se."
He who went to Koromante to fight to get an oath does not return and then waste his time saying, "I swear by my father."

2185. Nea ɔkɔ ne kwan na onim nea ɔbɛda.
He who takes his own way knows where he will sleep.

2186. Nea ɔkɔ anadwogoru nnya kaw a, nea ɔda anadwo dan mu na onya kaw ana? (Dea ɔkɔ agorɔ adadwo na onya ka; na dea ɔda ɔdane mu adadwo deɛ, onnya ka.)
When he who goes out all night to sing and dance does not incur a debt, will he who sleeps in his room incur a debt.

2187. Nea ɔkɔ anyan annya bi amma a, ofie mpa huhuhuhu.
The people in the house never stop murmuring when the person who went for firewood didn't get any to bring home.

2188. Nea ɔkɔ asu na ɔbɔ ahina. R. 92. Gr. p. 45.
He who goes for water breaks the pot.

2189. Nea ɔkɔ nnoma-nnoma mmisa berebuw.
We who always goes after birds does not ask about their nests.

-182-

2190. Nea ɔrekɔ anoma-kurom' nyi berebu ɔkwan mu.

He who goes to the birds' village does not take a bird's nest with him.

2191 Nea ɔkɔm gye ne me. R.155. Gr.p.45.

What hunger wants is satisfaction.

2192. Nea ɔkɔm akum no no, wommisa n'adaka. Z.104.

You don't ask for the food-box of someone who died of starvation.

2193. Nea wɔakum guan adi hɔ no, ɛhɔ na efuw wura.

The place where you have killed and eaten a sheep, there the grass grows well.

2194. Nea okum Tabirifo (pitini) na ɔfa ne ntokota (:ne mpaboa) R.99.

He who kills a leper gets his sandals.

2195. Nea wɔbekum wo nnɛ ne sɛ wɔbekum wo 'kyena no; ma wonkum wo nnɛ na kɔhome prɛko.

If those who are coming to kill you today say they will kill you tomorrow, let them kill you today and then you can rest immediately.

2196. Nea okura ntrama o, nea obefirii o, ɔdede se: ɔntɔn bio.

Whether you have cowries with which to pay or you want credit, the owner says he isn't selling any more.

2197. Nea akwatia bɛyɛ sɛ ɔtenten no, na ɔtenten de, ɔnsen wiase bio.

The short person can become like the tall person, but the tall person has nothing else he can excel in.

2198. Nea n'akyi apae no, ɛnyɛ nankasa na ɔpam.

If a man's back breaks, he can not stitch it up himself.

2199. Nea ɔman bi ka serew na ɔman bi ka su. Cf.32.2854.

What makes some people laugh, makes other people cry.

2200. Nea ɔman adu no so na wototo no mu a, obu wo nan mu.

When it is a man's turn to rule the state and you get in his way, he breaks your leg.

2201. Nea ɔnna na onim (:ɔhyia) nea ɔnna. Gr.p.45.

He who is not sleeping knows who isn't sleeping.

2202. Nea wonam foro (ɛhɔara) na wonam sian.

The path you climb up is the same one you must come down.

2203. Nea wo-ne no di akapimafwɛ, na ɔsɔre a, woka ne pim fwɛ, na ɔno nso sɔre a, ɔka wo pim fwɛ.=2366.

When someone you are intimate with gets up from bed you look at his buttocks and when he gets up he looks at yours.

2204. Nea ɔ-ne me goru na me-ne no goru.

If you play with me, I will play with you.

2205. Nea n'ani abere, wɔmmɔ n'ani so. (Osiadau.) R.98.

If someone's eyes are red (from being in trouble) you don't slap him in the face.

2206. Nea n'ani akyea (:akyew) na ɔfwɛ toa mu. Gr.p.45

He who can squint looks into the bottle.

2207. Nea wo ani nna hɔ no, ɛhɔ na wo funu si.

The place where you have not set your eyes on is where your corpse will be buried.

2208. Nea wo ani agye sen nea wɔawo wo. = 2310.

The place where you are happy is better than the place you were born.

2209. Nea onni bi dan nea ɔwɔ bi. (..., mɛkɔ makohu!)

He who has nothing depends on him who has something.

2210. Nea onni hɔ mfa tokwaw hɔ fwe.

He who is not present can't cause a fight.

2211. Nea onni hɔ kyɛn nea ɔwɔ hɔ adankyɛn.

The builder who is absent is better than the one who is present.

2212. Nea onni Apea ne Boakye wɔ Kumase no, onya n'asɛm a, odi.

If the person who doesn't stay with Apea and Boakye in Kumase gets in trouble, he has to bear it alone.

2213. Nea onim man asɛm (ase) na odi.

He who understands the affairs of the state inherits.

2214. Nea n'anim sɛ oguan, wode akokɔ ka n'anim asɛm a, wo ano fomfom.

If someone deserves a sheep, and you give him a chicken, you stutter.

2215. Nea n'anim sɛ nsa, womma no nsu.
He who deserves wine should not be given water.

2216. Nea onipa nim ne dinsɛe.
What man knows how to do is to ruin the good name of others.

2217. Nea ɔnoa aduan annya bi anni a, wommisa nea ɔ(tra ho) noae.
If the one who is preparing the food doesn't get any to eat, we don't ask her to give us some.

2218. Nea wɔnom (ho) wonnuare ho. Gr.p.45.
If one drinks from a river, he should not bathe there.

2219. Nea wanya nhui no, wanya (:onya) nkae. Cf.2528. Gr.p.58.
What you have not seen you don't remember.

2220. Nea woanya no, ma wo ani nsɔ.
Be satisfied with what you have.

2221. Nea ɔpanyin ada na ne nan gu adiwo.
When an elder is in bed, his feet are still outside the room.

2222. Nea ɔ(re)pɛ dabere nka nkyerɛ wo sɛ: mmɛdwensɔ (:nnwensɔ) kɛtɛ so.
He who is looking for a place to sleep doesn't tell you that he wets the bed.

2223. Nea ɔpɛ ade akɔ Asaman, wonni no aboro.
He who wants riches to go to the land of the dead is not envied.

2224. Nea ɔpɛ sika na onnya bi, wo de, wuse: wagyimi. Cf. 1346.
You tell the person who wants to get rich and doesn't: "you are stupid."

2225. Nea wompɛ, (wo)mfa nyɛ wo yɔnko.
What you don't like, don't do to your neighbor.

2226. Nea wɔmpɛ no, wonsan nkɔfa.
If you don't like something, you won't return to get it.

2227. Nea wompɛ, wotra no hia.
You stay in a place you don't like with reluctance.

-185-

2228. Nea ɔmpɛ wo suo, ɔmpɛ wo biribi.

He who doesn't like your character, dislikes whatever belong to you.

2229. Nea apem sɛ no na ɔma.

If a thousand people deserve something it should be given to them.

2230. Nea wo nsa da n'anom', wompa n'atifi. Cf.160.

If your hand is in someone's mouth, you don't hit him on the top of his head.

2231. Nea ɛsɛ sɛ wosu kyerɛ no na wosu kyerɛ no.

When it is necessary to complain to someone, you complain to him.

2232. Nea wose wada adaduasa akɔdu hɔ no, ɛyɛ obi afikyiri.

When we come to the place where you say you have stayed thirty days, we see that it is simply the back of someone's house.

2233. Nea okosee sɛ trɔm-merɛbo yɛ dɛ no, wonni nnya no. Z.90.

He who told you that the liver of the bush cow is delicious should not be left out when it is being eaten.

2234. Nea okosee ayi na ɔma yekum bayifo.

He who makes us kill the witch told us about the death (of a chief).

2235. Nea ɔsen wo fompɔw no ɔsen wo ntasu. = 423.

He whose cheeks are more puffed up than your's, can also spit more than you.

2236. Nea ɔsɛw kɛtɛ ɔkwan mu (:tempɔn mu) ne nea okotiaa so no, hena na ɔyɛɛ bone?

Who is in the wrong? - He who spread the mat on the path or he who walked on it?

2237. Nea woresie afu no na afu te hɔ resu.

If you are burying a hunch backed person, there will be another hunch backed person there crying.

2238. Nea wuresisi kwasea no, na onyansafo te hɔ fwɛ wo.

If you are taking advantage of a fool, there is a wise man there watching you.

2239. Néa ɔso aburow-pae mmisa Kankan hyɛn.

If you are carrying a bag of corn that breaks open, you don't ask the whereabouts of the Dutch ship.

2240. Nea ɔso kyene-kɛse wɔ biribi a, ne werɛ kyekye wɔ ho.
If he who is carrying a big load of salt has something, his consolation is there.

2241. Nea ɔso ne ti na onim mu asɛm.
The person who is stubborn knows the reason for being so.

2242. Nea ɔso na ɔmene ne yɔnko.
A big animal can swallow (kill) a small one.

2243. Nea aso te na ano bua.
That which the ear hears the mouth replys to.

2244. Nea ɛsono wui (wɔ) n'afikyiri no, ɛho ahaban nhina sae.
Wherever an elephant is killed, there won't be any leaves left.

2245. Nea asu afa no, wommisa n'ahode. Cf.3085.
You don't ask for the personal property of someone who has drowned.

2246. Nea nsu gyina no (ɛho na) egyina.
Where the water stands still, it stands still.

2247. Nea nsu ata ho no, dote nkyɛ ho ba.
Where water is standing, mud also soon comes.

2248. Nea osu akoso ne nsoremu.
Tears keep coming at the cemetery.

2249. Nea osu na wosu boa no.
When someone is crying, your crying helps him.

2250. Nea ɔta wo mmerɛ a, wo a wureguan wunse sɛ: mabere. R.161.
If he who is running after you is not tired, then you who are running away don't say: "I am tired."

2251. Nea ɔtan wo na ɔbɔ wo aboa ade.
He who hates you, insults you.

2252. Nea ɔte bamma ho nhyira ɔman.
The person who sits on a swish-seat can not bring prosperity to the nation.

2253. Nea ɔte gya ho aduan na ɛben kan.
He whose food is nearest the fire gets done first.

2254. Dea atentrehuo hyɛ no to nhuri ntra ogya.
If you have silk-cotton up your ass you don't jump over a fire.

2255. Nea ɔtɔ apata nwe n'ani ase abon.
He who buys fish does not eat the scales under his eyes.

2256. Nea watɔ ade na onim sɛ ɔde kaw.
He who has bought something knows that he has a debt to pay.

2257. Nea watɔ na ɔtɔ tia.
What you have already bought you add to your further buying.

2258. Nea watɔ asu mu nsuro awɔw.
If you jump into the water, it means you don't fear the cold.

2259. Dea wantɔ Bennaa wɔ ne tobere.
He who didn't die on Tuesday has his own time of dying.

2260. Nea wantɔ nkrumabere wɔ ne toda.
The vegetables that are not ripe during the okro season have their own season.

2261. Nea ɔtɔn mɛnsa de butuw, na nea ɔretɔ nso, ɔdan no.
Cf.2559.
He who sells the yams turns them over, and he who is buying also turns them over.

2262. Nea watra ɔprɛm so anom tawa no, wɔmfa akwadamma nyi no hu.
He who has sat on the mouth of a canon and smoked is not frightened when a gun is shot.

2263. Nea obetumi na ɔpagyaw.
The person who is strong is the one who can lift things.

2264. Nea ontumi dan nea otumi.
He who has no power depends on the one who has.

2265. Nea otwa ɔkwan nnim sɛ n'akyi akyea.
He who is cutting a path doesn't see that it is crooked behind him.

2266. Nea ɔwaduru pɛ ne tum tum.
What the mortar likes is the sound of pounding: tum,tum.

2267. Nea ɔwɔ din na wɔbɔ ne din.
He who is famous has his name often mentioned.

2268. Nea ɔwɔ dɔm nsam' na oyi ma. R.233.
That which is in the army's hand, they can give away.

2269. Nea ɛwɔ ahenkwa tirim na ɔsɔ ho dae.
What is in the mind of the chief's servant, he dreams about.

2270. Nea ɔwɔ no na wɔde ma no.
The thing is given to him to whom it belongs.

2271. Nea ɔwɔ akyirikyiri se 'kyenekɛse yɛ no dɛ' a, ɛnte sɛ
nea ne ti bɔ ho.
If he who is far behind says he likes the sound of the
big drum, it's not like him whose head it is hitting
against.

2272. Nea ɔwɔ yere na onim sɛnea ɔte.
The husband knows how his wife lives.

2273. Nea wawɔ n'aniwam' se 'ɔbɛwɔ ne serɛ mu' a, wunnye no
kyim.
If he who has poked his eye says he will stab his thigh,
don't doubt him.

2274. Nea ɔwɔ aka no suro sunson. R.100. Gr.p.45.
He whom a snake has bitten is afraid of an earth worm.

2275. Nea ɔwoo wo te-ase a, wɔmfrɛ wo agya-ba. = 3475.
If your mother is alive, you are not called your father's
son.

2276. Nea wawo ato Agyako ntwa aboba.
He who has named his child "stop fighting" does not make
bullets.

2277. Nea wɔ-ne no tu amu na wɔ-ne no ban mpɔw.
Those who help you dig holes for yams also help you
store the new tubers of yam.

2278. Nea wawu mfa nsa ho fwe. = 2761.
A person who has died doesn't care for palm wine.

2279. Nea wobɛwe nanka ayare tefwire no, fa sa we nankanini ua
wo se ntutu prɛko.

The way in which you will eat a gaboon viper that has
infection in the gap between his teeth, eat the male gaboon
viper in the same way and let your teeth come out at once.

2280. Nea ɛyɛ den hɔ na adwonkobɛn fi. B.

The place where it is really hard is the protuberance on the
hip-bone.

2281. Nea ɛyɛ wo wura dɛ na ɛyɛ wo dɛ.

The favorite food of your master is your favorite food.

2282. Nea anyɛ yiye, wɔmfa nka asɛm.

That which isn't good you don't talk about.

2283. Nea wo yonko ayɛ no, wususuw so yɛ bi.

That which your neighbor has made, you also think about
and make.

2284. Nneɛma nhina dan sua. = 802.

All things depend on learning.

2285. Nnɛ-mma se: tete asoɛe, wɔnsoɛ hɔ bio! na dɛn nti na
wontu tete 'muka abiɛsa no biako na ɛnka abien?

The present generation says: "We don't rest at the old
resting place any more!" then why don't you take away one
of the three stones used for a fireplace and cook on two?

2286. Anene-mmea wɔ ne kaeda.

The person who goes to toilet in the bush here and there
should remember where he has gone previously.

2287. Wo ni wu a, wunwu, na ɔfɛre a, na (wo nso) woafɛre. R.266.

If your mother dies, you won't die; but if she is disgraced
you are also disgraced.

2288. Wo ni wu na wobɔ kaw na woantua a, wose wo ayi da.

If your relative dies and you incur a debt and you don't
pay it, they talk about it at your funeral.

2289. Wo ani bere a, wofa aberekyi were we.

If you are angry, you chew on a goat's hide.

2290. Wo ani bere a, wofa ogya mu.

If you are angry (your eyes are red), you take it from
the fire.

2291. Wo ani bere wo yonko ade a, woyɛ bi, na wunwia. Cf.613.2283.

If you covet something belonging to your friend, you make one, but you don't steal it.

2292. Wo ani ammere na wutwa wo mene a, wontɔ.

If you are not serious and you cut your own throat, you won't die.

2293. Ani biako nfwɛ kra nfwɛ asibe. R.114.

One eye does not at the same time look at the "kra" monkey and the "asibe" monkey.

2294. M'ani abien a etua me tirim, biako atwa me nkontompo.

The two eyes in my head, one tells me lies.

2295. Wo ani rebɔ a, wunse sɛ: mikyi tɛ. R.196.

If you are losing your sight you don't say: "I don't like eye disease."

2296. Wo ani nnye a, wuse: meko Dawu asanom.

If you are not happy you say you are going to Dawu for a drink.

2297. Wo ani nnye wo kurom' a, ɛte sɛ wunni dan wo mu (:ho).

If you are not happy in your town, it means you don't have a room there.

2298. Wo ani nkum a, na wuse: minnya dabere. R.169.

When you are not sleepy you say: "I don't have a place to sleep."

2299. Wo ani ansɔ wo akwawa a, wuwia akwa-kɛse.

If you don't like your small farm, you steal a big farm.

2300. Wo ani so toto a, wuse "mikyi nkasagua"?

If you keep looking around, do you say you don't like grumbling?

2301. Wo ani so wɔ tɛ nti, wommɔ tɛ din bio ana?

Because you have a cataract, don't you ever pronounce the name cataract?

2302. Wo ani tra wo ntɔn a, woyera.

If your eyes are higher than your eyebrows, you get lost.

2303. Wo ani wu adwabirem' a, enwu bone.

If you are ashamed in the market, it is not a bad shame.

2304. M'ani ayɛ patuni, (na) ɛnkyere aboa.
My eye is like the eye of an owl, but it doesn't catch any animal.

2305. Enni babira a wotra we atadwe a, ɛnyɛ yiye.
Eating tiger-nuts goes well anywhere.

2306. Enni babiara a wotra we yisa hinam suman so a, ɛnyɛ nnam.
No matter where you chew on guinea pepper and squirt it on your talisman, it will be strong.

2307. Enni da biara a womfrɛ no "nna-no".
We are always saying: "Just the other day."

2308. Enni wo so a, wɔse: bɔ no powpaw ma yɛnkɔ!
Wonni.. Wunni...s.906-922.
If it doesn't affect you, you say, destroy it and let's go.

2309. Onifuraefo ntumi nkyerɛ onifuraefo kwan. Z.3.
The blind can't lead the blind.

2310. Anigyebea sen awobea. =2208.
The place of joy is better than the place one was born.

2311. Onihafo na ehia no a, ɔde wu kyekye ne werɛ.
If a lazy man is in want, he comforts himself with death.

2312. Onihafo na ose: ɔkyena mɛyɛ. Gr.p.156. Cf.2111.
The lazy man says, "tomorrow I will do it."

2313. Onihafo tam nhyia no da.
The lazy man's native cloth is always small.

2314. Anihaw mu nni biribi na ɛwɔ ntama-gow.
The only thing you get out of being lazy is a ragged cloth.

2315. Anihaw mu nni biribi sɛ ohia.
The only thing you get out of being lazy is poverty.

2316. Nikisa kum ni (:nipa).
Homesickness can kill a relative.

2317. Ani-kɔkɔ yɛ adeɛ a, anka obi nsene ayeremire sika.
If red eyes had any value, then no one would be richer than the "ayeremire" bird.

2318. "Nim" nim nnim..
The "know-all" knows nothing.

2319. "Nim-sa" biara nni kan da. - "Nim-sa" ka akyiri.
"Had I known that" is always late..

2320. Minim ade pae, na ɔkromfo na n'aso yɛ den.
I know how to shout (a curse), but the thief is hard of
hearing.

2321. Minim ko a, anka me na din de Kra?
If I knew how to fight, wouldn't my mother's name be Kra?

2322. Minim sɛ: m'agya wu a, obesi me; na enti oregyam no,
ɔpenten tia me. B.
I know that if my father dies his spirit will trouble me,
therefore when he is at the point of death, he flings his
limbs and body about stepping on me.

2323. Minim sɛ: me nko na meyɛ mumɔ.
I know that I am the only bodily misformed person.

2324. Minim sɛ ɔtane yam' yɔ yea (=hyehye no).
I know that hatred's conscience bothers him.

2325. Wonim sɛ, wode kyɛ hyɛ nankroma a, ɛbɛyɛ 'ye; na wode
hyɛ ti.
Even though you know that you can put your hat on your
knee, you still put it on your head.

2326. Wunim abara na wunim atugyaw a, wodada me akyere me,
medada wo miguan.
If you know deceit and desertion, you deceived me and
caught me, and I deceived you and fled.

2327. Wunim di a, di bi, na nni ne nhina. R.116.
If you know how to eat, eat some, but don't eat it all.

2328. Wunim how a, how wo serɛ Cf.2333.
If you know how to smoke animal meat, smoke your own thigh.

2329. Wunim nkontompo a, wunim tugya?
If you know how to tell lies, do you know how to run away?

2330. Wunim wo anome a, wunnyaw kora.
If you can still drink, you don't put down your calabash.

2331. Wunim nyansa bebrebe (:pi) a, woma akɔkɔ akye.
(Wunim ade nim ade a, woma aboa akye?)
If you are too clever, you say good morning to the cock.

2332. Wunim sɛ ɔfwento ne nkruma-kwane yɛ wo tane, na wokɔfaa
no waree yɛɛ dɛn?
You know that a noseless person and okro soup don't agree
with you, so why did you go and marry her.

2333. Wunim tu a, tu wo dwen. (Obuobi Atwede,...) R.24.
If you know how to pull, pull out your own gray hair.

2334. Wunnim a, ɔmanni kyerɛ. Cf.265.532.
If you don't understand, a native will teach you.

2335. Wunnim kurow bi mu a, wonka mu asɛm.
If you don't know anything about a town, you don't tell
anything about it.

2336. Wunnim nipa a, wo-ne no nsi kɔsow.
If you don't know a person, you don't join him in a joint
business enterprise.

2337. Wunnim asaw a, na wuse: akyene nyɛ dɛ. R.213.
If you don't know how to dance, you say you don't like the
sound of the drum.

2338. Wunnim sɛnea wote a, fwɛ kora mu!
If you don't know how you are living, look into the calabash.

2339. Wunnim wo to a, wommene adobɛ aba.
If you don't know your rear, you don't swallow the nuts
of the "adobɛ" palm tree.

2340. Wunnim owu a, fwɛ nna!
If you don't know what death is like, look at someone sleepin

2341. Wonnim onipa tirim asɛm a, ɛnyɛ wɔnne Otu a ɔte Datɛ.
If you don't know a man's thoughts, how much more those
of Otu who lives in Date.

2342. Yenim oguan fwɛfo, na yennim ne wura.
We know the one who looks after the sheep, but we don't
know their owners.

2343.   Yenim sɛ kontromfi kon wo hɔ, na yɛde hama to n'asenmu.

We know the monkey has a neck, but we tie a rope around
its waist.

2344.   Yenim sɛ Koromante bɛbere a, anka yɛantete no abunu
ansɛe no. (Mp.)

If we knew that "Koromante" would become ripe then we would
not have picked its unripe fruit and spoiled it.

2345.   Yenim sɛ kyemi na ɛte nkwan, nanso wɔtɔ no afikyiri,
ansa-na wɔde abɛto sanya mu.

We know the "stink fish" give the soup a scent but we
put them behind the house before we put them in the
nice pewter dish.

2346.   Yenim sɛ nkyene yɛ dɛ; na yɛkɔ gua so a, yɛtɔ mako.

We know that salt is tasty, but when we go to the market
we buy pepper.

2347.   Yenim sɛ 'mogya wɔ yɛn anom', na yɛfe ntasu.   R.20. Z. 58.

We think that there is blood in our mouth, but we only
spit out saliva.

2348.   Yenim sɛ nnoma dɔso (:nnoma-nnoma nhina aduasa), na
anoma werɛmfoɔ (=ɔkɔre) na yɛrepɛ no.

We know there are many kinds of birds, but we want the
eagle.

2349.   Yenim sɛ nsu nhina dɔso, na bosonopo ne panyin.

We know that there are many rivers but the ocean is the
biggest.

2350.   Yenim sɛ wɔde gya bɛkɔ akogu sumana so; nanso wɔde fi
wuram' ba a, wɔde ba ofie ansa.

We know that firewood will be taken and thrown out on the
dump when it turns to ashes, but when it is brought from
the bush it is first taken to the house.

2351.   Anim a anyɛ nyam na ɛbɛyɛ sɛ nammɔnmu.

A face which is not beautiful is like the sole of a
person's foot.

2352.   Anim nkyene, akyiri mako, wokyi.

Salt in a person's presence and pepper in his absence,
you hate this.

-195-

2353. Wo anim nkyene, atiko wusa (:yisa)!

To your face salt, to the back of your head guinea-pepper.

2354. Anim nte sɛ foto mu.
Anim nyɛ bonsua...s.2405.

Your face is not like the inside of a bag.

2355. Nimdeɛ firi obi ano.

Wisdom comes from a person's mouth.

2356. Nimfi nimfi akɔfrɛ nanka nanka. B.

The one who is from the place shouts,"gaboon viper, gaboon viper."

2357. Nnimmo nnimmo (:Nnimmo-dodow) yɛ owu.

Always mentioning a person's name in a derogatory way causes his death.

2358. Nim-yɛ di bi, na onni ne nhina.

Knowing how to do something accomplishes some things, but not everything.

2359. Anini abien nna bon mu. R. 177. Z.44.

Two male animals don't live in the same den.

2360. Ninkunu yɛ kɔm a, ɛde mmarima nhina.

If jealousy caused hunger, then all men would be hungry.

2361. Aninyanne, wonhu no abien.

You don't have two severe pains at the same time.

2362. Onipa a wɔde sanya mu aduan ayɛn no no, ohu asanka mu aduan a, ne werɛ how.

The person who was raised eating from a tin plate is grieved when he has to eat food from a black earthware dish.

2363. Onipa a wanyin sen oduefoɔ.

An experienced old man knows more than a fetish priest.

2364. Onipa a ɔmpɛ sɛ ne yonko yɛ yiye no, ɔnyɛ yiye. Cf. 2451.

The person who doesn't want his neighbor to prosper, doesn't prosper himself.

2365. Onipa a ɔmpɛ wo no, ɔmpɛ wo ho fwɛ.

If a person doesn't like you, he doesn't like anything about you.

2366. Onipa a wo-ne no di akapimfwe no na osore a, woka ne pim
fwe na ono nso ka wo de fwe. = 2203.
When someone you are intimate with gets up from bed,
you look at his buttocks and he looks at yours.

2367. Onipa reba a, wunse no se: bera! R. 43.
When a person is already coming you don't say to him,
"come!"

2368. Onipa bi se 'obenya wo' a, na o-ne yares.
If some one says he will get even with you, he gets sick.

2369. Onipa bi wu afe bi, na wo nso woko afe bi.
If someone has died one year, you will also die another
year.

2370. Onipa-bone biako te man mu a, ne nkoa ne nnipa nhina.
When there is a wicked person in the town all the other
people become his slaves.

2371. Onipa de ade sie a, ode sie nea ope a obenu.
If a man preserves something, he puts it where he can
find it when he wants it.

2372. Onipa de fere (:aniwu) na ewu. Cf. 2451.
Man dies because of disgrace.

2373. Onipa de ne kotoku se a, ode se nea ne nsa beso.
If a man is carrying a purse, he carries it where his hand
can reach it.

2374. Onipa de anibere na ewia ade.
Man steals because of covetousness.

2375. Onipa odesani te ho, ofie nwansana nkeka no huno; ewo
nea aka no nti na eka no.
If a man is sitting and the house flies bit him for no
reason, it is because of what is on him that they bit
him.

2376. Onipa didi wie a, na onkasa (:onka asem) nwie. Cf.2394.
2417.
If a man has finished eating, he doesn't finish talking.

2377. Onipa bedidi a, obisa kotokuo. (Abrokwaw.)
If a man wants to eat, he asks his purse.

2378. Onipa, wonno no nna nhina. R. 10. Gr. #201,5.
Man is not loved at all times.

-197-

2379. Onipa dom gyina hɔ a, wommisa dua ɔdom.

When a great number of people are present you don't ask the oduɑ tree.

2380. Onipa firi soro na obesi a, obesi nnipa kuro so.

If a man comes from heaven to land, he will land in a town of humans.

2381. Onipa afiri, wosua no tempɔn mu, na wonsua no kwankyɛn.

You learn how to trap people on the main street, not on the roadside.

2382. Onipa afiri, wosum a, wɔnkata so.

If you set a trap to catch a person, you don't cover it.

2383. Onipa mfɔn kwa: ɔkɔm nne no a, na ɔde kaw. R. 7. Z.32.

One does not lose weight without a cause: the cause may be hunger of debt.

2384. Onipa annyae mmɔbɔ-yɛ a, wonnyae no mmɔbɔhu. Cf.1255. Gr. p. 69.

When a person's misery doesn't stop, you don't stop pitying him.

2385. Onipa (be)gye nkanare a, ɔsen dade.

When a man gets rusty, he is worse than iron.

2386. Onipa ogyigyefo na ɔma onipa horan.

A flatterer makes man become proud.

2387. Onipa ogyigyefo sen bonsam. F.

A flatterer is worse than the devil.

2388. Onipa nnyimi nsi ase.

Man's foolishness never ends.

2389. Onipa hiani gyasefoɔ ne nwansana.

The poor man's attendants are house flies.

2390. Onipa ho antɔ no a, (na) efi n'asɛm.

If a man is unhappy, his conduct is the cause.

2391. Onipa ho yɛ den a, efi ne kotodwe.

If a man is strong, it is because of his knees.

2392. Onipa ho nyɛ fɛ nkosi ase.

Man is not handsome when he becomes old.

2393. Onipa honam na wode hu n'afitra mu nsɛm.

A man's personal appearance shows how things are going in his home.

2394. Onipa nkasa nwie ɔsa. Cf. 202. 2376. 2417.

Man does not talk if he hasn't finished drinking his palm wine.

2395. Onipa nkowtow kwa.

Man doesn't bow for no reason at all.

2396. Onipa me da a, anka ɔte sɛ sono.

If man ate his fill every day, he would be as big as an elephant.

2397. Onipa-mu mfa n'anuonyam nsie ne to.

An honourable person doesn't keep his glory in his rear.

2398. Onipa mudua ne aduan.

The staff of life for man is food.

2399. Onipa na ɔma onipa yɛ yiye.

Man makes his fellow man prosper.

2400. Onipa na onyin, na ɔdan nnyin.

A man grows up, a house can't grow up.

2401. Onipa nam na o(re)siane amoa. Gr. p. 154.

Man is always walking near his own grave.

2402. Onipa ne ne din na ɛnam.

A person takes his name with him wherever he goes.

2403. Onipa ne asɛm: mefrɛ sika a, sika nnye so: mefrɛ ntama a, ntama nnye so; onipa ne asɛm. (Amoakwa.)

A human being is important: if I call gold, it does not respond, if I call a native cloth, it does not respond; a human being is important.

2404. Onipa anim te sɛ ewi (:owia) anim; wuhu a, na wo bo adwo.

Man's face is like the face of the sun, when you see it, you are appeased.

2405. Onipa anim nyɛ bonsua na wɔapun mu da.

Man's face is not an oil pot which should be smoked black everyday.

2406. Onipa anim nyɛ burodua na wɔde agye ahohora.
Man's face is not a corn cob; which you use for a disgraceful purpose.

2407. Onipa nya amanne da; na woanhyia wo gyigyefo a, na wuse:m'ase adwo me. Cf. 2435.
A human being always has troubles, if you don't meet a flatterer you say, I have peace today.

2408. Onipa patuw pow? (Boaten a ofi Dwaben baa Akyem.)
Does man become civilized all at once?

2409. Onipa si bone kwan mu a, afotu yɛ no ɔsɛmɔdɛ.
When a man is setting out to do evil, advice is a joke to him.

2410. Onipa soa ade a obetumi.
Man carries the load he can.

2411. Onipa nsu kwa; wohu asude a, na wosu.
Man cries for a reason; if you see something worth crying about, you cry.

2412. Onipa te sɛ sare; na sɛ wɔyɛ no yiye a, na ayɛ yiye, na sɛ wɔyɛ no bone a, na asɛe.
Man is like grass, if you look after it, it grows well, and if you don't look after it, it spoils.

2413. Onipa nti na wobɔ afoa.
It is because of man we wear swords.

2414. Onipa wu a, na ne nam wɔ hɔ.
When man dies, his flesh remains behind.

2415. Onipa wu a, ne tɛkrɛma mporɔw.
When a man dies his tongue does not rot.

2416. Onipa wu (wɔ) samampow mu a, wɔmfa no mma ofie bio.
When man dies in the cemetry, he is not brought back home again.

2417. Onipa wie didi, na onwie asɛm ka. = 2376.
Man finishes eating but not talking.

2418. Onipa yɛ abogyaboa.
Man is a red blooded animal.

-200-

2419. Nyimpa yɛ fɛw sen sika. Mf. Gr. p. 165.
A good name is better than riches.

2420. Onipa yɛ wo yiye a, mfa bone nyɛ no.
If someone does good to you, don't do evil to him.

2421. Onipa yɛ yiye a, ɔyɛ gyaw ne mma.
If a man becomes rich, he leaves it behind for his children.

2422. Onipa bɛyɛ bi, na wammɛyɛ ne nhina.
A man can only do some things, not all of them.

2423. Onipa nyɛ abɛ na ne ho ahyia ne ho.
Man is not like the palm tree which is surrounded by its branches.

2424. Nnipa banu ko a, nea otia abiɛsa na ɔpatafo ne no.
If two men fight, the third one is the peacemaker.

2425. Nnipa banu mpata nyɛ bone. Cf. 2430.
Two people are not bad at the same time.

2426. Nnipa banu so dua a, emmia. = 45.
If two people carry a log, it doesn't press hard on their heads.

2427. Nnipa nhina de anka guare a, wɔn ho yɛ huam; na ahohow se: ɔkɔda so,-na ne ho bɔn. R. 139.
If all people would use lemon when they bathe, they would smell sweet: but the red ant says he lives in the lemon tree, and he still stinks.

2428. Nnipa nhina-nhina bewu; na owu pa na yɛrepɛ.
All people will die, but we want a good death.

2429. Nnipa nhina na 'yɛde sae hyɛ 'yɛne nsa a, 'yetumi bɔ dadeɛ soɔ?
If we put a hammer in every person's hand, could they all become blacksmiths?

2430. Nnipa nhina mpatuw nyɛ bone. Cf. 2425.
All people are not bad at the same time.

2431. Nnipa nhina pɛ Aburokyiri akɔ; na onya na wonnya! Gr. # 247,2.
Everyone wants to go to Europe, but the opportunity doesn't come to everyone.

2432. Nnipa nnina pɛ ɔhene ayɛ; na wɔannya a, na wose: mpo
ahenni yɛ yaw.

All men want to become chiefs, and if they don't become
chiefs then they say chieftancy is a burden.

2433. Nnipa nhina pɛ makye meda-ase,-ɛkaw asɛm ntia.

Because of debts everyone likes to say good morning,
thank you.

2434. Nnipa nhina soa (:sum) nyankopɔn a, ɔbiakofo mmerɛ (:nnuru
mu afu). = 2755.

If everyone helps to hold up the sky, then one person
does not become tired.

2435. Nnipa nhina yɛ nnipa-bone, na wo nko de fi a, na nkurofo
se: akoa yi yɛ onipa bone! Cf. 2407.

All men are sinful, but if your sins come to light, then
poeple say, "this is a wicked person."

2436. Nnipa nhina yɛ Onyame mma; obi nye asase ba.

Everyone is a child of God, no one is a child of the earth.

2437. Nnipa nhina yɛ ti biako, (na)nso wɔn ti nsɛ.

Everyone has a head, but there is no one exactly like
the other.

2438. Nnipa-pa bi ko 'sa, wɔanhu ano, na gyama Kutroku! R. 187.

Good men go to war and they don't see the end, and what
of the coward!

2439. Nnipa tirim asɛm yɛ mmiako-'miako.

Every person has his own ideas.

2440. Anisuatɛtɛ sene abogyesɛ panyin.

Man's eyelashes came before his beard.

2441. Nitɔre se 'ɔbɛda' a, wonnye no kyim.

If the one-eyed person says he is sleepy, we do not
argue with him.

2442. Niwa niwa na ɛyɛ niwa abien. (... atiri du.)

One eye and one eye makes two eyes.

2443. Niwa nso yɛ ade.

The eye is valuable.

2444. Aniwa fufu nkum anoma. R. 81.
A white eye does not kill a bird.

2445. Aniwa hu ade a, ano di bi.
If your eye sees something, your mouth eats some of it.

2446. Aniwa na εtan nipa, na aso de εntan nipa. R. 221.
It is the eye that dislikes people, not the ear.

2447. Aniwa nnim awerεhow. R. 117.
The eye does not know (can not be overcome by) grief.

2448. Aniwa nya a, na fwene anya. =1198. Gr. # 202, 2.
If your eye finds something, your nose also finds it.

2449. Aniwa wu a, etuatua tirim ho ara.
Even if your eye dies, it still stays in your head.

2450. Aniwa nyε abura, nso emu nsu nsa da.
The eye is not a well, but its water never dries up.

2451. Aniwa ne wu, na εfanim wu. Cf. 2372.
Of the two, shame and death, death is preferable.

2452. Ano berεberε ma adae tɔ.
Peaceful talk makes one live to see the "Adae" festival.

2453. Ano-bone yε ɔkrabiri. (Ohenewa) Cf. 1531.
To have a quarrelsome mouth is to be unlucky.

2454. Ano-kεse na ese asεn-kεse.
It is the big mouth that says big things.

2455. Ano-kurokuro twa neho adafi.
The talkative person reveals things about himself.

2456. Ano ne ano goru a, na ntoto ba; na nan ne nan goru a,
na ntoto mma. = 2093.
If mouth and mouth plays, discord comes, if leg and leg
play, discord doesn't come.

2457. Ano annya adwuma ayε a, enya asεm di.
If the mouth doesn't get work to do, it gets into trouble.

2458. Ano-pa gya owura kwan.
A good mouth guides its master.

-203-

2459. Ano-pa hyira ne ho. (:ne wura).
A good mouth brings blessings upon itself.

2460. Ano-pa ma ade kye (:owura).
A good mouth gives its master long life.

2461. Ano patiriw a, ɛsen nammɔn. R. 151.
A slip of the tongue is worse than a slip of the foot.

2462. Ano se 'onim aduan'a, ɛnte sɛ tɛkrɛma a ɛda mu.
When the mouth says it knows a food, it is not like the
tongue on which the food is lying.

2463. Wo ano so a, womfa nhyɛn ɔwaduru, na wode hyɛn abɛn.
Even if your mouth is big. you don't blow a mortar for
pounding fufu with it, but a horn.

2464. Wo anom' asɛm sa a, na wo adeɛ asa.
If you have nothing to say, your wealth is finished.

2465. Wo anom' asɛm asa a, na wose: Kini a ɔwɔ Aburokyiri yɛ
ɔhene. Nea n'atomfo tono aprɛm no, wɔkamfo no bio?
If you have nothing to say, then you say: "The king who
is is in Europe is a king indeed." He whose blacksmith
makes the cannon, does he need any more praise?

2466. Wo anom' asɛm nsa a, (ma) wuse: minni yere, minni ba
(:mma). =2658.
If you still want to talk, you say: "I don't have a wife,
I don't have any children."

2467. Wonoa akokɔ-kesua ma me a, miyi mu kɔkɔ (:kɔkrobotɔ)
metwene (=mekyene).
If you boil a chicken's egg for me, I take the yellow of
the egg and throw away the rest.

2468. Wonoa ma nea ɔde (WWɔnoa no nea ɛyɛ ne dea, nea wame),
na wɔnnoa mma nea ɔkɔm de no.
We cook well for he who has some (:we cook for the person
whose food it is for he who is satisfied), we don't cook
well for those who are hungry.

2469. Wonoa ɔsa na nkontompo gya hyɛ ase a, ɛmmen.
If you are cooking the war medicine and there is fire of
untruth under it, it will never be well cooked.

-204-

2470. Wonoa ntorewa di, na wommene n'aba.

You cook garden eggs and eat them, but you don't swallow the seeds.

2471. "Wonnoa mperennu" ye nkyene-see.

We don't cook food twice, and thus spoil the salt.

2472. Anɔfranako sore abrɔde ase na ɔdwehene awo nta. Cf. 2075.

The "anofranko" (a medicinal plant whose flowers are poisonous to animals), grows at the base of the plantain, but the ram still gave birth to twins.

2473. Anokorampɔn n'ase fi soro na obi nnim n'ase.

The "anokorampon" (a parasitical plant growing on trees), its roots are from above, and so no one knows the source of its life.

2474. Ɔnokwafo mo ne tam a, ɔmo no akwan-akwan.

If the truthful man puts on his native cloth, he puts it on while walking (to hear the case).

2475. Nokware mu nni abra.

There can be no deceit in telling the truth.

2476. Nokware ye ahe na wodi mu atoro yi?

How many truths are there that you can tell lies about some of them?

2477. Nokware nye ahe (:nnɔsɔ) na wɔatwa mu nkontompo!

There is not so much of truth that it should be lessened by falsehood!

2478. Wonom nsu a, wofwe ne nkwammanoa.

When you drink water, you look at its sides.

2479. Anoma a ɔda afirim' nko ne ne kasa.
(Anoma a ɔte afirim' no, ɛsono ne kasa nko.) R. 260.

The cry of a bird which is lying in a trap is not the same as its usual cry. (A bird which is caught in a trap doesn't make its usual sound.)

2480. Anoma biako wɔ wo nsam' a, ɛyɛ sen abien a ɛwɔ wuram'
(:nnoma du a ɛwɔ ahunum').

One bird in the hand is better than two in the bush.

2481. Anoma (biara) wu wɔ soro a, (ɛnyɛ dɛn ara a,) ne ntakara ba (:gu) fam'.

If a bird dies in the sky, no matter what happens, its feathers fall to the ground.

-205-

2482. Anoma-bone na ɔsɛe ne berebuw (mu). (...ɔyɛ ne b. mu fi.)
       It is a bad bird that makes its own nest dirty.

2483. Anoma de akɔ-ne-aba na ɛnwene (bere)buw. R. 191. Gr. #
       237c.
       It is by coming and going that a bird weaves its nest.

2484. Anoma kɛse antu a, obua da.
       When a full-grown bird does not fly in search of food, it
       goes to sleep hungry.

2485. Anoma kɔ asu a, ɔde n'ano.
       If the bird goes to get water, he gets it with his beak.

2486. Anoma kɔreɛ, onni anammono a, ɔnna.
       If the eagle doesn't eat raw meat, it doesn't sleep.

2487. Anoma koro di awi a, otiatia so.
       When one bird is eating grain all alone, it steps all
       over the grain.

2488. Anoma kyɛ dua so a, ogye bo.
       If a bird remains too long in a tree, someone hits it
       with a stone.

2489. Anoma nam nkɔso kyɛ. F.
       There is not enough meat in a bird to divide up.

2490. Anoma ne nua ne nea ɔ-ne no da.
       It is one of its own family that a bird roosts with.

2491. Anoma niferefo, wode mposae na eyi no. R. 242.
       The cunning bird is caught by placing the withered bark
       of a plantain tree over a trap.

2492. Anoma ano ware a, ɔde didi: asuogya na ɔmfa ntwa asu
       (:ntware asuo nkodidi).
       When a bird has a long beak, it uses it for eating on its
       own side of the river and not for stretching across the
       river.

2493. Anoma ano yɛ den a, aboa bi nkyere no nwe.
       If a bird can shout loudly, it can not be caught and eaten
       by a wild animal.

2494. Ɔnomdɛfo na nsɔe hia no.
       A dainty eater is troubled by fish bones.

2495. Anom hohoro nti na Akyenkwa bɔɔ, otuo.

It is because of the rite of "rinsing one's mouth' that Akyenkwa shot himself.

2496. Anɔpa-nom' bɔn, na asɛmpa na ɛwom'. R. 181. Z. 190.

One's mouth stinks in the morning, but there is truth in it.

2497. Anɔpa dwuma ankɔ, na bɔnnɔ?

If work done in the morning doesn't go well, then what about work done in leisure time?

2498. Anosɛmfo biara nni ahooden.

People who boast have no power.

2499. Anosɛmfo biara nnya ɔyere da.
Wonnuu... Wunnuu...s. 989. 990.

People who boast never find a wife.

2500. Wunu mu nu mu a, egyen.

If you keep stirring it up, it becomes tasteless.

2501. Onua-panyin yɛ owura.

The senior brother is the one in charge.

2502. Wo nua a ɔtan wo no ɔte se oni ne nua a ɔdɔ wo.

Your brother who hates you is like someone else's brother who loves you.

2503. Wo nua ho yɛ fɛ a, ɛnyɛ mma wo.

If your sister is beautiful, she is not so for you.

2504. Wo nua serɛ so a, na ɛnyɛ wo na woda so.

If your sister's thighs are gib, it is not you who lie on them.

2505. Wununu kokora a, nunu bamfo bi.

If you blame the thorny climber "kokora", also blame the thorny plant called "bamfo".

2506. Wununu akura a, nunu nkankan-mma bi.

If you blame the mouse, blame also the termites.

2507. Onunum ho annwo na efi ɔmanni.

If the "nunum" plant doesn't have peace it is because of the people (plucking its leaves).

2508. Nusu yɛ abura a, anka obi nsaw obi de da.

If tears were a well, then no one would ever go to collect
water from some one else.

2509. Manya wo mayɛ a, (na) woanya asamaradwo atoto awe, na
wuse: namkɔm de me (:sakɔm de wo)?

If I were in your place, and you got beetles to roast
and eat, I would say, "I'm hungry for meat?"

2510. Wonya a, wonwia.

If people get what they need, they don't steal.

2511. Wunya a, na wopere (:woserɛ) ntoso. Z. 23.

If you get a good bargain, you still fight for a bonus
in addition.

2512. Wunya obi na ɔtɔ ama wo na wudi a, ɛte sɛ wonne kaw.

If you come upon someone and he buys for you and you eat,
it is like you have no debts.

2513. Wunya adeɛ a, di bi; "ennwo, ennwo" dwo wo yɔnko anom'.
Cf. 1064. 2525.

If you get rich, enjoy your riches; if you say it is not
cool, then it cools off in your friend's mouth.

2514. Wunya ade a, na obi gu mu.

If you have riches, someone is added to your care.

2515. Wunya ade a, na wode bi kyɛ.

If you get rich, you share some of your wealth with others.

2516. Wunya ade a, wɔtan wo; wunnya ade a, wɔfrɛ wo bone.

If you get rich, they hate you; if you are not rich, they
call you a bad man.

2517. Wunya aginaye a, (na) wuhuro ɔpanamiri.

If you get a good place to stand, you make fun of the
cobra.

2518. Wunya ɔkɔ a, na wunya (woanya) ɔba.

If you get a chance to go, you also get a chance to come.

2519. Wunya nkwa a, na wunya akwahosan.

If you have life, you have life and health.

2520. Wunya asɛnkɛse a, wonka nkyerɛ ɔbea; mmea kum nnipa.

If you get an important matter, don't tell a woman; women
kill people.

2521. Woanya foforo atow dedaw akyene, (Koko ne amankani.)
When you get something new you throw the old one away.

2522. Woanya me Kofi Millo abɛ?
Do you get me Kofi Millo's palm wine?

2523. Woanya ano a, nya nsa!
If you have a mouth, get some palm wine!

2524. Woanya woho a, to wo pon mu da.   (... mua wo ano)
R. 25.   Gr. # 237. 239c. 276, 1.
If you become rich, sleep with your door shut.

2525. Wunnya nnwo a, wudwo obi anom'.   Cf. 1064. 2513.
If the food hasn't cooled down, it cools down in someone
else's mouth.

2526. Woanya adagyew anyare a, wunya adayew wu.
If you have no time to take care of your sickness, you
get time to die.

2527. Woannya yɔnko-pa a, wofwefwɛ foforo.
If you don't have a good friend you look for another one.

2528. Wpannya nhui a, wpannya nkae. Cf. 2219.   Gr. p. 68.
What you haven't seen you don't remember.

2529. Wunnyaa nkɔfaa kontromfia tibi nkɔyɛɛ adwuma (:nkɔdɔw
afuw) na ose obedi yi, na menne sɛ wobenya (:wobɛkɔ)
akɔfa (n'atibi akɔyɛ adwuma a, anka afuw no gye obekuku)!
You weren't able to take any of the monkey's soldiers to
go and work in his farm and yet he says he will eat some
of the produce, so what if you did get some of his
soldiers to help you.

2530. Wonnya awuru a, wontew no so hama.   R. 192.
If you haven't caught a turtle, you don't cut a rope to
tie it up.

2531. Yenya ko a, yɛbɛko; nkisiwa resɛeko.
If we get a war, we will fight; the worthless person
spoils the war.

2532. "Benya ade o, bewu ntɛm!" wokyi.
"Get rich, die quickly!" is not said.

2533. Anua-me-nyɛe twɛre, wotow a, ɛpae.
I got some to grind, if you throw it, it breaks.

2534. Onya nya neho a, ɔnom nyankonsu. R. 197.
When a slave becomes free, he drinks rain water.

2535. Anya-duasa nso bayifo (:bonsam) di.
Even thrity slaves are not too much for a witch to eat.

2536. Onya se: ɔkɔsow nkruma; afei ɔkɔpae a, tenterehu!
The slave says he produces okra pods, but when they
burst open it is silk-cotton!

2537. Onya tu a, hunhon na efi anaṅmu.
If the slave flees, the "hunhon" vegetable grows in his
footsteps.

2538. Onyame nkrabea nni kwatibea. Cf. 1763.
The destiny God has assigned to you cannot be evaded.

2539. Onyame anku wo a, wunwu. Cf. 2546.
If God has not decreed your death, you won't die.

2540. Onyame ma wo yare a, ɔma wo aduru.
If God gives you an illness, he also gives you the cure.

2541. Onyame na ɔwɔ basin fufuo ma no.
It is God who pounds fufu for the one-armed man.

2542. Onyame ne panyin. Cf. 2787.
God is greater than anyone else (the Creator).

2543. Onyame pɛ sɛ ogye yɛn yiye nti, na ɔde Mankata besii
agye yɛn.
Because God wants to protect us well, he put the state
umbrella on earth to protect us.

2544. Onyankopɔn ba de Mpatuw-nwu.
The child of God is called sudden death.

2545. Onyankopɔn hyɛ wo nsa kora-ma na ɔteasefo ka gu a (Ony.
ma wo sakora-ma na ɔdesani fwie gu a), ohyia wo so (bio).
If God gives you a calabash full of palm wine and an evil
man knɔcks it over, he fills it up again.

2546. Onyankopɔn nkum wo na ɔdasani (ɔdesani, onipa ɔteasefo) kum wo a, wunwu (da). Cf. 2539.

If God has not decreed your death, and a human being tries to kill you, you will not die.

2547. Onyankopɔn amma asonomfoa katakyi biribi a, ɔmaa no ahodannan.

If God gave the swallow no other gift, he at least gave it agility.

2548. Onyankopɔn mpɛ asɛmmone nti na ɔkyɛ din mmiako-ʼmiako. Cf. 789. Gr. p. 157.

Because God doesn't like evil he gave every creature a name.

2549. Nyankommerebere (biara) nka ahunmu (ahunmʼ ani, ɔsoro) da.

The noise produced by the rain in the air before falling on the earth never touches the storm (wind).

2550. Nyankommeretere ne panyin.

The Bavbab is the greatest of all trees.

2551. Nyankonsoroma, menne wɔn ka, ɔsrane na efiri a, ɛnna ehia me.

The stars remain, but if the moon comes out, then they are in trouble.

2552. Nyankonsoroma, ɔmane wɔ no da; ɔsrane de, ɛnnɛ-nnansa pɛ na wawu.

The stars are always shinning over the town, but the moon is only there a few days before it dies.

2553. Nyankonnuru nnuru po mu da.

The "Nyankonnuru" plant (growing on trees) never reaches the sea.

2554. Nyansa nyɛ sika na wɔankyekyere asie.

Wisdom is not like money which you can bundle up and store away.

2555. Onyansafe de pɛsewa gye ɔkwasea nsamʼ pereguan.

The wise person uses a pesewa to get thirty six dollars from a foolish person.

2556. Onyansafe na ɔto asawa.

The wise person spins cotton.

2557. Onyansafo na etwa akwammew. (...ɔkwan pa.) R. 220.

The wise person can cross over the roots of trees running across the road (any obstacle).

2558. Anyansafo banu gɔru a, ntoto ba.

If two wise people play together confusion comes.

2559. Anyansafo banu kyɛ mɛnsa; ɔbako dan si hɔ, na ɔbako redan butuw hɔ. Cf. 2261.

If two wise persons are dividing a yam between them, one stands and turns it over, and the other squats and turns it over.

2560. Anyansafo banu kyɛ niwa abiɛɛsa a, ɛnyɛ 'ye. (: to ba).

If two wise people divide three eyes, it doesn't go well.

2561. Wunyin a, na wunhu; na woyɛ bɔne de a, wuhu.

If you are growing up you don't understand, but if you do something bad, you understand.

2562. Wurenyini na wo mmusuo renyin.

You are growing up, so also are your misfortunes.

2563. Onyin awie, 'kyiri (mpabotwaw).

"Stop growing" doesn't like "mpabotwaw".

2564. Onyinkyerɛ, ade wɔ mu.

There is something good in a long life.

2565. Nnuannya mfa kyim ho fwe. B.

The sheep's leg is not involved in the preparation of the food that is prepared with its blood.

2566. Ɔnwam di bi a, opurow di bi. =2728.

If the toucan eats some, so does the squirrel.

2567. Ɔnwam ho wɔ ade a, anka ontu.

If the toucan had something, then he wouldn't fly away.

2568. Ɔnwam nim ne to nti na ɔmene adobɛ-aba.

Because the toucan know his anus, he swallows the nuts of the palm tree.

2569. Ɔnwam, wusu bɛn? akyenkyena na ose: asuakua mmɔ me!

Toucan, what are you crying about? Akyenkyena says: "asuakwa don't hit me."

2570. Nwansana (de ne nsa gu n'akyi a, o) se:nea aka akyiri na ɛdɔso. R. 33.

When the fly stretches it legs behind him, he says, "what is left behind is a lot."

2571. Nwansana ɛmpa funu ho a, wɔde no sie. Z. 20.

If a fly does not get up off a dead body, he is buried with it.

2572. Nwansana pobi, onni ano, na ɔtwɛre bebun.

The fly has no mouth, but it can strip unripe palm nuts.

2573. Nwansana pobi si abeya mu a, wotafore mu. Cf. 465.

Even though the fly lands in the dish, you still lick inside it.

2574. Nwansana nso fa mmɛrɔsa ho dɛn?

What does the housefly want to do with the brandy?

2575. Nwansana yɛ sisi a, onsi gya mu.

Wherever the fly is going to land, it doesn't land on the fire.

2576. Anwenhema pɛ adansɛɛ ti, na hyirɛ si ne nwene soo.

The white-nosed monkey likes the witnesses head, so there is white clay on his braids.

2577. Onwini adwo a, na yehu nea ayi wɔ no.

When it is evening, we see where the funeral is.

2578. Wɔpa wo ho tam (wɔ) abɔnten so na wɔde befura (wo) ofie a, ɛnye fɛ.

If you take off your cloth in the main street and put it on at home, it is not good manners.

2579. Wopa ɔpayare a, ɔyarɛ pa gye wo mu.

When you pretend to be sick, a real sickness comes upon you.

2580. "Pae mu se" yɛ fɛre, nso ɛyɛ ahodwo. Gr. # 251, d.

We are shy to tell things plainly, but it brings peace of mind.

2581. Mpafe nti na wɔntow funu bo.

It is because of pains in the side that people don't stone a dead body.

2582. Apakyi, wɔammɔ wo a, wummue! Cf. 1849.

Gourd, it they don't hit your cover, you don't open!

2583. Apakyi akyi nkyerɛkyerɛwa dodo kyiri obiako asɛm.
Cf. 949.

The many figu es on the back of a gourd bear the problem
one person has.

2584. Wopam aboa no na woamma ne kwan a, oguan fa wo so.
Cf. 2587. 31501. Z. 208.

If you chase an animal away and you don't give him room to
flee, he will run over you.

2585. Wopam mmoa no ansa-na woatu mmofra fo.

You chase the animals away before you advise children.

2586. Wopam guam-mɔne a, oguam-pa guan.

If you drive away a troublesome sheep, the good one also
runs away.

2587. Wopam hufo na woamma no aguanbea a, oyi ne barima kyerɛ wo.
Cf. 2584.

If you chase away a coward and you don't give him room
to glee, he snows you his strength.

2588. Ɔpampam nyɛ dua bi, nso wɔde no di asikadivini. (Ɔp, nyɛ
ogya bi nanso wɔde no nan sika.)

The "ɔpampam" tree is not just any tree, but the one used
in doing gold-smith's work.

2589. Ɔpampan-nya, wonyɛ ogya bi, na wɔde wo nan sika a, wɔde
wo yɛ nnesma nhina.

"Ɔpampan" tree, you are not just any kind of fire-wood,
but when you are melting gold, you are used to make many
things.

2590. Pane nim pam a, anka ne to nna tokuru. R. 122.

If the needle knew how to sew, then it would not have a
hole in the back.

2591. Pane se 'onim ade-pam', nanso ne to da tokuru.

The needle says it knows how to sew, but it has a hole
in its back.

2592. Pane, wunim pam a, pam wo to.

Needle, if you know how to sew, sew your own buttocks.

2593. Ɔpani nnim ta a awu.

If the hired labourer doesn't know tobacco which has died. (dried)

2594. Apantwewa nim dades bɔ a, ankara onni afuo?

If the "apantwewa" bat knows how to smith, then wouldn't he have a farm?

2595. Ɔpanyin a wanyin dan mma.

An elder who has grown very old depends on his children.

2596. Ɔpanyin a wanyin ne nea wakɔ Asante aba ne nea wakɔ Aburokyiri aba, atorofo a ɔwɔ ɔman mu nen. (Anakwa a ɔte Mamfe).

The elder who has grown very old, and the elder who has gone to Ashanti and returned, and the elder who has been to Europe and returned, all these are the liars of the nation.

2597. Ɔpanyin di nsɛm nhina akyi a, ɔman bɔ. Cf. 2601.

If an elder were to follow up every offense in order to inflict punishment, the country would go to ruin.

2598. Ɔpanyin nni abansosɛm akyi. =2615.

An elder pays no attention to rumors.

2599. Ɔpanyin nni biribi a ɔwɔ batwɔw (ɔwɔ "hɔ o"). Cf. 2611.

If an elder has nothing, at least he has his riches.

2600. Ɔpanyin didi adibone a, oyi n'asanka.

If the elder eats greedily, (not leaving any of the food behind) he has to remove (and wash) his own dish.

2601. Opanyin due, mante, mante. R. 106.

The elder uses as a preventive to evade accusation or responsibility by saying; "I haven't heard it, I know nothing about it."

2602. Ɔpanina fɛre ne mma a, na ne mma suro no.

When an elder is strict with his children, they have a respectful fear for him.

2603. (Sɛ) opanyin begye me nsam' akonnua, onnye asase a mete so.

Though an elder may take away from me the stool I am sitting on, he cannot take away from me the ground I sit on.

2604. Opanyin nko na odi amim?
It is it elder alone who oppresses others?

2605. Opanyin Kwakye a obɛdɔw ama Agyimakofo adi, na wawu; na me de, mintumi nnɔw ketewa na mmoa mmedi.
The elder Kwakye, who weeded for people of Agyimako to eat, has died, as for me, I am not able to weed a little for the animals to eat.

2606. Opanyin kyɛ a, edwo.
(Tie poanyin de; op. kyɛ a, edwo.)
If a grown-up divides things, there is peace.

2607. Opanyin me nsono.
An elder satisfies his hunger with his intestines.

2608. Opanyin ne mmofra hu nantew a, wosoa ne botɔ.
When an elder and his children know how to walk together, the children carry his (money) bag.

2609. Opanyin anim asɛm yɛ ɔka-na.
It is not an easy to tell one's case before an elder.

2610. Opanyin ano sen suman.
The words from the mouth of a grown-up are more powerful than an amulet.

2611. Opanyin nyin (wɔ) ne batwɛw. Cf. 2599.
The elder becomes rich. (grows at the elbow).

2612. Opanyin pere gye agua, na ɛnye bamma.
The elder struggles to get a chair, but not to get a swish seat.

2613. Opanyin se na wanyɛ a, mmofra nsuro no.
When a grown-up says something but doesn't do it, the children no longer fear him.

2614. Opanyin nsoma abofra afirifwɛ na anoma nkasa no. Cf. 340.
The elder doesn't send a child to check the trap without the bird giving him away by his shouting.

2615. Opanyin ntie abansosɛm. 2598. Z. 187.
A grown-up doesn't listen to gossip.

2616. Opanyin tirim na wohon akuma.
It is on a grown-up's head that the axe head is pulled from the handle.

2617. Ɔpanyin to asa a, na ɛwɔ mmofra de mu.

When an elder becomes thin, his fatness has gone into his children.

2618. Ɔpanyin nto bo-hyew nto abofra nsam'.

A grown-up does not roast a hot stone and put it in the hand of a child.

2619. Ɔpanyin ntra ofie na asadua (:asebia) mfɔw.

A grown-up does not sit in the house when it rains and let his loom get wet.

2620. Ɔpanyin wɔ nkwa a, enni mfensa (mfe apem). =1878.

Even though an old man is strong and healthy, he won't live forever.

2621. Ɔpanyin wu yɛ mmusu.

An adult's death is a misfortune.

2622. Mpanyimfo na ebu bɛ se: Gya me nan, na wonse sɛ: Gya me ti.

Experienced elders have a saying, "Leave my legs alone" but they don't say, "Leave my head alone."

2623. Mpanyimfo se: mayɛ sɛ wo pɛn.

The elders say; "once upon a time I was like you."

2624. Sɛ mpanyimfe pɛ wo atoto awe a, wunhuru ntra ogya.

If the grown ups want to roast and eat you, you don't jump over a fire.

2625. Mpanyimfo yɛ wo guannuan, na sɛ woguan a, akyiri no wɔserew wo. Cf. 1850.

If old people frighten you to make you run off, and you do so, afterwards they laugh at you.

2626. Papa asusuw de rekɔ no, na kontonkyɛ kura di n'akyi de rebɛbɔ mu.

When goodness is planning to do something, then crookedness follows him seeking to join.

2627. Apapafwekwa taforo befua ho a, na wame.

If an unmarried person licks a palm nut, he is satisfied.

2628. Ɛpare wo a, wusua.

If it passes you by, you are too small.

2629. Ampasakyi se: mewɔ oni a, anka mente-ase.

The "ampasakyi" animal says: "If I had a relative I would not understand."

2630. Wo mpasua si atɛkyɛ mu a, ɛhɔ ara na wofa.

If your part of the battlefield is stuck in the mud, then that is where you must also pass.

2631. Wo mpasua si wo nnuarem'a, wunnyaw nkodi nea eye.

If your part of the battlefield is in a difficult situation, you don't leave it and go to where it is easy.

2632. Pata ase wɔ hene.

Under every shed there is a chief.

2633. Wo pata bua a, aginamoa nnan wo.

If your shed falls down, the cat no longer comes to you for his living.

2634. Wopata adaban abien hyɛ gyam' a, biako hyew. R. 72.
Cf. 3348.

If you put two bars of iron together into the fire, one will get burnt.

2635. Yɛmpata kra mpata asibe na ɔkwaku nko nto gyam'. B.

We don't passify the monkey but the kwaku monkey also is not thrown into the fire.

2636. Mpata kɔ a, ansa na abodwo aba.

The means for pacification goes to the person before peace comes.

2637. Ɔpatafo di aba.

The peace-maker receives blows.

2638. Wo patafo sa wo anim a, wokyi (:na wo anim agu ase).

If your peace-makers pass away in front of you, you don't like it.

2639. Apatipere da nyɛ da-na.

If is not difficult to dig a grave for the "apatipere" bird.

2640. Apatipere gyansakyi, odi mako, ɛnyɛ no ya a, ɔde yɛ ne to aduru. (Brafo ap, di mako a myɛ no dɛ, na ɔde yɛ...)

The bird (apatipere gyansakyi) eats pepper, if it is not painful, it uses some as an enema.

-218-

2641. Apatiperɛ kosi mako so na ɔtetew bi di, na wobisa no sɛ
"ɛdɛn na wonyɛ soe soe?" na ose;efisɛ memene no amu-amu
ntia!

The "apatiperɛ" bird lands on the pepper plant and picks
at some and eats it and you ask him,"why do you shout
soe soe? and he says,"because I have swallowed them whole."

2642. Apatiperɛ se: obi nnim a, obi kyerɛ. Cf. 265. 1407

The "apatiperɛ" bird says: "If one doesn't know, someone
teaches him."

2643. Wopatuw bereku (anɔpa) a, ɔbɔ wa. Cf. 315.

If you come upon the "bereku" bird suddenly, it coughs.

2644. Wopatuw kɔ kwan a, wo anim gu ase.

If you go on a trip unexpectedly, you are embarrassed.

2645. Wopatuw (we dua) pɔw wo se (apo-mono) a, efi bogya (:etu).

If you clean your teeth with a chewing stick in a hurry,
they will bleed.

2646. Ɔpatuwu yaw nti na wokyere akokɔ a, osu.

Because of a sudden death, if you catch a chicken it
cries.

2647. Pɛ babi atra bɔ wo bra yiye.

If you want to stay in a place, watch your conduct.

2648. Wopɛ babi atra a, ɛhɔ na eye.

If you are looking for a good place to live, the place
where you already are is good.

2649. Mepɛ obi makra Saben (a), na biribi nte sɛ nankasa
(:Agyaben) nam.

If I like someone, I send for so-and-so, for nothing is like
his flesh.

2650. Mepɛ osu nti na medi funu akyi.

It is because I like crying that I follow the corpse.

2651. Mempɛ obi ti matwa na obi atwa me de.

I didn't like to cut off anyone's head, but someone
has cut my head off.

2652. Wopɛ obi ti atwa a, na wotwa wo de.

If you want to cut off someone's head, you lose your own.

2653. Wopɛ abɔfo adi a, na wokeka.

If you like to eat the carcass of a animal you put it up and boil it with salt, pepper, tomatoes, okro etc.

2654. Wopɛ abusua bi abɔ na woannya a, na woware mu yere.

If you want to be taken into the extended family, but aren't, you marry into your wife's family.

2655. Wopɛ habansɛm a, wutua ka-perennu.

If you like an agreement decided upon in the bush without a witness, you pay twice.

2656. Wopɛ aka asɛm aka kayerɛ Onyandopɔn a, ka kyerɛ mframa.
R. 79.

If you want to tell God anything, tell it to the wind.

2657. Wopɛ akasakasa a, na woware yerenom bebrebe.

It you want to have frequent quarrels, then you marry many wives.

2658. Wopɛ kasame (:kasamim) a, na wuse:minni yere, minni ba.
= 2466.

If you like to talk a lot, you say: "I have no wife, I have no child."

2659. Wopɛ kurow bi mu atra a, wututu mu nnunsin, na wonhyɛ mu mpam

If you want to live in a certain town, you dig up the tree stumps, but you don't put stakes next to the yams.

2660. Wopɛ pɛsewa atumpan a, wunya; na wɔde ma wɔ dammirifua a, (na) wonte.

If you want a penny's worth of drumming you get it, but when the drummers beat out condolences on their drums for you, you can't hear it.

2661. Wopɛ sɛ egu wo yɔnko so a, egu wo so.

If you want something bad to come to your neighbor, it rather comes to you.

2662. Wopɛ asɛm a, na wote asɛm.

If you want trouble, you listen to trouble.

2663. Wopɛ ɔsom bebrebe a, ɔsom ka wo kɔn mu.

If you like servitude too much, it (chains) stay on your neck.

2664. Wopɛ mtɛm kɔ wo agya amamfo so a, wɔtew so hama kyere wo.

If you are in a hurry to arrive at your father's deserted village, they stretch a rope to catch you.

2665. Wopɛ wo akyekyere mogya-dodow a, wunya.

If you like your tortoise with much blood, you get it.

2666. Wompɛ ɔbea bi a, na wubisa ne kunu.

If you don't want to have intercourse with a woman, you ask who her husband is.

2667. Wompɛ wo yere ako no a, na wuse: migye aduasa-abien. (Dwaben Boaten.)

If you don't like your wife's fighting you say: "I'll take thrity two."

2668. Wopɛ aketewa a ɔyɛ ade, na wompɛ okokuroko a odi amim.

People like a small person who is kind, they don't like a big man who bullies others.

2669. Wopɛ wo atoto awe a, wunkyini gya ho.
(Wopɛ wo akum wo a, nhuruw ntra ogya.)

If they are looking for you to roast and eat, you do not wander around the fire. (jump over the fire.)

2670. Yɛpɛ a yebuhu nti na yɛkyekyere boa. R. 222.
(Wopɛ a wob...woky. b.) Gr. p. 174.

In order to find what we need when we want it, we put it together in a bundle.

2671. Ɔpɛ fi dompem'.

Love comes from the core of one's heart.

2672. Ɔpɛ mmae no na yɛhata ade.

If the harmattan has not yet come, then we have to hang up things to dry them.

2673. Ɔpɛ kurom' yɛ bɛ na ɔkɔm na ɛwɔ hɔ.

Harmattan town is beautiful, but there is a famine there.

2674. Apeanimma burohono se: magye nim mama Kankuwa.

The husk of maize in the horn used for drawing blood from a swelling says: "I have won glory for the horn."

2675. Apeawa nim su a, yɛnhyɛ ammoro no.

If Apeawa knows how to cry, we don't beat him.

2676. Apem dada wo kyere a, wodada apem ɡuan.

If a thousand people are deceiving you to catch you, you also deceive a thousand in running away from them.

2677. Mpempɛnso yɛ wo dɛ a, wo asɛm ho nwini.

If you like hints, your trouble leaks out.

2678. Pen nyɛ ayan.
Pentemerefo ...s. 1172.

A single stroke on the drum is not drumming.

2679. Mepere abɔnten (a), nnyedua (na ɛ)sen me tenten.

If I walk along the street, the shade trees are taller than me.

2680. Ɔperɛfwɛ yɛ yaw sen nkam.

Being made fun of is more painful, than having one's body all cut up.

2681. Pereguan a ɛda hɔ na minni bi; na nea ɛnennam hɔ de, ebi wɔ hɔ.

An amount of gold dust equal to thirty six dollars is lying there and I have none, and that which is travelling there I have some of it.

2682. Pereguan da man mu, ɛwɔ amansan.

The amount of gold dust equal to thirty six dollars is in the country, it is for the whole country.

2683. Peredwane fwete abusua mu.

Gold dust equal to thirty six dollars is spread among the relatives.

2684. Peredwane nya ananne a, asuasa nna.

If gold dust equal to thirty six dollars suffers, the gold dust equal to twenty seven dollars does not sleep.

2685. Pɛsɛwa nti na Dankyira-man bɔe. Cf. 1068

It is because of a pesewa worth of gold dust that the Dankyira state was destroyed.

2686. Pɛsɛwa yi amanne a, pereguan ntumi ntua.

If a pesewa worth of gold dust gets itself into trouble, the gold dust equal to thirty six dollars can't pay it debt.

2687. Opete ho na ɛyɛ nkwasea, nanso okyi aguare-anni.

The vulture's body is a foolish looking thing, yet even he does not eat with someone who doesn't bathe.

2688. Opete kwakye kasa kyerɛ obonukyereɛo a, ɔte. =513.
If the vulture gives advice to the wolf, he takes it.

2689. Opete ne anene kara nsɛ.
The vulture and raven have different destinies.

2690. Opete, wudi bi bin, na obi nni wo de. =517. R. 39.
Vulture, you eat anybody's excreetment but nobody eats yours.

2691. Opete-takara twa owira nkontompo a, otu twene.
When a vulture's feathers tell its master a lie, he plucks
them out and throws them away.

2692. Apetebi kwakye-agyei: mete bin, mete ta.
Squirrel "kwakye agyei" says: "I smell excreetment, I smell
fart."

2693. Apeterebi-akura (Opeterebiekuru se): akɔnnɔ bekum ohiani.
The squirrel says: "Desire will kill the poor man."

2694. Opitri memene a, ɔmemɛne ma owura. R. 200.
If the "opitiri" fish swallows anything, he swallows it
for his master.

2695. Opititofo anyi brofere ayɛ.
A fainting person does not praise the paw-paw.

2696. Po-sorɔ-samini se: ɔfwɛ sakraka ne ne mma akewa a woregoru.
The large "po-soro-samini" sea fish is looking for a big
sea fish and its little children who are playing around.

2697. Mpoano kotɔ guan kɔ mpo mu, na onnuan nkɔ sareso.
The sea coast crabs run into the sea, they don't run into the
bush.

2698. Mpoatwa na ɛde ko ba.
Insulting brings about fighting.

2699. Mpoatwa nti na ɛma ohene tu sa.
It is because of being insulted that a chief goes to war.

2700. Mpoatwa nti na ɛma asafohen ko tɔ.
It is because of insult that the head of the army fights and
dies in battle.

2701. Mpobi di tɔ ne mene mu regono (=regow).
Mpobi eats mashed yams and his voice becomes deep.

2702. Ɔpɔdɔ kakraka si hɔ a, obi nkɔ asu mfa nnu toa mu.
If there is a very large water pot sitting there, no one goes
to the river for water to put in his gourd.

2703. Ɔpofoni se 'ɔbɛkɔ po' a, wunnye no kyim.
If a fisherman says he is going to sea, we don't doubt him.

2704. Opoku Frɛdefrɛde na ose: biribi reba, biribi reba; ɛnyɛ
ɔko a, na ɛyɛ ade.
Opoku Frɛdeprɛde says: "Something is coming, something
is coming, if it is not war, it is riches."

2705. Opoku anim ne dɔm anim.-na ɛfanim dɔm anim (Kwaku Saforotwie.
Coming before Opoku and coming before an army, I prefer to
be before an army.

2706. "Pon tra kwan mu!" Wokyi.
If you have finished your work, you shouldn't sit on the
road.

2707. Ɔpɔnkɔ mman kwa (:teta, hunu).
A horse does not turn to the right or left without a reason.

2708. Ɔpɔnkɔ agyimi a, nea ɔte no so nnyimɛ ɛ.   R. 143. Z. 12.
Although the horse is stupid, it does not follow that the
rider is stupid.

2709. Ɔpɔnkɔ ankɔ ɔsa a, ne dua kɔ.
If the horse does not go to war, its tail does.

2710. Ɔpɔnkɔ wɔ dua, ɛsono wɔ dua, na ɔpɔnkɔ de kyɛn sono de kakra.
The horse and elephant have tails, but that of the horse is
a little larger than that of the elephant.

2711. Aponnwa sunti dea ɔwɔ no, na ensunti amane nhina.
The door step causes the one who is on it to stumble, it
doesn't cause everyone to stumble,

2712. Aponkyerɛn se ne na sɛ: manyi(n) kakraka! na ne na se: na
me ɛ! B.
The frog tells his mother: "I've grown very big! but his
mother says: "what about me!"

2713. Aponkyersn wɔ abafan-nuru a, anka ne ba mmutuw fam'.

If the frog had medicine to cure rachitis, then his children wouldn't be crouching on the ground.

2714. Wopopa wo ani a, wode kyerɛ wo ani.

If you clean your eye, you show it to your eye.

2715. Mpopa-dodow na abɛ de yɛ kɛse. Cf. 67.

Many palm branches make the palm tree great.

2716. Apopokyikyi fi nsu ase bɛka sɛ ɔdɛnkyem yare a, wonnye no akyinnye.

If the "apopokyikyi" fish comes from the bottom of the river and the alligator is ill, nobody doubts him.

2717. Potɔ-gum' ne fwie-gum' nhina hyia kwansɛn koro mu.

"Grind it and put it in, and pour it in," they both meet in the same pot.

2718. Wɔpra pata so ansa-na wɔapra fam'.

The ceiling is swept before the floor.

2719. Wo mpra serɛ bɔ ne nsam' a, na wawie wo asɛnka.

If your girl friend hits her thighs with her hand, it means she has stopped your speaking.

2720. Ɔprada nyɛ biribi (nhye afuo) a, (nanso) esi mpono nkɔnom' S.

If lightning has no value, at least it strikes the crotch of a tree.

2721. Prammafo yɛɛ ɔnokoro no, wotumi dii mmɔre-kutu. Cf. 1146.

If people living in a large compound are in unanimous agreement, they can eat a pot full of dough.

2722. Ɔprammiri fi amoa mu fi a, na aboa bi nni mu bio.

If a cobra comes out of a hole, it means there is no other animal in it.

2723. Ɔprɛm nfwere nnam.

A cannon never loses its power.

2724. Mprɛmpren nni aduru.

Medicine that is prepared quickly is not good medicine.

2725. Prokuo wo nta.
He who has had teeth gives birth to twins.

2726. Pumpunu (se e)mpunu a (ɛn)na epunu.
If the store room allows itself to be blackened, then it
is black.

2727. Apupu a ɔkɔbɔɔ ne nsu, ɔda nsu nkakye.   B.
The fish which created the water is lying on the bank.

2728. Opuro di bi a, ɔnwam di bi. = 2566. Z. 14.
If the squirrel eats some, the toucan also eats some.

2729. Sa tow, sa tow! (:Merekɔ, merekɔ!) ama Akodwa at'n n'akoa.
I'm going, I'm going, did not allow the lazy man to sell
his slave.

2730. Ɔsa, wɔkɔ nɔ nkatae dodo.
A war is fought with many gun-lock covers.

2731. Ɔsa, wɔkɔ no wɔn agya mma.
When one goes to war, it is with one's brothers.

2732. Ɔsa, wɔtwe no berɛberɛ.
You go to war slowly.

2733. Nsa berɛ kwa, ano na ebedi.
The hands are tired for nothing, the mouth is doing
the eating.

2734. Wo nsa da ɔbɔn mu a, ɛmmra wo.
If your hand is already in the hold, you can't be forbidden
to put it in.

2735. Wo nsa da mu a, wonni nnyaw wo. R.30. Gr. # 202, 2.
If your hands are in the dish, people do not eat everything
and leave nothing for you.

2736. Wo nsa yɛ den a, na wobu mu.
If your hand is strong, it can still get broken.

2737. Nsa yɛ ɔdɔkye. B. Nsa-nsa...s. 2778.
The hand is the lover who gives gifts.

2738. Wo nsam' nni biribi a, mmua, na mma mmofra nntiti akyiri.=468.
If there is nothing in your hand, don't close it let the
children scratch the back of your hand.

2739. Wo nsam' nni biribi a, wofrɛ wo eyinom ne ade.
If you are not rich, people don't value what you say.

2740. Wo nsam' yɛ den na woko a, wunyi dom.
If you are unkind and get involved in a fight, you won't
get many supporters.

2741. Nsam' ayɛ fi a, ɛnte sɛ ɔnammɔnmu.
If your hands are dirty, they are not as dirty as the
soles of your feet.

2742. Nsa kon, asɛm kon.
Where there are people drinking, there is much chatter.

2743. Nsa mu nni dompe na wɔawosaw.
In palm wine there are no bones to be chewed.

2744. Nsa mu wɔ biribi a, anka asamanadwo nhome mfa n'ankyi.Cf. 2271.
If there was any value in drinking, the bettle would not
breathe through his back.

2745. Nsa nnim ayemfo.
When a person drinks palm wine he doesn't remain quiet.

2746. Nsa neo ba-pa.
Alcohol does not bring forth good children.

2747. Sabarima (:Ɔsabofo) tow twerɛ a, ɔhwe ase.
If a drunkard throws a punch, he falls down.

2748. Sadweam ne Tadweam kɔ Aburokyiri, obi amma. Cf. 3157.
The drunkard and the smoker went to Europe, but neither of
them returned home.

2749. Ɔsafo nsa neho.
The doctor cannot heal himself.

2750. Ɔsafo (a ofi) Adanse nim sɛ ɔbɛware Gyamawa a, anka wanton
n'aberewa.
If Ɔsafo Adanse knew he would marry Gyamawa, he would not
have sold her mother.

2751. Ɔsafo Adanse se okiri suonwini; manso 'yɛde ba a, ɔnoara na ɔnom kane.

Ɔsafo Adanse says he doesn't like cold water, but if some comes, he is the first one to drink it.

2752. Ɔsafo Adanse se: 'yɛwoo no ne asɛm, na mammesua.

Ɔsafo Adanse says he was born with elequence, he didn't learn it by study.

2753. Ɔsafo te hɔ yi, na wɔka akyene na ogyina hɔ a, na ne nan mu keka no.

A dancer is always stimulated to dance when the drums are beaten.

2754. Asafo ani sa akura. R. 102.

The army always directs its efforts toward the smallest village (to obtain food from it).

2755. Asafo so nyankopɔn a, ɔbake nnuru mu afu. = 2434.

If the whole of mankind holds up the sky, one person does not become humpbacked by bearing the weight alone.

2756. Ɔsafohene nsua na wakɔ.

The warrier does not swear oaths before going to war.

2757. Asahina ntu neho ase nkyɛ.

If the palm wine pot is knocked over, it is quickly set upright.

2758. Nsa-ka-ano nsa nsa.

The tasting of palm wine does not finish the palm wine.

2759. Ɔsaman-pa hyira ne ba.

A good ghost blesses her child.

27C0. Nsamampɔw mu soduro: wo ni wu a, wo abusua asa. Cf. 2068.

When your mother is dead, that is the end of the family.

2761. Ɔsaman mfa nsa ho fwe. Cf. 2278.

The ghost doesn't care for palm wine.

2762. Ɔsamane ahoofwam ne nunum.

The smell of a ghost is like the smell of the "Nunum" shrub.

2763. Ɔsaman teɛ ne nsa kyia wo a, wopono wo de mu.

When a ghost puts out its hand to greet you, you draw yours back.

2764.   Osaman ntwɛn teasefo ansa-na wadidi.

A ghost does not wait for the living to begin to eat before it partakes.

2765.   Asaman nni biribi a, ɛwɔ nhyehye-wo-akyi.

If the spirit world posesses nothing else, at least it has boasting.

2766.   Asaman nni man (:kurow bi), yɛde hyehye yɛn akyi.)

The ghosts have no town to boast about.

2767.   Asaman, wɔnkɔ nsan mma.

No one goes to the land of the dead and returns.

2768.   Asaman, wɔmmana.

Things cannot be sent to the spirit world.

2769.   Asamantawa se: enim pae a, ɛte sɛ atawa pa.

When the "asamantawa" tree declares it knows how to burst, at best it can hope to do so (only) like the real "tawa" tree.

2770.   Asamanadwo a ɔda nsa mu na ammow, na wo a wokɔ ho no na wobow?

Even the bettle that lies in palm wine is not drunk, what about you who merely go near it and get drunk?

2771.   Asamanadwo home n'akyi.   Cf. 2744.

The bettle breathes through its back.

2772.   Sanna fi a, efi ma odwumayɛfo.

If August comes, it comes for the farm workers.

2773.   Nsanehɔ na asu nam.

The water travels in a track.

2774.   Osani biara nnya anuonyam da.

A habitial drunkard is never respected.

2775.   Osansa firi ahunum' reba se: mekɔkyere nipa ma di, na afei okowia akokɔ.

The hawk comes from the sky and says: "I am going to catch a human being to eat and then goes and steals a chicken."

2776.   Osansa kɔ abuw a, ɔde n'akyi gyaw akroma.

When the hen-harrier goes to hatch her eggs, the hawk keeps watch.

2777. Ɔsansa se: ade a Onyame ayɛ nhina ye (:na ɛyɛ).
The hawk says: "everything that God made is good."

2778. Nsa-nsa-dodow kyere banin-koro.
Many hands catch even a strong person.

2779. Asautefo te sɛ osebɔkora: wɔnkyere aboa, nso aboa biara ntwam' wɔ wɔn anim.
The Ashantis are like an old leopard, they don't catch animals, but no animal passes in front of them.

2780. Wo santen mu yɛ tia a, wunnyae nkɔdi tenten mu.
If you are in a short line, you don't stop and go in a long one.

2781. Asantrofi din de takyiampoben, na asɛm tɔɔ ne fi na wanhu di nti na wɔde no tɔɔ asantrofi.
The "asantrofi" bird is really called "takyiampoben," but he had trouble at home and because he couldn't settle it, we call him "asantrofi."

2782. Sasabonsam kɔ ayi a, ɔsɔɛ obayifo fi. R.45. Z.46.
When the monstrous "sasabonsam" goes to attend a funeral; he lodges at a witch's house.

2783. Sasabonsam te-ase, wose ɔyɛ ɔbayifo, na menne sɛ osi odum atifi na odum nso sow mmoatia!
If the monstrous "sasabonsam" is down on the ground he is called a wizard, how much more when he is perched on top of an odum tree and the odum tree is also bearing a crop of dwarfs as its fruits!

2784. Asase biara nkyi funu. Z.8.
No land refuses a corpse.

2785. Asase duru efu a, na wɔfrɛ no siw.
If the earth has a hunchback, it is called an ant hill.

2786. Asase ano ara ne babi a amoa da.
The entrance into the earth is where there is a hole.

2787. Asase terɛw, na Onyame ne panyin. Cf. 2542.
The world is a big place but God is the Creator.

2788. Asaseboa, 'yɛde wanterema na eyi no.
The sand-worm is taken off with "wanterema" grass.

2789. Nsaseboa ka wo na woantu no anto gyau' a, woda a, wo ani nkum.

If the sand-worm bites you and you don't throw it off into the fire, when you go to bed, you won't sleep.

2790. Sasonnoto (kusu, Sasono-doto busufo) bɛka(ɛbɛhye) yɛn nhina na yɛahu.

A thicket of nettles will burn us all and we will feel it.

2791. Sasonnoto, wonto no abamma.

A thicket of nettles is not put on a swish seat.

2792. Nsatea biako nkuru ade (nkyere dwiw).

One finger can not lift a heavy load. (catch lice).

2793. Nsatea biako butuw fa ade wo fam' a, entumi.

If one finger tries to pick up something from the ground, it cannot.

2794. Nsatea biako na aka srade ode asra honam nhina.

One finger touches the pomade but it is rubbed on the whole body.

2795. Nsatea koro sa agohina.

The oil in the pot is cleaned out with only one finger.

2796. Nsatea yɛ kuru a, wontwa nkyene.

If there is a sore on your finger, you don't cut if off and throw it away.

2797. Nsateawa nyɛ pono-na nyɛ tene-na (:nso ɛnyɛ teɛna). Gr.p. 184.

The small finger is not difficult to bend, nor difficult to straighten.

2798. Ɔsatofo nnim animka.

The swindler does not understand reproof.

2799. Wonsaw nsu a, wonsaw adwene.
*Sɛ occurs, but may be omitted, at the head of the following proverbs: 487. 1861. 2055. 2603. 2624. 3582.

If you don't gather up and throw out water, you don't gather up fish.

2800. Sɛ agyenkuku bɛbɔ abusua ara ni.

The "agyenkuku" dove really belongs to a family (clan).

2801. Sɛ oketew nsa te ara nen na ode saw (nkyene ma ne yere ne ne mma).

No matter what the size of the hand of the lizard is, he uses it to give out salt to his wife and children.

-231-

2802. Ose ne ne bua.
Every saying or question has its appropriate answer.

2803. "Mase, mase" a, na ɛyɛ ahi.
"I said that, I said that," is annoying.

2804. Woase a mate nti na me tiri dwen (:gwen) fita.
It is because of "I have heard what you say" that I have grey hair.

2805. Wose "biribi reba" a, na wode nea aba pɛn. Cf. 2115.
If they say something is coming, they mean what has come before.

2806. Wose "ade bɛkye" a, wonne kyena.
If they say the morning will come, they mean tommorrow.

2807. Wose "gye boa di na boa me." (Twifo.)
They say take this bundle and eat what is inside it, and then help me.

2808. Wose "gye na soa me" (:soɛ me na gye), na wonse sɛ: soa me na gye.
They say, take and load me, you don't say, load and take.

2809. Wose: ohun-kyɛree, na wonse sɛ: nnam-kyɛree.
The saying is: "Fear has long life," and not, "Courage has long life."

2810. Wose: mahyɛ wo sram, na wonse no sɛ: mahyɛ wo nsoroma.
They say,"I made an appointment by the moon,"you don't say,"I made an appointment by the stars."

2811. Wose: kɔ man koto, na wonse sɛ: kɔ man kɔsen. R.153.
They say: "Go to a town and settle there," they don't say: "Go to a town to boast that you are better than its citizens."

2812. Wose ko ansa-na woase 'nu. Z.219.
We say one before saying two.

2813. Wose okokuroko a ɔda akoe mu, na wonse sɛ: ɔkankrantan a ɔda akoe mu. Cf.1683.
We talk about the strong man who is lying in the field of battle, and not a tall man who is lying in the field of battle.

2814. Wose: akonta-gye, na wonse sɛ: akonta tane me. (As.)

The saying is: "Brother-in-law who saves me," not, "Brother-in-law who hates me."

2815. Wose: ɔkwantenten akwaba, na wonse: ɔkwantia akwaba.

We welcome someone returning from a long journey, and not from a short journey.

2816. Wose: manya, na wonse no sɛ: yɛanya. R.67.

The saying is, "I got some," and not, "We've got some."

2817. Wose (:Wɔrese) sɛ wɔnne wo na wubua a, woadi fɔ.=2076. 2914. (As.)

If they are uttering insults and don't mean you, and yet you reply, you have condemned yourself.

2818. Wose wo bi a, tie, na kyenkyentakyi-kurow wotu so pɛ a, wonwie da.

They tell you something, listen, for as soon as the town of obstinate people throw you out, your troubles never end.

2819. Wuse wo ba (:abofra) sɛ ɔnkɔ sumana so, na (sɛ) ɔkɔ na ɔwɔ ka no a, wonyɛ no aduru ana? (:woyɛ hɔ aduru na wuntwa hɔ nkyene.)

You tell your child he shouldn't go to the dump, but if he goes and a snake bites him, won't you give him medicine? (You will put medicine on it and not cut it off.)

2820. Wuse: wode wo nsa bɛtew...s. 778.

2821. Wuse: wobedi ampesi, na anka fufu!

You say you will eat boiled yam, how much more so fufu!

2822. Wuse 'wopɛ ɔkyensoafo' a, ɔkyekye nse sɛ: me na me tiri ho wɔ apɔw nti me na mɛsoa.

If you say you want a drum carrier, the iguana does not say: "I have a bump on my head so I will do it."

2823. Wuse: wopɛ amirika atu; na wo ase nantwi atew. Cf. 1771.

You say you like to run, and your mother-in-law's cow has broken loose.

2824. (Wo na) wuse: Apenten atuo apem; afei wuse: emu ahannum de, atwɛrebo nni ano!

You say: "Apenten shot one thousand times," now you say, "Of all those the flint only struck 500 times."

2825. Wuse wobɛsom Nyankopɔn a, som no prɛko, na mfa biribi
mmata ho.

If you say you will serve God, serve him alone, and don't
add anything else.

2826. Wuse wonyɛ (bone) a, wopɛ pa bi yɛ.

If you say you will not do anything bad, you must then
try to do something good.

2827. Mese donno a, (:na) memmɔ.

Should I not beat the donno drum if it is hung on my shoulder

2828. Wose fruntum se matatwene a, wuse: wugye kwabɛten akyekyere wo akyi?

If you say the rubber tree is hanging on the creeper do
you say you will get a tall palm tree to tie up your back?

2829. Ɛse anna a, ɛyare kekaw.

If the teeth do not sleep, they will get toothache.

2830. Ɛse hu ne serefo a, ɛsere.

If the teeth sees who is smiling at it, it also smiles.

2831. Ɛse nhyia a, na wofrɛ no gyaw. R.163.

If the teeth do not meet, it is called a gap.

2832. Ɛse tenten ne se kwatia didi biako (:pɛ). R.235.

Tall and short teeth all eat the same way.

2833. Wo se nye a, nea wotaforo akyiri ara nen. R.44.

Though your teeth are bad, they are what you lick.

2834. Wo asɛ ansow yiye a, na wontew no yiye.

If your beans don't produce well, you can't pick many.

2835. Wo ase di wo atɛm a, di no bi; na ogye ne ba a, wobegye
wo sika.

If your mother-in-law insults you, insult her, for if she
takes her daughter back, she will charge you.

2836. Seante guare Nkran. = 2906.

The stubborn person bathes in Accra.

2837. Osebere-bo-ntu se: owo ne mma na ɔde ayɛ n'afɛ.

The goat says he has his children and he makes them
his playmates.

2838. Osebere-bo-ntu, ɔte Amporemfie anom' asɛm a, na odi
ahurusie.

The goat says that if he hears what Amporemfie is saying, he
rejoices.

2839. Aseberekyi fra nnuanten (mu) a, woyi no (mu).

If goats are mixed in with sheep, you take them out.

2840. Aseberekyie na ɔde dwantene kodidie. Aky.

It is the goat that lead the sheep to go and eat.

2841. Ɔsɛe bekum wo a, ennim akamatwe.

If the chief of Ashanti will kill you, there is no casting
lots.

2842. Ɔsɛe anku wo a, na woakɔ awuasisi. S.

If the chief of Ashanti hasn't killed you, you will die
a sudden death.

2843. Ɔsɛe ani ase nkama, onipa na ɔsae.

The cut under the eye of the chief of Ashanti, was made by
a man.

2844. Ɔsɛe asɛm te sɛ kontonkurowi: ɛda amansan nhina
kɔnmu. Cf.1712.

Problems with the chief of Ashanti are like the halo
around the moon, everyone in the nation are involved.

2845. Ɔsekan a ɛnyɛ nnam na ɛte sɛ mpopa. = 2848.2851.

A knife that is not sharp is like the long mid rib of the
palm leaf.

2846. Ɔsekan-fua na egye neho abofra nsam'. R.157.

The knife that doesn't have a handle frees itself from the
hand of a child.

2847. Ɔsekan hyɛ boham' a, na ɛho yɛ hu.

The knife is fearful when it is in the sheaf.

2848. Ɔsekan ano anyɛ nnam a, na ɛbɛyɛ sɛ akyiri. Cf.2845.

If the knife's edge is not sharp, it will become like its
back.

2849. Ɔsekan koro nnua wi nnua batafo na ɛnsan mmetwa ne wura
nsa bio.

One little knife which cannot skin an antelope or a wild
boar, can cut its master's hand.

2850. Ɔsekan-tia biakɔ nnua ɛsono nnua ko nnua ɔdenkyɛm-
mirɛmpɔn (:asuboa), na wasan agua ɔnanka (:bɔre) na wasann
atwa wo wura nsa na wɔnhɔn wo nto ade mu ana?

One little knife cannot skin an elephant, a buffalo, a
big-throated crocodile, and yet you have gone out of your
way to skin a python, and cut your master's hand, will
you not be taken from your handle and cast out of the way?

2851. Ɔsekan konaboagye, m'anim anyɛ nyam a, ɛte sɛ mpopa.
Cf. 2845.2848.

Knife without a handle says: "If my face is not shinny and
sharp, it is like a palm branch."

2852. Asɛm a ɔhene betie no, ɔkyeame te a, ɔserew.

The case which the chief hears, when the chief's spokesman
hears it, he laughs.

2853. Asɛm a meka mekyerɛ wo yi ntɔ nkyea, ɛte sɛ adwennimmɛn.

The matter which I am telling you is not crooked, it is
like ram horns.

2854. Asɛm a wɔka serew wɔ babi na wɔka su wɔ babi. Cf.32.2199.

A matter which is in one place causes laughter, at another
place causes tears.

2855. Asɛm a Onyame adi asie no, ɔteasefo nnan no. (As.)

What God has foreordained, no human being can change.

2856. Asɛm a wobese na wobɛsan no, fa sa ma ɛnka wo tirim.

A word that when spoken you would wish back, let it remain
unspoken in your head.

2857. Asɛm a ɛsen hene wɔ hɔ.

There are some problems even a chief can't solve.

2858. Asɛm a wontumi nka no abɔnten so no, wo-ne wo yere te
fie a, nka nkyerɛ no.

You should not tell your wife a story which you would not
like to be known to the general public.

2859. Asɛm ba a, na (n')abebu (a)ba. R.257.

When the occassion comes, the proverb comes.

2860. Asɛm mma a, abebu mma.

If the situation has not arisen, the proverb does not come.

2861. Asɛm amma a. anka nkeka amma.

If trouble does not come, then a stain would not come.

2862. "Asɛm mmera na wonni" wɔ hɔ yi, enye.
To invite a lawsuit is bad.

2863. Wo asɛm ba a, na wuhu wo dɔfo. (:wo tamfo.)
When you are in trouble, you see your true friend (enemy).

2864. Asɛm-mone fata ohiani. R.8.
Bad things are always attributed to the poor.

2865. Asɛm-mone na wɔde soma odi.
You use someone to send a bad message.

2866. Asɛm-mone nyɛ di-na.
Wrong-doing is not difficult.

2867. Asɛm nnyae ba a, wonnyae di.
If cases don't stop coming you don't stop sitting in
judgement.

2868. Ɔsɛm-hyeɛ (:Asɛm a ɛhye) yɛ obua-na. (Asirifi, Ky.)
A difficult case is difficult to answer.

2869. Asɛm nko, nyansa nko. Gr. 248,3b.
Words are not the same as wisdom.

2870. Asɛm kyɛ a, nyansa ba ho.
If the case takes a long time, wisdom comes to it.

2871. Asɛm nam ani so na ɛkɔ (:ansa-na akɔ) aso mu.
It is through your eyes that you hear what is being said.

2872. Asɛm nantsew sen (:kyɛne) anomba. Mf. Gr. p.165.
A case walks more than a bird.

2873. Asɛm-pa nyɛ ɔka-na.
A good case is not difficult to state.

2874. Asɛm nsa (da).
Troubles never end.

2875. Asɛm-sasono hye wo aso na woanka bi a, enye. (:ɛbo wo
yare.)
If you have **heard** something that irritates you and you
don't say it, it is not good.

2876. Asɛm sɛ afitiam' a, wɔmfa nkɔ ahemfi.

If the problem is purely private, it is not taken to the chief's palace.

2877. Asɛm nsɛ asɛm a, wɔmfa nto (asɛm) ho nka. (:mmu bɛ.)

If one case is not like the other, you don't compare them.

2878. Asɛm sen wo panyin na wubua ho bi a, wunhu ne ka-su (:ne kabea, =wunnya no aka-ye).

If a case is greater than your wisdom and you give an answer to it, you usually don't get the right solutions to it.

2879. Asɛm asoɛ asɛm fi. Cf.3542.

Trouble always lodges in the house of trouble.

2880. Asɛm suro bogyesɛ (=panyin).

Trouble is afraid of the beard (an adult).

2881. Asɛm te hɔ yi, wosina no sɛ ahene.

Stating a case is like stringing beads.

2882. Asɛm te sɛ afwefwɛ.

A case is like a mirror.

2883. Asɛm te sɛ anoma, ɛnkyɛ otu. Gr.p.150e.

News is like a bird, it flies quickly.

2884. Asɛm tɔ wo so a, wo nyansa yera.

When trouble comes upon you, you lose your wisdom.

2885. Asɛm antwa antwa a, etwa.

If the case is difficult to be solved, it will be solved.

2886. Asɛm nyɛ kesua na wɔatow amana.

Trouble is not an egg that you can throw in a hole.

2887. Ɔsɛmpɛfo na ɔnam na ɔbɔ ntwɔm.

When a quarrelsome person walks he clicks his tongue in annoyance.

2888. Sɛm-ansa afuw nyɛɛ kɛse da.

The farm of the endless talker never produces much.

2889. Ɛsɛn fwee ase ara pɛ na fokyɛw kaa fam'.

When the herald fell to the ground the hat made of monkey's skin stayed on the ground.

2890. Ɛsen: mete ɔhene akonnua ho kwa; ade na nkwamanfo awie
di.
The herald says, "I am sitting near the chief's stool for
nothing, for the common people have taken all his wealth."

2891. Ɔsen, wɔsen no fie ansa-na wɔde afi-adi (:afi guam').
The cooking pot is hung up at home before you go out.

2892. Wosen me adidi a, mesen wo nna. R.71. Gr.#235c.
You can eat more than me, but I can sleep more than you.

2893. Sɛnea afoa te na boha te. R.73.
The sheath is always like the sword.

2894. Sɛnea ɔtwekyɛw yeraa mpoano no, sa nso na borɔkyɛw yeraa
kwaem'. Gr. p.165.
Just as the antelope's hat got lost on the seashore,
so the European hat got lost in the forest.

2895. Sɛnea ɔwɔ nam no, sɛ ɔda ara nen. Gr. p.166.
As the snake walks, so also he sleeps.

2896. Ɔsɛnnahɔ wo mmofra.
Examples have children.

2897. Asɛn-nɛw nti na aberewa kotra dan-akyi.
Because of good news, the old lady goes and sits at
the back of the house.

2898. Ɔsɛn-nɛw nti na obiakofo kɔ ɔman kodi asɛm a, odi bem.
Because of pleasant words, if one person goes to the
state to settle a case, he is judged innocent.

2899. Asɛnka te sɛ ahene-sina.
A good talk is like beads that are beautifully strung.

2900. Ɔsɛn-kam yɛ yaw sen kam-pa.
An offensive word hurts more than a flesh wound.

2901. Asɛn-kɛse bɛba a, ɔfranka nsi so.
A really great event does not come with the waving of flags.

2902. Asɛn-kɛse da ho na asɛn-ketewa akonyan no.
When a big affair is asleep, a small affair goes to awake it.

2903. Asɛn-kɛse, wonni no nsɛmma-nsɛmma.

An important matter is not treated as a small thing.

2904. Ɔsen-kɛse nni wura ade bi.

A large cooking pot does not partake of the master's wealth.

2905. Sɛnkyerɛase bebrebe yɛ amammɔe.

Too much tale bearing destroys the state.

2906. Ɔserantefoɔ dware Nkran. = 2836.

The stubborn person bathes in Accra.

2907. Woserɛ na wobenya a, wontɔ.

If you beg and you get it, you don't have to buy it.

2908. Wokɔserɛ obi ntwoma a, fwɛ ne bamma ho!

If you go and beg for someone's red clay, look at his swish seat!

2909. Aseredowa atakru te ne berebuw ano, na ɛnyɛ ɔno na ɔyɛe a, na wɔyɛ gyaw no. Cf.1436.3308.

The "aseredowa atakru" bird sits at the opening of his nest but it is not he who made it, it was made and left behind for him.

2910. Aserɛnɛ: madi wo hukan.

The mat says: "I saw you first."

2911. Ɔsereserefo se wo ayi a, wunsu.

If a person who is fond of laughing informs you of a relative death, you do not weep.

2912. Aserewa su agyenkuku su a, ne menewam' pae.

If the "aserewa" bird tries to sing like the "agyenkuku" bird, its voice breaks.

2913. Wosesa woho nhina a, wofwere dabere.

If you change yourself completely, you lose your sleeping place.

2914. Wosese wɔnne wo na wubua a, wudi fɔ. = 2817.

If someone is uttering abuse and has not specially referred to you, and you reply, you have condemned yourself.

2915. Osese: me nnaase ne gya!
The hut says: "My thanks is to be made into firewood."

2916. Osese-bone a 'yɛbɔ adabane tweri mu de me?
Is a poorly built hut which we beat with an iron bar
placed to lean against me?

2917. Osesea akurampɔn, ɔno na odii afuw so kan, nso wannya
adukuro.
The "osesea" tree was the first one in the farm but it does
not have buttresses.

2918. "Esi babi a asi" yɛ amammɔe.
"Come what may" causes the destruction of a country.

2919. Wosi, wosi, wonsi akaperɛ.
You say you can stop, but you can't stop putting off the
payment of a debt.

2920. Woansi no (:wo dan) yiye a, na wusunsum ase.
If you don't build your house well, you have to support it.

2921. Woansi no yiye a, na wusuro mu nna.
If you don't build your house well, you are afraid to sleep
in it.

2922. Wusianka aberewa a, mpere nsa wɔ no ho.
If you hold back an old woman, don't fight for the palm
wine she has.

2923. Asiamoa gye adwogu a, yennunu no; efiri dea ɛka no.
If Asiamoa receives the fish trap, we do not blame him
because he did so for some purpose.

2924. Asiananta twene, wosa a, wo aberewa awu; nsoso woansa a,
wo yere aka babi.
The "asiananta" drum, if you dance to it your mother will die
and if you don't, your wife will die.

2925. Sibiri-denkye: ɔtan fi fie.
Sibiridenkye says: "Hatred comes from ones home."

2926. Sie ne kagya nni aseda. = 2971.
The ant hill and the "kagya" plant do not thank one other.

-241-

2927. Asie na ɔfa.
The one who keeps it (hidden), takes it.

2928. Woresie afu no, na afu te ho resu.
You bury a hump-backed person, another hump-backed person
is sitting there crying.

2929. Osigyafo didi aberaw-aberaw. Cf.1363.
The unmarried person eats scantily.

2930. Osigyafo sɛw ne kɛtɛ ansa-na wabow nsa.
The unmarried person prepares his bed before he gets drunk.

2931. Sika bɛn wo a, ɛhoa. R.9.
When gold comes near you, it becomes white.

2932. Sika dabere nyɛ ahe?
How many places are there where gold can be found?

2933. Sika wɔde tɔ dɔnkɔ na wɔde gye ɔdehye awowa.
It is the money which is used in buying a slave that is used
in keeping an heir to the throne as a hostage.

2934. Sika di ntomu, na enni ntewso.
Money requires addition not reduction.

2935. Sika nni adagyew a, wɔmfa mpɛ bosea.
When one has just sufficient money for ones own needs, one
does not let it out as a loan.

2936. Sika nni "ka wo nsa pɛ!"
With money it is not a case of, "I got it immediately."

2937. Sika hia me nti minni fwe, afei worepɛ me ho bosea ana?
Because I am in need of money I have nothing, and then do
you want me to give you a loan?

2938. Sika nkɔ adidi nsan mma kwa.
Money does not go out to earn it's livelihood and come back
empty-handed.

2939. Sika kyɛn (:Asikamono sen) nkrante nnam.
Ready cash is sharper than a sharp cutlass.

2940. Sika, wonya, na wɔmpɛ.
Money is always obtained, but we don't want to keep it.

2941. Sika nyin wura foto mu.
Money grows in the bank of its owner.

2942. Sika pereguan da kurom' a, ɛwɔ amansan.
If there is a pereguan worth of gold dust in a town, it is
for all the people.

2943. Sika pereguan mu wɔ domponini. (:nni domponin?)
In every pereguan worth of gold dust, there is sufficient
money to bring something to eat.

2944. Wo sika resa a, na wo ani tew.
You become wise when you begin to run out of money.

2945. Sika sene, biribi ansen bio. Cf.942.
Wealth is the most important thing.

2946. Sika te sɛ akoa: woanhu no so fwɛ a, oguan.
Money is like a slave, if you don't treat it well, it flees.

2947. Sika nti na ɔdehye dan akoa (:yɛ onya). Gr. p.80.
Because of (lack of) money a free person becomes a slave.

2948. Sika nti na ɔkɔmfo de ne ti pem dan.
It is because of money that the fetish priest knocks his
head against a building.

2949. Sika nti na akomfo di nkontoro (:mene agyan).
For the sake of money the fetish priest prophesises falsely
(swallows arrows).

2950. Sika yɛ fɛ na ɔpɛgyafo yɛ na. R.183.
Wealth is a fine thing, but to find an heir is not easy.

2951. Wo sika yɛ wo yaw a, ɔkɔm de wo.
If spending your money gives you pain, you will go hungry.

2952. Wo sika yɛ wo yaw na woko a, wunyi dɔm. R.227.
If spending your money gives you pain when you go to war,
you will not win.

2953. Sika-dwuma biara nyɛ aniwu. R.179.
It is no shame at all to work for money.

2954. Osikafo nom nsa bow a, wɔfrɛ no yare. Cf.834.
When a rich man is drunk, people say he is sick.

2955. Osikafo wɔ hɔ yi, ofura ntamagow.
When a man is wealthy, he may wear any old cloth he likes.

2956. Osikafo wɔ hɔ, onya neho a, ɔnnserew funo, na onhu nea
ɔfa.
If a wealthy person is present and he comes upon riches
he should not laugh at the corpse, for he doesn't know
where he is also going.

2957. Osikani de, wɔnnwansi no bone ara da.
As for a rich man, he is never sneezed at unluckily.

2958. Osikani (:-fo) na odi ade a ɛyɛ dɛ.
A rich man eats delicious foods.

2959. Osikani ne hiani goru a, ɛnsɔ.
If a wealthy man befriends a poor man, the friendship
does not last.

2960. Osikani (:-fo) ne panyin.
The rich man is the man of importance.

2961. Sikanibere na ɛde bone nhina ba.
Love of money is the root of all eveil.

2962. Sikanibere nti na akɔmfo de won ti pem nnua.
Because of the love of money the fetish priests knock their
heads against trees.

2963. Sikanibere nti na ɔkɔmfo mene agyan.
Because of love of money, the fetish priest swallows arrows.

2964. Sikasin n'yɛ atida.
Incomplete payment does not give satisfaction.

2965. Asi-pɛ-ntama: mafi mmerɛsono!
The small ant hill says it has grown enormous mushrooms.

2966. Wo sisi yɛ den a, na wudi abaguade.
If you have a strong waist, you earn money from settling
cases.

2967. Wo sisɪ yɛ den a, na wupirew hase.
If your waist is strong, you can roll a barrel.

2968. Woresisi atwe na woredi ara nen.
As you are in the act of shaving food you are in the act
of eating it.

2969. Sisiriku na obetumi Kwanoku? Cf.3278.
Can Sisiriku a strong person, be beaten by Kwanoku a weak
person?

2970. Siw ho ba ɔkwan (:S. mu ba tokuru) a, mmoadoma nhina
kɔda mu (:hyɛn mu).
If there is a hole in an ant hill, all animals go and
sleep in it.

2971. Esiw ne kagya nni aseda. = 2926.
The ant hill and kagya plant do not thank one another.

2972. "So me ba mu ma me" a, "meda aye-nnya?" B.
Do I say, "Hold my child for me, for I am sleeping?"

2973. Meso me de, mintumi, na wuse: gye me!
I am not able to carry my load, and yet you say, "help
me!"

2974. Woso dua na tɛtea fam ho a, pɔn no; na ɔwɔ mu na ɔma
ɛyɛ duru.
If you carry a log and ants are clinging to it, let it
fall down, for they are making it heavy.

2975. Woso pantene na wuntumi a, wonkɔfa ɔnanka mmɔ kahiri.
If you are not able to carry a python, you don't go and get
a gabon viper for a head pad.

2976. Wɔso adaka a, na wɔso ne mu (:emu) ade.
When a box is carried, what is inside the box is also
carried.

2977. Woso, wunhu mu; wobere no ase a, wunhu mu; na wufwie
gu ɛ? Z.85.
You are carrying something and you can't see what is in it,
and if it is set down you still can't see what is in it, then
what if you pour it out?

2978. Woansɔ ofuru ano na wutwa a, egugu. B.
If you don't seal the opening of an animals stomach and you
cut it, its insides fall out.

2979. Woso dam a, na wobɔ.
If you are the type of person to be crazy you become crazy.

2980. Aso da a, na afotosan reba.
If the ear is sleeping, the opening of the money bag is coming.

2981. Aso nhina mu wɔ kwan, na ɛnyɛ ne nhina na ɛte asɛm.
There is an opening in every ear, but some ears don't hear.

2982. Aso haw anɔ. Z.220.
The ear troubles the mouth.

2983. Aso mu nni nkwanta. R.189.
There are no cross-roads in the ear.

2984. Aso si abien, na ɛnte asɛm abien. Gr. # 251. d. Z. 10.
Man has two ears, but they don't hear the same thing in two different ways.

2985. Aso siw a, dua na wode yi mu, na ɛnyɛ fitii.
If your ear is stopped up, you clean it out with a stick, you don't pierce it.

2986. Aso te sɛ nsɛnea: woto mu to mu a, ɛda.
The ear is like a pair of scales, if you put too much weight into it, it goes down.

2987. Aso nte na abogye nyera.
If the ear listens the jaw gets lost.

2988. Wo aso ankɔ adidi a, wo ti yera.
If your ear didn't go to eat, your head is lost.

2989. Wo aso yɛ den a, yɛde afare begu mu na ayɛ 'merɛw.
If your ear is hard, (if you are disobedient) we put the "afare" herb in it and it becomes soft.

2990. "Soa kodi!" nyɛ akommu.
"Carry your load and go and eat," does not break one's neck.

2991. Wosoa onipa adesoa a, wosoa no nea obetumi.
If you carry someone's load, you carry it as far as he can.

2992. Woansoa no tuntum so a, wosoa no fufu (:dwen) so.

If you don't have to carry a load when your hair is black, you will have to carry one when your hair is gray.

2993. Wobɛsoa aboa no (:aberekyi) a, soa no ntɛm, na mma ɔmmfa neho nnyɛ fi (:dote) ansa.

If you are going to carry an animal, do it quickly don't let him make himself dirty before you carry him.

2994. Nsoaforo yɛ sika a, anka nnipa nhina anya bi pɛn.   Cf.28.

If youthful arrogance were wealth, every one of us would have been wealthy.

2995. Nsoko* nni abɛne bi nhyɛne. Aky. *Asante kuro bi.

The people of Nsoko have no horns to blow!

2996. "Som woho" nyɛ akoa (:anyadimo).   Gr. p.156.

"Serve yourself," doesn't make you a slave.

2997. Mesom ɔhene, minsuro bi; n'akoa ara ne me.

I serve the chief; I don't fear anyone for I am his slave.

2998. Wosom Akɛse a, wokyia Awa.

If you serve great people, you greet Awa.

2999. Wosom wo fukwan so a, obi nhu wo hia.

If someone serves you on the path to the farm, no one sees your poverty.

3000. Mesoma wo anoma-to, woannya ogya a, ne nan hyew?

I sent you to knock down a bird, and if you don't get a piece of wood, does the bird's foot become warm?

3001. Wosoma obi akoa a, wo atifi dwo wo, na wo yam' na ennwo wo.

If you send someone's slave on an errand, the top of your head is cool, but your stomach is not at peace (cool).

3002. Wosoma me soro huan m'ase antweri!

You send me to the top and then pull away my father's ladder.

3003. Wosoma ɔnammontenten a, wobɔ pa-perennu.

If you send a person who is good walker, you hire two times.

3004. Wosoma wo ba Nkran a, nhyε no da, na n'akwanhyεde sa a, ɔbεba.

If you send your child on an errand to Accra, don't give him time to return for when his money to buy food is finished he will come back.

3005. Wɔsoma ɔbanimdefo, na wɔnsoma nammɔntenten. R. 211.

One sends a wise person, not a long-legged person.

3006. Wosoma wo dupɔn-tow a, kɔtow, na tokuru da mu.

If you are sent to fell a tree, go and fell it, because it may be a hollow tree.

3007. Ɔsomankafo bin yε ketewa.

The excreement of one who doesn't go when he is sent is small.

3008. Asomma nsen ne na ta da.

The fart of a baby elephant is never louder than its mother's.

3009. Asommεn fi sono yam'.

An elephant's trunk comes from within the elephant.

3010. Asomdwee ne ɔman-nyina.

Peace makes for the stability of the state.

3011. Ɔsonkrobia se: ɔkɔsow bise; wannya ansow, wasow abemmen.

The "ɔsonkrobi" tree says he bears bettle nuts, and if he doesn't get any to bear he bears hot (red) fruits.

3012. Εsono binom adɔkonni nko.

Every state has its own way of eating kenkey.

3013. Εsono dawuro, εsono dawuro, na εsono Akonnɔ-kuma dawuro.

Every gong-gong is different from Akonnɔ-kuma gong-gong.

3014. Εsono afuo dotɔ, εsono kwae dotɔ.

The thicket in the farm and the one in the bush are not the same.

3015. Εsono akoa, na εsono akɔba.

The slave and his child are not the same.

3016. Ɛsono kɔsɛ-kam, na ɛsono kam-pa.

A wound by accident and a real wound are not the same.

3017. Ɛsono ɛpɔ (:apo) nko, ɛsono abete nko.

The "ɛpɔ" (food made of a herb) and the "abete" (roasted maize flour boiled) are different.

3018. Ɛsono sɛ aboa no rekɔtɔ nko, na ɛsono sɛ ɔrekɔnom nsu.

The animal that is falling asleep is different from the one drinking water.

3019. Ɛsono ntanto nko, na ɛsono agorufɛw nko. (Ɔheneba Bampo, †1868.)

The disregard of an oath, and beautiful drumming and dancing are not the same.

3020. Ɛsono "wo ho yɛ tan!" na ɛsono "wo ho yɛ tan papa!"

"You are ugly" is different from "you are very ugly."

3021. Ɛsono di ade, ogyaw go.

The elephant eats everything, but he leaves behind the reeds.

3022. Ɛsono di asawa. Z.80.

The elephant eats the little "asawa" berries.

3023. Ɛsono nni wuram' a, anka ɛko (nso) yɛ ɔbɔpɔn bi. Z.213.

If the elephant were not in the forest, then the buffalo would be one of the biggest animals.

3024. Ɛsono afɔn a, wɔnne mpakam-ma ɔha. Z.154.

Even if the elephant is thin, its meat will fill a hundred baskets.

3025. Ɛsono afɔn a, wonnua no berɛw (:apa) so. R.76.

Even if an elephant is thin, it is not skinned on a palm leaf.

3026. Ɛsono ho na wɔbɔ apuruwa (=nankum).

It is from the elephant that big hunks of meat are cut.

3027. Ɛsono kakra, (:kuntann, na) adowa na ɔde ne ha (:ad. di panyin).

The elephant is a huge animal, but it is the tiny antelope that is the chief of the forest.

3028. Ɛsono akyi aboa ne bɔmmɔfo.

After the elephant there is a still greater animal, the hunter!

3029. Ɛsono akyi nni (aboa).

There is no other animal as big or as strong as an elephant.

3030. Ɛsono nya wo a, adowa bɔ wo me.

When the elephant has caught you, the tiny antelope comes up and slaps you in the face.

3031. Ɛsono tia afiri so a, ɛnhuan. R.126.

If an elephant steps on a trap that is set, it doesn't spring back.

3032. Ɛsono woo no, ɔkotɔ kum no.

The elephant gave birth to an elephant, but the crab can kill it.

3033. Nsono mmoa ɔyafuno (aduan na ɛboa yafunu).

Intestines don't help the stomach (food helps the stomach).

3034. Asontakum nyɛ biribi a, ɔwo nsaseboa. Cf.3469.

If the "asontakum" (small sand worm in the ground sucking blood from man's feet) has no value, at least it gives birth to sand worms.

3035. Sɔprɔpo ne nyinya reperepere amamfo, na ɔpanyin ne hena?

The "sɔprɔpo" herb and the "nyinya" trailing plant (the sour leaves of which are used against fever), are fighting over the deserted town, who is more important?

3036. Ɔsoro ade yɛ duru a, ɛnyɛ wɔnne tentrehu.

If things from the sky are heavy, it is certainly not silk cotton.

3037. Ɔsoro gye tɛ a, na ɛfam' gye tum.
(Ɔsoro (a)gye tɛ ansa-na fam' agye tim.)

If the sky receives the sound of tearing the ground receives the sound of landing (tum)

3038. Wososo a, wode kɔma owura.

If you carry a lot, you carry to give it to the owner.

3039. Ɔsosow ammu, akuma ammu a, kwae si nea esi.

The long handled hoe did not break and the axe did not break, the forest is still lying there untouched.

3040. Ɔsosow ntow abɛ na (:mma) akuma mpene.

The long-handled digging-iron does not cut down the palm tree and then the axe groans.

3041. Asotɔre abien yɛ anikrakra.

Two slaps in the face cause bewilderment.

3042. Nsɔw abien gu adem' a, ɛbɔm'.

If two mattocks are sticking in something, they come together.

3043. Ɔsram de berɛbere na etwa ɔman mu.

The moon slowly passes over the town.

3044. Ɔsram mfi dakoro ntwa ɔman mu.   R.48 Z.197.

The new moon does not pass over the town in one day.

3045. Su nkwa, na nsu sika.

Cry for life, don't cry for money.

3046. Wusu woho a, nsu hia.

If you weep for yourself, don't cry because of poverty.

3047. Misu mefrɛ hena bio?

Whom can I implore again?

3048. Mesu wo berɛbere, na minse sɛ: wuwu a, fa me kɔ.

I am weeping for you because of your hardships; but I didn't say, "If you die, take me along."

3049. Osu yɛ mfono.

Too much crying is detestable.

3050. Osu ahu me, na Datɛ nhuu me ɛ.

Rain water has seen me, and Date has not seen me.

3051. Osu a ɛtɔ Krobow no, (na) ebi atɔ Siade.

Some of the rain which falls in the Krobo, also falls in the Shai hills.

3052. Osu a ɛbɛtɔ nnim abo-sɛn.

The heavy rain storm doesn't know that there are stones hanging up to ward it off.

3053. Osu borɔ bo a, etim nea etim.
(Osu aboro bo: esi nea esi.)

Though the rain beats on a stone, the stone remains where it is.

3054. Osu fwe sebɔ a, ne ho na ɛfɔw, na ne nwaran-nwaran de, ɛmpopa.

If rain beats a leopard he becomes wet, but the spots of his body are not washed off.

3055. Osu fwe wo a, wuse: wafwe me, na wunse sɛ: ɔpetee me so.

When the rain beats you, you say, "It has beaten me," you don't say, "It has drizzled on me."

3056. Osu tɔ a, wokum kɔmfo; osu antɔ a, wokum kɔmfo. Cf.1696. 3285.

If the rain comes, the fetish priest is killed, and if the rain does not come, the fetish is also killed.

3057. Osu bɛtɔ a, mframa na edi kan.

If it is going to rain, the wind comes first.

3058. Osu antɔ a, ade sa.

Even if it doesn't rain, night comes.

3059. Osu atɔ aboro asensɛ: monnserew me; me ho bɛwo.

The rain has fallen and beaten on the "asensɛ" fowl, and she says: "You don't have to laugh at me, I'll dry off."

3060. Osu tɔ fwe wo na owia fi hye wo a, na wuhu abrabɔ yaw.

When the rain falls and beats upon you and the sun comes forth and scorches you, then you experience the troubles of life.

3061. Osu tɔ gu po mu.
(Yenim sɛ ɛpo so, nanso nsu tɔ gum.)

The rain falls on the ocean. Even though there is plenty of water in the ocean, the rain still falls on the ocean.

3062. Osu tɔ na ɔbɔmmofo bekum aboa a, efi ne katae.

If the rain falls and the hunter kills an animal, that is
because of the cover of his (dry) gun lock.

3063. Osu tɔ na egu biribi so ansa-na ɛka wo a, ɛnyɛ yaw.

When the rain falls and drops on something else first
before touching you, it does not hurt.

3064. Osu tɔ na wonyiyi nneɛma (:ade wɔ sum') a, ɛnyɛ wɔnne bo.
R.49.

When it rains and things exposed to the rain must be removed,
you don't have to remove stones.

3065. Osu tɔ anadwo na woanhu a, adekyee, woanhu fam' ana? -
Osu tɔe anadwo, woante a, anɔpa adiwo fɔwe no, woanhu
(:adekyee nso, woanhu adiwo)?

When the rains fall at night and you do not hear it, don't
you see from the ground the next day?

3066. Asu a wonni mu adwene no, wɔmfa mu adwokufo (:nsɔwafo).

We do not trap fish in the river whose fish we don't eat.

3067. Asu a yenni mu adwene no, yɛmfa mu pow (sika-pow, pokoa).
= 3083.

We do not take gold nuggets from the river whose fish we
do not eat.

3068. Asu a wonnuare no, wɔnnom.

Water which you would not bathe in is not drunk.

3069. Asu a ɛta hɔ dinn na ɛfa onipa.

It is the still water that drowns a man.

3070. Asu(-kɛse) a ɛte sɛ bosoropo na nkyene atwam' yi, na
ɛwɔ ase.

If there is a body of water like the ocean without salt
there must be a reason for it.

3071. Asu biara bɔ po mu a, na ne din ayera.

Every river that runs into the sea loses its name.

3072. Asu (:Nsu) bɔ biribi din na ɛwow.

Water utters a spell and then dries up.

3073. Asu (:Nsu) fa wo a, (na) ɛho nhama (:nnerma) nhina tan wo.

If you are drowning, then all the creepers on the bank
of the river hate you.

-253-

3074. Asu fono ansa-na aɡyen.
The river gets muddy before it becomes clean.

3075. Asuo ho nni biribi a, ɛwɔ dware-hofiriɛ (:aguare-ahofi).
If water has no other value, at least it can wash the dirt from our bodies.

3075a. Asu-mu wɔ "soa me!" R. 32.
At the water-hole they say, "help me put it on my head."

3076. Asu annya ɔpatafo na etwaa ɔkwan mu.
If the stream is not checked it will cross the road.

3077. Asuo panyin ne kɔtɔ.
The chief of the river is the crab.

3078. Asu tware kwan, ɔkwan tware asu, na ɔpanyin ne hena? (Ɔkwan kɔtoo asu, asu fi tete, efi Ɔdomankama bɔɔ ade.)
The river crosses the road, the road crosses his river, which is older? (The road met the river, the river is very old, it is from the time God created the world.)

3079. Asu ɲyiri nwam.
The river does not flood out the toucans (which roost on the top of high trees).

3080. Nsu a wɔde redum gya (no), wɔmpɛ no kronkron. Z. 13.
Clean water is not needed to quench a fire.

3081. Nsu a ɛdɔ wo (:Nsu dɔ wo a,) na ɛkɔ wo ahina mu. Cf. 123.
The water which like you goes into your pot.

3082. Nsu ba ɔwɛn a, wɔwɛn.
If water calls for vigilance, we are alert.

3083. Nsu bi a wɔnni mu adwene no, wɔmfa mu pɔw. =3067.
We do not take gold nuggets from the river whose fish we don't eat.

3084. Nsu bɔ asu mu a, na adan abɔmma.
If one river runs into another, it changes into a tributary stream.

3085. Nsu fa Kramo a, wɔmmisa n'adurade. R. 96.
If a soothsayer is drowned, you don't ask for his clothes.

3086. Nsu fa wo a, wonom bi. Cf. 3073.
When water is drowning you, you drink some of it.

3087. Nsu-hunu yɛ ɔme a, anka aka mfa darewa (:wɔrenka d. da).
If plain water was satisfying enough, then the fish would
not take the hook.

3088. Nsu ketewa dɔ a, ɛso aguare.
If a small stream is deep, it is big enough to swim in.

3089. Nsu kyɛ toam' a, ɛbɔn.
When water remains too long in a bottle, it stinks.

3090. Nsu potopoto! tiatia mu na kɔsaw nsu-pa!
Muddy water! pass through it and go and fetch clean water.

3091. Nsu asa asum' nti na ɔsansa refa apata.
Because the water has dried up in the river, the eagle is
catching the fish.

3092. Nsu sen na egyina fako a, na wɔfrɛ no tare.
If the river flows and stands in one place, it is called
a pond.

3093. Nsu anso aguare a, ɛso nom.
Water which is not sufficient for bathing in, is sufficient
for drinking.

3094. Nsu-nsu nhina dɔso; na bosonopo ne panyin.
Of all the many rivers the sea is the biggest.

3095. Nsu ta dote so.
Water makes the ground level.

3096. Nsu ta aponkyerɛn a, ogye wo!
If the water runs after the frog, he welcomes it!

3097. Nsu yiri a, na apata ayɛ ahantan.
When the river floods over, the fish become daring.

3098. Nsua nyɛ ɔko.
Swearing a promise is not fighting.

3099. Wusua asɛmpa a, wunya anuonyam.
If you learn to behave properly you will be praised.

3100. Osua(biri ba) nwo foɔ. Cf.1740.
The "osua" monkey doesn't give birth to the "foɔ" (white-
tail) monkey.

3101. Osua nom nsu sie afedan.
The monkey drinks water for the new year.

3102. Osua tew anadwofa a, ɔntew nhyɛ ne ba ano.   811.
If the monkey picks fruit in the night, he doesn't give
them to his child.

3103. Osua turu ba a, oturu n'anim.
If the monkey carries its child, it carries it in the front.

3104. Osuboafo antɔn neho a, ɔtramatofo ntɔn neho da.
If the one who joins others in weeping doesn't sell himself,
then the player for cowries never sells himself.

3105. Osubodom nkowe akyɛ (:mmɔbo adwoku) na wontwitwa ɔbayifo
(:ɔkwarifua) aso (ntua ka).
The water dog chews on the fishing net, but he doesn't
tear up the ears of a witch (rat) to pay for it.

3106. Osufo nyɛ ɔna, na ɔkommuafo na ehia.
Mourners are not difficult to get but the provider against
hunger is scarce.

3107. Asuogya nko ne n'asase nko.
The other side of a river and its soil are not the same.

3108. Asuogya wɔ afa-nu.
The other side of a river pertains to both directions.

3109. Asuhina bɔ a, na kora atwe neho.
If the water pot breaks, the calabash pulls itself away.

3110. Osuhyɛfa, wommua.   R.167.
You don't put a half roof on a house.

3111. Osukwase anoma nkodi Krobɔ awi, na wɔnkyere Osanteni
ntua ka.   R.94.
If a bird from Sukwase eats the Krobo farmer's wheat, you
don't catch a man from Ashanti and make him pay by it.

3112. Wusum brɔde a, sum kwadu (bi), na obi nim nea obegu kɔm
(:wunnim nea obegye wo ɔkɔm mu).
If you plant plaintain, plant banana also, for you don't
know which of them will save you in famine.

3113. Wusum nkɔmpow afiri a, wuyi akasakasa.
If you set a trap and keep turning back to look at it,
you catch only the sound of animals.

-256-

3114. Suman kofirima nye biribi a, na eye amiade.

If the "kofirima" amulet is good for nothing else, it is at least a piece of armour.

3115. Sumana na skora adebone.

The garbage heap covers a bad thing.

3116. Sumana so koko se: osu to fwe no a, enye no yaw se mpetema.

The bird in the refuse heap says: "If it rains and beats him, it is not as painful as the spots on him from being splashed with water."

3117. Sumana so ntonko se: se onya agyinaye a, anka obssow nnenkyenema.

The large pepper plant on the refuse heap says: "If only I had a place to stand, I would produce enormous fruits."

3118. Sumana so nye a, na efi fie.

If what is in the dump is not good, it's source is from the house.

3119. Osunson se: obenyin ansa-na wafi ani; onyini, na ode ne ti pempem. R.112.

The worm said it would get eyes when it grew up, but when it grew up it just felt its way about by knocking its head against things.

3120. Sunsuan mfaa onipa nkoe da.

The water from a heavy rainfall flowing the over ground can not carry a person away.

3121. Sunsuan (biara) mforo bepow (da).

The water from a heavy rainfall can never climb a hill.

3122. Sunsuan mu denkyem ara ne apotoro.
(S. ne d. ne aponkyeren.)

The crocodile in a heavy down pour is the frog.

3123. Supurupu dom aberewa, na aberewa (nso) dom supurupu. Cf.101.

The "supurupu" turtle grants favours to the old woman, and the old woman grants favours to it.

3124. Suro nea oben wo.

Fear the person who is near to you.

3125. Suro nea ose: obegye, na nsuro nea ose: merema wo.

Fear him who says he will take from you, but do not fear
him who says I will give to you.

3126. Misuro kum nti na mayɛ me kɔn tia. (Kwasi Ta.) =610.

Because I am afraid of being killed, I have made my neck
short.

3127. Yensuro dɔm anim, na (menne) asɛm anim!

We do not fear the front line of battle, how much less the
court where only words are used!

3128. Wusuro nnimmo a, wɔde wo sekan gua ɔnanka.

If you are afraid of becoming unpopular, your knife is used
in skinning a rhinocerous viper.

3129. Wusuro adɔna a, wɔde wo sekan gua apetebi. Cf.3568.

If you are afraid of giving displeasure, your knife is
used in skinning a vulture.

3130. Wusuro ɔdonkɔ bin a, wofwɛ no mperɛnsa.

When you fear to remove a slave's excreetment you have look
at it many times.

3131. Wusuro guamsɛm a, wo abaguade yɛ ketewa.

If you fear to take part in court cases, your share of the
fees is small.

3132. Wusuro ahenware, a, wowo nnofowa ba.

If you are afraid to marry a chief, you will give birth to
a child who is not a member of the royal family.

3133. Wusuro wo ho asɛm na wunya amanne a, wunya no ketewa.

If you are afraid of your own problems and you get troubles,
you get a small trouble.

3134. Wusuro n'ani a, wunni ne nam.

If you fear the (eye) presence of the animal, you don't eat
his meat.

3135. Wusuro wo ase a, wo yere nware wo. Cf.1116.

If you fear your mother-in-law, your wife does not marry
you (treat you well).

3136. Nsusoa se: m'ani mmere atoropo.

The land by the side of a river says, "I am not covetous
of garden eggs."

-258-

3137. Asusow, wodi no tofɔe.
       The first great rainy season (April-July), is the time you
       get wet buttocks.

3138. Asusow tue a, wonkyi wansan.
       When the rainy season sets in, you can't avoid house flies.

3139. Wosusuw aboa no kɔn mu na ɛbɔ hama.
       You measure the animal's neck and then tie it up.

3140. Wosusuw aboa so na wɔbɔ no aba.
       You estimate the size of an animal before you hit it with
       a stick.

3141. Wonsusuw sono yam' na wobu ahaban.   Cf.346.
       You don't measure the elephant's belly before you gather
       leaves for it to eat.

3142. Nsuwa-nsuwa bom' a, na wofrɛ no asukɛse.
       If small streams come together it is called a river.

3143. Nsuwa-nsuwa na ɛma ɛpo yɛ kɛse.
       Many small rivers make the ocean big.

3144. Ata ne Ata a wɔnka no, ɛbɛyɛ sɛ Tawia.
       (A. ne A. nka a, na ɛnte sɛ T.)
       If twins don't go together, it is like Tawia.

3145. Ata (ne Ata) ntra ho na Tawia nni ade.
       If twins are alive, the one follows the twins does not
       inherit.

3146. Nta ne Nta nnim wɔnho a, ɛnte sɛ Tawia.
       If twins don't know one another, it is not like Tawia.

3147. Nta ne Nta se 'wonim wonho' a, ɛnte sɛ Ɔbempɔn ne Ntiamoa.
       If twins say they know one another, it is not like
       Ɔbempong and Ntiamoa.

3148. Ata-panyin nni nkyene mma ɛntere Ata-kuma anom'.
       The elder twin does not eat salt that it may trickle into
       the younger twin's mouth.

3149. Ta fata ofufu.
       Farting suits the white man.

3150. Wota aboa no na woamma no aguanbea a, oguan fa wo so.
Cf.2584. 2587.

If you chase an animal and don't give it room to flee, it
runs over you.

3151. Wota aboa no na woanto no a, na wuse: ne ho bɔn.

If you chase an animal and don't catch it, you say it
stinks.

3152. Wota abofra na oguan kɔ fasu ase a, na ɔkwan asiw no.

If you are chasing a child and he goes under the wall, his
way is blocked.

3153. Ɔtabira wɔ ne fafo.

Even the "ɔtabira" snails have someone who likes to eat
them.

3154. Ɔtabirifo (:ɔtobrafo, ɔkwatafo?) ne akyere nna.
Cf.636. (Ɔbrafo...)

A leper (executioner) and a person destined to be killed
do not sleep.

3155. Ɔtabon se bnim nsu ase' a, ɛnte sɛ darewa.

If the paddle says it knows the bottom of the river, it
doesn't know it as well as the fish hook.

3156. Tadua kyenkyen (:tenten) gya anoma.

A trap whose string is too stiff lets the bird escape.

3157. Tadweam kɔ Aburokyiri; wamfa fwe (:biribi) amma. Cf.2748.

If an excessive smoker goes to Europe, he doesn't bring
anything back.

3158. Ntafoɔ karakyerɛ ne seres.

The Northerners "soul-money" (gold and precious beads
fastened to the wrist of the right hand in thanks to the
soul for having enriched the person) is grass.

3159. Taforobɔtɔ se: fwɛ nea owu ayɛ me!

The plate says: "look at what death has done to me!"

3160. Ntakara-pa na ɛma anoma ho yɛ fɛ. Cf.1658.

Good feathers are what makes a bird beautiful.

3161. Ntam nti na aberewa di nya.

Because of an oath the old lady possesses a slave.

3162. Otam abiri a, ɛnhyewe. R.199.

Even though your cloth is dirty, it is not burned.

3163. Wo ntama biri a, wohoro, na wonhyew.

If your cloth is dirty, you wash it, you don't burn it.

3164. Otam ano pow (wɔ hɔ yi), wonsi no kwa.

The knot at the corner of a cloth is not made for nothing.

3165. Wo tam ano yɛ duru a, na woboa akobɔfo ano. (:wopon akobɔfo.)

If you have a big knot at the corner of your cloth (are rich), you collect runaway slaves.

3166. Otam-pa ne nwera.

A good cloth is white calico.

3167. Otamasifoɔ nni biribi a, ne bowerɛ mu yɛ fita.

If the washer man has nothing, at least his finger-nails are clean.

3168. Otamfoɔ kwane, yegya no dako.

We seldom see off enemies when they visit us.

3169. Wo atamfo abiɛsa kɔ agyina, na hena na abebu wo bem?

When three of your enemies go aside to deliberate on the verdict to be given you, who is going to find you innocent?

3170. Wo tamfo di wo asɛm ase kan a, woka nkyene a, ɛdan mako.

If your enemy gets the first chance to state a case he has with you, then if you say salt it is turned to pepper.

3171. Wo tamfo kɔ agyina mu.

The one who hates you goes to deliberate on the verdict to be given you.

3172. Wo tamfo nya amanne a, di ma no; na ɔda wo ase a, na nnye so.
Wo tamfo asɛm ba a, wudi ma no; na ɔda wo ase a, wunnye no so. R.268.

If your enemy is in trouble, help him, but if he thanks you, don't reply.

3173. Wo tamfo sua wo asaw a, ɔkyeakyea ne pa.

When your enemy imitates your dancing, he twists his hips in an awkward manner.

3174. Otan nni aduru. Z.111.
There is no medicine for hatred.

3175. Wotan bi a, na wofa ne yere.
When you hate someone, then you seduce his wife.

3176. Wotan wo ni a, womfa no mma dom. R.158.
Even if you hate your mother, you do not hand her over
to the enemy.

3177. Wotan wo sapow a, wo anom' bon. R.265.
If you hate your sponge, your mouth stinks.

3178. Wotan wo yonko a, wunnya wo ho anuonyam (ara) da. (Kofi
Akwatia.)
If you hate your neighbor you will never be a respected
by others.

3179. Wotan wo yonko ba a, wo ba wu awusin.
If you hate your neighbor's child, your own child dies a
sudden death.

3180. Wotan nipa a, woma oyɛ nneɛma nhina.
If a person is disliked, he is made to do everything.

3181. Otan ne ne ba mpae.
Hatred and its child never separate.

3182. Otan a owoo ba na onim abadae.
The mother who bore her child knows what it is to yearn
for him.

3183. Otan woo ne ba na onim sɛ ɔkɔm de no.
It is the mother who bore the child who knows when the
child is hungry.

3184. Ntanhare yɛ mfaso.
Quick breeding is profitable.

3185. Ntan-kyinnye nti na ohene kum nipa.
If someone does not keep his oath, the chief kills him.

3186. Atannuru Abena: m'afɛ kyiri me.
Medicine tree Abena says: "My mates hate me."

3187. Ntansa annya din, na asuasa na ɛbɛyɛ dɛn?

If a gold weight of one hundred and eight dollars doesn't have a name, then what will the gold weight of twenty seven dollars do?

3188. Tanseserewa nkyiri biribi a, ɛnyɛ 'yɛnne tasɛnfi.

If dirty cowries do not shun anything, how much more so a dirty pipe.

3189. Ntantia dodow kum dom.

It is the many caps of the flint-lock gun that kill the enemy.

3190. Tapo nni aban mu. R.40.

There is not even a halfpenny in the palace.

3191. Tapori, wo anɔ (:woho) yɛ dɛn a, potɔw nnwea!

If the grinding stick says it is strong, it should grind palm kernels.

3192. Wotase pi a, ɛtotɔ.

If you pick up too much, some falls down.

3193. Ntasu nko nnantew.

Spit doesn't go anywhere on its own.

3194. Ntasuo mpa (:nsa) onipa anom'.

Spittle is never absent from the mouth of a person.

3195. Mete Dankyira, minni amiade.

I live in Dankyira, I have no war dress.

3196. Mete akura mifura ntama-gow, na afei meda kɛtɛgow so ana? (Yaw Purow se...)

I live in a village and I wear a tattered cloth, and now do I also sleep on a tattered mat?

3197. Wote bi korow mu na enwini a, wonsesaw mu nsu?

When you are staying in someone's town and his roof is leaking, don't you keep drawing up water?

3198. Wote fako a, wote wo ade so; nso wonam nam a, wuhyia.

If you stay in one place you sit on your wealth, but if you travel you meet something.

3199. Wote Kumase na wɔbekum wo a, woara na wunim.

If you live in Kumasi and they are going to kill you, you yourself know it.

3200. Wote kuro-bone mu a, wo ani na ewu.

If you live in a bad town, you are disgraced.

3201. Wote man mu a, wokotɔ serɛ, na woanya biribi adi.

If you live in a town and you beg, you get something to eat.

3202. Wote nsu ho reguare na ɔbɔdamfo fa wo tam a, fwefwɛ bi ansa-na woatiw no; na wumfura bi a, obi besusuw sɛ mo banu yɛ abɔdamfo.

If a madman takes away your cloth while you are at the water bathing, put on a cloth before pursuing him; for if you are naked people will think you are both mad.

3203. Mate masie (me tirim).

I thought so beforehand.

3204. Wote sɛ wɔretow atuo (:atuo totow fi bepɔw so reba) a, mpɛ ntɛm nserew, na ebia (wunnim sɛ) wɔde wo agya funnu reba (:na ɛyɛ bi a wɔso wo na reba).

If you hear a gun shot, (a gun shot comes from the hill) don't be in a hurry to laugh, for perhaps (you don't know) they are bringing your father's dead body (it is someone coming carrying your mother's dead body.)

3205. Wonte obi asɛm ase a, wonyɛ no yayaya.

If you don't understand what someone is saying, don't cause trouble to him.

3206. Wontee afrɛse a, womfa abufuw.

If you don't understand the reason for being called, you shouldn't become angry.

3207. "Ate a, bisa" ne agorɔ.

If you hear something (bad about yourself) go and ask, for this brings good relationships.

3208. "Ate a, ma mente" te Korantiri anafo.

"If you know, let me know," is how it is at the feet of the bed of Korantiri.

3209. Ote se: ne ho ate, na osi nwuram'.
The "ote" tree says it is well, for it is still in the bush.

3210. Te-were tuatua nsatea ano.
The skin on the tips of the fingers is fastened to the tips
of the finger.

3211. Te anko te.
Honesty is not always immediately evident.

3212. Wotew aduan na efi wo nsa to asanka mu a, enkoo babi mmae.
If you pick up some food and it falls from your hand into
a bowl, its not going anywhere.

3213. Wotew so a, wotew gye amono.
If you reduce the price of something, you do so to collect
ready cash.

3214. Oteasefo nfwe ase.
The person who is sitting on the ground can't fall down.

3215. Oteasefo na oma osaman kon do oto. Cf.3453.
It is the living who cause the ghosts to long for mashed
yams.

3216. Tekrekyi-gow wofa no hiada.
If you become poor, you use an old cotton net.

3217. Tekrema a wode tutu kaw no, enye no na wode pe bosea.
Cf. 3620.
The tongue with which the debtor puts off a debt is
different from that with which he asks for a loan.

3218. Tekrema bogya, wofe bi gu, na womene bi.
The blood on the tongue, one spits some out and swallows
some.

3219. Tekrema (din) de sakrama. = 3228.
The tongue is called an advocate.

3220. Tekrema adi guan-nam, na osekan atwa mu.
The tongue ate the sheep meat, but the knife cut it.

3221. Tekyerema ahoodene ne abogye.
The strength of the tongue is in the chin.

3222. Tɛkrɛma-kam yɛ yaw sen kam-pa.
Cutting words are more painful than an ordinary cut.

3223. Tɛkrɛma-koro hyia tɛkrɛma apem a, ɛtɔ piti. R.83. Z.16.
If one tongue meets a thousand tongues, it faints.

3224. Tɛkrɛma na ekum nipa, na tɛkrɛma na egya nipa. R.5.
Gr. p.150.
The tongue kills people, and it also saves them.

3225. Tɛkrɛma-pa na wɔde wɛn ti.
The head is protected by a good tongue.

3226. Tɛkrɛma soa nea ɛyɛ hare.
The tongue carries that which is light.

3227. Tɛkrɛma nsoa ade a ɛyɛ duru.
The tongue does not carry that which is heavy.

3228. Tɛkrɛma wɔ hɔ yi, wɔfrɛ no sakrama. = 3219.
The tongue is called an advocate.

3229. Ɔtɛkrɛmafo nyɛ (:nwie) yiye da.
A liar never prospers.

3230. Ɔtempɔn da hɔ a, akwamma da hɔ.
If there is a main road, there is also a short cut.

3231. Ɔtɛn si aguam'.
The tsetse fly lands on the chair.

3232. Tenten-teatea ne tiatia-pipripi nhina sɛ (:bɔ so).
(Tenten ɛne tiawa nhina bɔ so.)
Tall and thin, and short and fat, are all equal.

3233. Ɔtenten-tea ne akwatia pipripi: ɔtenten pono ne mu a,
na ɔ-ne akwatia sɛ; akwatia nso teɛ ne mu a, na ɔ-ne
ɔtenten sɛ.
Tall and thin, and short and fat; if the tall person
bends then he and the short person are the same, and if the
short person stretches then he and the tall person are
the same.

3234. Wɔteta gyatɔ a, wɔteta ogyatofo gyaw ofofifo.
If they dress yaws, they dress the person having yaws
rather than those who didn't go to farm.

3235. Tɛtɛ frene yɛ dua. (Woyɛ biribi na ɛtra so a, ɛnyɛ fɛ.)
The big town of Tɛtɛ is like a small tree. (If you make
something and it is too big, it is not beautiful.

3236. Tɛtɛ abɛ, womfa nyɛ nkwan.
Old palm nuts are not used to make soup.

3237. Tɛtɛ adewafo ampue ntɛm, na efi atansɛrɛ.
The women engaged in the "adewa" play didn't make their
appearance quickly because they had to go and look for cloths
that they could borrow.

3238. Tɛtɛ ka asom'.
The past remains in the ears (traditions survive).

3239. Tɛtɛ ara ne nnɛ.
The olden times are what we see today.

3240. Tɛtɛ asoɛe, wonsoɛ hɔ bio. R.267.
We no longer rest at the place where our ancestors put
down their head loads to rest.

3241. Atetew a, na Brɔfo na ɛnwenee.
If it is torn in many pieces, the European have woven it.

3242. Wotetew ahaban tua kaw na wɔbegye a, wogye nea ɛso ano.
If you pick leaves to pay your debt and they receive them
they receive what is sufficient for the mouth.

3243. Ntɛtea bɔn mu tɔ ade a, wɔn ara na woyi.
If something falls into the nest of the small black ants,
they take it out themselves.

3244. Ntɛtea na obu ne bɛ se: Kosɛ (:m'asɛm) wɔ me tirim.
The small black ant says, "My grievance is in my head."

3245. Ntɛtea nsen, ɔdowa nsen, na nsa no resa.
The little black ant does not go away and the bee does not
to away, but the palm wine is getting finished.

3246. Ntɛtea, ɛnyɛ ne yɔnko ne nkrane.
The little black ant is not a friend of the warrior ant.

3247. Atetekwa we dua a, ɔde wɔ ne se akyi.
If a foolish person chews on a stick, he chews on it with
his back teeth.

3248. Ti a edi kan ne panyin.
The head which comes first is the elder.

3249. Ti a ɛso dae ne panyin.
The head which has dreams is superior.

3250. Eti aben, na berɛbo yɛ amono!
The head is well cooked, but the liver is raw.

3251. Wo ti ben wo na wunya wo twɛre a, wɔde bom' hɔ ara.
R.175.
Even though your head aches, when you are going to
receive blows, that is exactly where you will be hit.

3252. Ti bi ne ti bi nsɛ a, wonni atwɛrebo.
If one head is not like the other, you don't strike the
flint-stones.

3253. Ti-bone, wɔfa no fam', na wɔmfa nwo.
A bad head is taken to the ground, it is not taken to give
birth.

3254. Ti-dɛnsow mmɔ aguabum.
A well known person does not cause a disturbance.

3255. Ti nhina sɛ, na emu asɛm nyɛ pɛ.
All heads are the same but the thoughts in them are not
the same.

3256. Ti koro nkɔ agyina. R.168. Z.206.
One head can not hold a consultation.

3257. Wo ti anyin a, na wudi akotopene.
If your head has grown, you play blindman's bluff.

3258. Eti, wopere no mmako-'mako. R.238.
Each person defends his own head (life).

3259. Wo ti nsɛ Tete (sama) a, wonse sɛ: twa me Tete sama.
If your head is not like Tete's, you don't say, "cut the
figures on my hair like Tete's."

3260. Ti sɛe dakoro.
A head becomes useless in one day.

3261. Ti te sɛ adesoa: wɔnfwefwɛ mu ade nhu dakoro. Cf. 2001.
A head is like a head load, you can't look in and see it
all at one glance.

3262. Eti te-ase a, nankroma nso kyɛ. Z.76.
(Eti te hɔ a, wɔmfa kyɛw nsoa nankroma.)
If the head is there, the hat is not put on the knee.

3263. Eti ntetewe a, wonnyae kyɛw soa. R.85.
If your head is not torn to pieces, you don't stop wearing
a hat.

3264. Eti te hɔ yi, wɔmpae mu nfwɛ.
We do not cut open someone's head to see what is in it.

3265. Eti nyɛ brofere na wɔapae mu ahu mu asɛm.
A head is not like a pawpaw which can be cut open to see
what is inside it.

3266. Ntia ntia na ɛbɔ ntow.
Addition makes a clod of mud.

3267. Ntiamoa Sampanimakɔ soa abusuboa (:obusufo) kyɛ, wokyi.
Ntiamoa Sampanimakɔ is not allowed to carry the hat of an
animal of ill omen.

3268. Wutiatia obi de so fwefwɛ wo de a, wunhu.
If you trample on another person's things in looking for
your own, you never find them.

3269. Wotie obi fi tum tum a, wobua da? Cf.349.
If you hear tum, tum, (the pounding of fufu) at someone's
house do you fast?

3270. Atiko nte ntwiri.
One is not affected by calumny in his absence.

3271. Ntim Gyakari wui, wɔka kyerɛɛ Ɔbansua.
When Ntim Gyakari died, they told Ɔbansua.

3272. Timɔbɔ nti na woyi awirikwaw.
Because of compassion you catch a green parrot.

3273. Atipae nyɛ biribi a, ɛyɛ aniadam.
If headache does nothing, at least it gives you red eyes.

-269-

3274. Tirim' fɛre sen fɛre-pa.

Shyness in expressing one's thoughts is better than real
shyness.

3275. Wo tirim yɛ den a, wunnya otubrafo.

If you are cruel, no one wants to settle with you.

3276. Otirimɔdenfo na ɔsom asra.

It is the cruel person who takes snuff.

3277. Atirimusɛm 'ti na ɛma adwene ani yɛ nkuma.

Some secret thoughts make the eyes of fish small.

3278. Titiriku na obetumi Kwadwoku? Cf.2969.

Can Titiriku challenge Kwadwoku?

3279. Titiriku se: ɔkɔpɛ twɛ adi, na wannya a, ne kuru mmore.

Titiriku says he is looking for a vagina to have intercourse
with, and if he doesn't get one, his sore doesn't
become any bigger.

3280. Atiti-ati-brafo-ati, obi mpɛ wo agoru (:woantumi ati)
a, tra wo ase; na ɔkɔtɔ bɔ pemmɔ a, ɔsan n'akyi. Cf.415.

Player of the "atiti-ati-brafo-ati" game, if no one
likes your game, sit down, if the crab falls on its back
it turns around.

3281. "Ɛtɔ babi a, edum, etɔ babi a, ɛhyew" nyɛ amammu -pa.

If the fire (of the law) dies in one place, and burns
in another place, there is something wrong with the law.

3282. Ɛtɔ-dabi-a onipa-bone ho yɛ na.

Sometimes a bad man is hard to find.

3283. Tɔɔ akyeame nko a, anka yenso mpomatiri ansa-na yebu
atɛn.

If only the chief's linguists were concerned, then we
would not discuss the case in front of the chief before
we condemned someone.

3284. Ɛtɔ nea onni tam nko a,...s.1478.

3285. Ɛtɔ sikyi o, ɛtɔ mfuate o, yenya ɔkomfo kum no.
Cf.1696.3056.

Whether the die falls "sikyi" or whether it falls "mfuate"
the fetish priest will be killed.

3286. Ɛtɔ nwaw ne akyekyere nko a,...s.1479. Z.149.181.

3287. Woto asum' a, wudu ase prɛko.

If you jump into the river, you go to the bottom
immediately.

3288. Onto dwen na ohyia nkwanta, na nkwanta hyia apagya, na
apagya hyia osewuo.

He is not seized as a slave, and he meets the cross roads,
and the crossroads meets the steel for striking fire, and
the steel for striking fire meets the company of warriors
in Akem.

3289. Woto awere-mono a, wotere ho.

If you put a new linen in water, the water just runs over it.

3290. Woto obabasia a, to no adooden, na kuro da ne yam'.

If you buy a woman, buy her for a high price, for there is
a village in her stomach.

3291. Moto adeɛ a, muntua ka, nso mubisa a, na 'yɛde rebɔ mo
aboɔ.

If you buy something you don't pay for, but if you ask,
we give you the price.

3292. Woto adeɛ de sika-mono tua ka, a, ɛnyɛ sɛ woatɔ biribi.

If you buy something and pay for it with ready cash, it is
as if you bought nothing.

3293. Woto adeɛ na wutua ka a, 'yɛrefrɛ wo kunini.

If you buy something and pay for it, you are called a
distinguished person.

3294. Woto adeɛ na wutua ka na afifiri firi wo a, ɛyɛ wo dɛ.

If you buy something and have to sweat before you pay for
it, then you are pleased with yourself.

3295. Woto tam sie wo ni na woantua kaw a, wonnyaw wo ayi se da.

If you buy a cloth to bury your mother and don't pay for it,
they never stop reminding you of your mother's death.

3296. Woto otɔtobrɔfo ade na wuntua no kaw a, nse sɛ woanya no
fow.

If you buy something from an idiot and don't pay him for
it, don't say you got it cheaply.

3297. Wokɔtɔ onipa na woannya bi a, wosan wo akyi.

If you go to buy slaves and you don't get one, you return
back home.

3298. Atɔ-nkyene-akyɛ: wɔde mako ayi me ayɛ.

I bought salt for my neighbors, but I was thanked with pepper.

3299. Wotɔ wo bo ase a, woware ɔhene awowa (ayowa, yere). Cf. 3558.

If you are patient, you can marry one of the chief's female slaves.

3300. Wotɔ wo bo ase gua ntɛtea a, wuhu ne nsono. Cf. 734.

If you skin the ant with patience, you see its intestines.

3301. Wotɔ wo bo ase na nsu gyen na wofwefwɛ ase ade a, wuhu.

If you are patient and wait till the water becomes clear, you will find what you are looking for at the bottom of the water.

3302. "To wo bo ase, to wo bo ase" (nti) na ɛmaa ɔketew bo yɛɛ traa.

Because of "put your chest down" the lizards chest became flat.

3303. "To wo bo ase, to wo bo ase" nti na anka ɔketew nsono refi ne kɔn ayki.

Under other circumstances always saying, "put your chest down", "put your chest down" would have caused the lizard's intestines to come out from behind his neck.

3304. Woto dom-mone a, ɛbra wo.

If you say evil things about others, it becomes a habit.

3305. Wɔto ɔhene bɛ ansa-na wɔ ayaw no.

You give the chief a proverb before you insult him.

3306. Woto anhwea-ban a, wo nsa mpa ho.

If you build a sand fence, your hand never stops caring for it.

3307. Wokɔtɔ kwadwofo wɔ afum' a, ma no amo, na onyɛ biribi a, owia rehye no.

If you met a lazy person n the farm, congratulate him, for even if he is doing nothing, the sun is still burning him.

3308. Wokɔtɔ asredowa wɔ ne buw ano na ɛnyɛ ono na ɔnwenee a, na wonwenee gyaw no. Cf. 1436.

You meet the "aseredowa" bird at the opening of its nest, but it did not weave it, it was left behind for it.

-272-

3309. Woto pampim a, na woato kuro.

If you come upon a barrier across the path, that means you have reached the town.

3310. Woto pra a, woato nam. R. 237.

If you come upon the armadillo, you have come upon meat.

3311. Woto sɛbe (:tafrakyɛ) na wuse (:woka) asɛm bi a, wonkyi.

If you apologize before saying something bad, it will not be taken badly.

3312. Mato meho sere, na mese: wonnsere me. S.

I have exposed myself to laughter, and I say they shouldn't laugh at me.

3313. Anto wo a, da.

If it has not happened to you, sleep.

3314. Woto dua na anwu a, ɛsɛ wo ara.

If you make a fire around a tree to kill it and it doesn't die, it deserves you right.

3315. Woto aduru a, ebi ka wo ano. R. 2. Gr. p. 170.

If you poison someone, some of the poison goes into you mouth.

3316. Woto hene ntam mpɛn aduasa a, wuyi no prɛko.

If you transgress a cheif's oath thirty times, you give satisfaction for the transgressions all one time.

3317. Wonto ɔhene mmara a, ɛte sɛ ɔ-ne wo ka. (:ɔdɔ wo).

If you don't transgress the chief's laws it is like you and he are good friends.

3318. Wo to sa a, wosakra wo nantew.

If you are tied around the waist, you change your way of walking.

3319. Toa-fufu abɔ, na gyirase! Cf. 727.

A white bottle of wine was broken, then what about a wine glass!

3320. Toa ho yɛ hyɛhyɛ a, na nsu na ɛwɔ mu. Cf. 1383.

If a bottle is hot, there is hot water in it.

3321. Toa mu wɔ ade a, Amakye na onim.

If calabashes bring wealth, Amakye knows.

3322. Toa na ɔpɛ na hama sa ne kɔn.

The gourd has a string tied around its neck because it likes it that way.

3323. Nto-ana mfa sɛne mmutu pa. =358.
Ɔtobrɛfo ...s. 636. 3154.

No one gives his geneology by turning a new cooking pot upside down.

3324. Ɔtʊfoɔ ba nyini akora.

The child of a person who has fallen in battle or who has been killed by an accident grows to be an old man.

3325. Atokoro sɛe nokwapem.

One lie destroys a thousand truths.

3326. Tɔkwa-bo sɔ yɛ toro.

The surface of the stones used for fighting are flat and slippery.

3327. Tɔkwa-mirika wɔ menease.

Running in fighting carries a grudge.

3328. Ɔtomfo bɔ mpontɛre a, ɔbɔ sosɔw bi.

If a blacksmith makes door hinges, he also makes a long-handled digging-iron.

3329. Ɔtomfoɔ tono a, ɔde asae bɔ nea ehia no.

If a smith is forging, he strikes with his hammer where it is needed.

3330. Metɔn ne matɔ ahyia.

"I offer it for sale," and "I have bought it" have met.

3331. Wotɔn wo a, wontɔ tuo. R. 93.

If you are being sold, you don't buy a gun.

3332. Wotɔn wo aso di a, wode wo anuonyam tew guaha.

If you sell your ear, you complete the bargain with your honor.

3333. Ntɔn wo kɛtɛ apem a, biako pɛ so na woda.

If you sold your thousand mats, it is only one you sleep on.

3334. Ntonko: mesen bɛw koko.

The large pepper says, "I am greater than the red palm nut."

3335. Ntontom pɛ Ada akɔ, na mframa anu no mu.

The mosquito wants to go to Ada and is blown there by the wind.

3336. Atɔperɛ yɛ mpatuw.

A play in which the victim is cruelly killed happens all of a sudden.

3337. Ɔtɔperɛfo na oyi neho agyama mu.

A cruel person clears himself in the "agyama" shrub.

3338. Ɔtorofo de mfe apem tu kwan a, ɔnokwafo' de dakoro tiw no to no.

When the liar has travelled a thousand years, the one who speaks the truth chases him and overtakes him in one day.

3339. Ɔtorofo gye agua; ose manya ɔbo.

If a liar takes a sheep he says: "I have a stone."

3340. Ɔtorofo mma osensin.

The liar doesn't give an uncompleted law suit.

3341. Ɔtorofo na ose: me dansefo wɔ Aburokyiri.

The liar says: "My witness is in Europe."

3342. Ɔtotɔ mfɔn.

The buyer does not starve.

3343. Atotɔ-nsa nnom nsu.

The one who buys wine does not drink water.

3344. Wototo akɔkono a, wuyi no benabena. B.

If you roast snails, they are given out on sticks.

3345. Ɛtoto a, mesan, ne ɛba a, mewaw ano: ɛba-a-mewaw-ano ne panyin. =2.

If it is entangled I untangle it, and if it comes, I prevent it, if it comes, I prevent it is the best.

3346. Wototow kyene(kyene) a, wuhu no hia-da.

If you keep throwing your things away, you'll find them when you are poor.

3347. Atotobɛ, wowe no akɔnnɔ.

A roasted palm nut is eatenly greedily, but not for satisfaction.

3348. Wotow abo abien kɔ soro a, ne sɔw yɛ sɔw-na. Cf. 2634.
If you throw two stones into the air, it is difficult to catch them both.

3349. Wotow aboa tuo na oguan ba fie a, ɔsoa wo nam abia.
If you shoot at an animal and it runs to your house, it helps you carry your meat.

3350. Wɔtow kyene na wɔsan kɔfa a, wokyi.
You should not throw anything away and then go back to take it again.

3351. Wɔnkɔto nkyene a, wɔmfa nkosie adaka mu. Cf. 816. 3640.
If you have to throw away something, you don't store it in a box.

3352. Wotow mmɛta a, wɔpae mu.
('Yɛto mmɛta a, 'yɛmpalm!
If a bunch of palm nuts are thrown down it breaks up.

3353. Wotow sunson kyene a, na ne dua di akyiri.
When you throw a worm away, its tail will follow.

3354. Wotow ɔware a, abɔ ano.
If you play "ɔware" game, you try to prevent your fellow from going ahead.

3355. Tra nea midui!
Accomplish more than I have accomplished!

3356. Wotra twa a, egu wo ani so.
If you cut beyond your reach, it falls into your eyes.

3357. Atra, wuhu a, ɛte sɛ gow, nso sɛ wɔyɛ no ara nen.
If you see a fishing net, it is like something tattered, but that is how it is made.

3358. Trabea nhina nsɛ.
Not all seatings (positions) are the same.

3359. Atra-nnufua retra nkonnua, na yɛbɛyɛ no dɛn?
Those who sit on seats made of wooden blocks say they are sitting on chairs, what will we do?

3360. Ntrama niwa hia wo a, ɛsen apem.
If you need a single cowry, it is like needing more than a thousand.

3361. Otua abura nsa (=nsaw).
He dug a well to fetch water.

3362. Wutu de a, na wo nsa yɛ fa.
If you dig out the ripe yam, your hands become dirty.

3363. Wutu kwan a, yɛ woho yiye, na nea woahyia no no, wurenhyia no bio.
When you travel, do good for when you meet somebody you may not meet him again.

3364. "Tu kyene! tu kyene!" - na ɛka nso.
Take it out take it out!" and then only the ashes remain.

3365. "Wontu nkyene! wontu nkyene!" - na yɛreda ntuw. R. 50.
Take it out! take it out! or we shall sleep without a fire.

3366. Wutu nsu a, wuse: ma me tefo nte na mente!
If you are walking in water you say: "My hearer doesn't hear but I hear."

3367. "Kotu bɛtɛ!" anyɛ ye, n'ɛma (ne-mma, na ɛmma?) "kotwa bɛtɛw!"
"Go and pluck the tender ones!" and if you can't pluck them then "Go and cut the tender ones!"

3368. Etua wo yonko ho a, etua dua. R. 229.
Pain in your neighbour's body is like pain in a tree.

3369. Wutua owufo ho akaw a, wuwie; na ɔteasefo de, wutua no ho akaw a, ɛnsa da.
If you pay a debt incurred by a dead person, you have finished paying, but if you pay that of a living being, you never finish.

3370. Otubrafo na nti na apopobibiri fam bo ho.
It is because of settlers that there is moss on the rocks.

3371. Atuduru asa a, ɛnyɛ wɔnne Akowua ntoa mu. R. 111.
If there is no more gunpowder, this does not refer to the gunpowder in Akowua's pouch.

3372. Atufanu hyia a, asamankwan nna ntuw.
If guns from opposing camps meet, the toad to the land of the dead is never deserted.

3373. Otugya nti na ntam ba.
It is because of inheritance oaths have come.

3374. Otumfo woro ka a, oworo fa wo 'mati, R. 113.
When a strong person takes off your ring, he takes it off via your shoulder.

3375. Mintumi aban-nye nit na manware aberewa nana.
Because I can not build fences, I did not marry the old lady's grand-daughter.

3376. Mintumi akonnua-soa nti na makum m'agya ne me na.
Because I wasn't able to carry stools I killed my father and my mother.

3377. Mintumi mmorosa-nom a, menom ahai.
If I cannot drink wine, I shall drink pito.

3378. Yentumi biribi a, na yemmo kahiri nnye.
If we can't carry a load, we do not put a pad for carrying loads on our head.

3379. Woantumi hu-se a, tumi wo fwene ano nso-si.
If you weren't able to see and tell about the event, something got stuck in your nostrils.

3380. Wobetumi Korofoa Adowa adobo-si a, na wokogye ne ba Adoma Anku aware. (:woware ne ba).
If you can match Korofoa Adowa in the way she observes the custom at the death of one her husband's relatives, then you can have her child Adoma Anku to marry.

3381. Wuntumi akokono-bo a, na wuse: ako ne tirim.
If you can't get grubs from a palm tree by splitting it, you say they have gone into the head of the palm.

3382. Wuntumi anantenantew a, wonne ha ne Abiriw.
If you are not able to walk a lot, much less so from here to Abiriw.

3383. Wuntumi nsi dan a, na wodan wo yonko.
If you cannot build your own house, you depend on your neighbor.

3384. Wuntumi nto a, (en)na wuse: enye de.
If you can't buy, you say it is not delicious.

3385. Otuntuma bebu, na ɔdan afere!
If the wall of a house falls down, the house is disgraced.

3386. Atuo ben (:dɔ) a, na etweri mmarima kokom!
If a gun is hot, it is from leaning against a man's chest.

3387. Otuo kantamma nni biako so.
The cock of a gun does not rule only one person.

3388. Otuo nya ɔtiafo, na odi abaninsɛm. Cf. 3422.
It is when a gun has a man to cock it that it performs
warlike deeds.

3389. Otuo pae ka ɔbommofo a, wommisa nea odi ɔbofo nam.
When the gun bursts and wounds the hunter, don't ask his
assistant who has eaten the meat.

3390. Otuo mpae Aburokyiri mmɛka onipa wɔ Abibirim! Z. 73.
A gun fired in Europe does not hit someone in Africa.

3391. Wo atuo sua a, na wo asɛm sua.
When your guns are few, your words are few.

3392. Otuo ta huan a,. na ɛ-ne poma sɛ pɛ.
When the lock of a gun is out of order, it is just like a
stick.

3393. Otuo tantia, wutia a, esi mmerɛ esi.
The cap of a flint lock gun, if you cock it, it rests on
the mushrooms.

3394. Otuo ntow aboa bi nnyae nkɔhyehye aboa bi were mu.
A gun shot does not wound one animal and cause pain to the
skin of another animal.

3395. Otuo yera nifa mu na ekofi adɔnten mu a, na ɛnkɔɔ babi ɛ.
When a gun is missing from the fight flank of the battle
and appears in the forefront of the battle, it did not
go astray.

3396. Aturukuku fa ɔberɛ berɛ.
The turtle-dove grows tired.

3397. Yetutu abirika ako, yennu na berɛberɛ bɛyɛ dɛn?
We have gone running and we have reached our destination,
so what is the use of going slowly now.

3398. Wututu ka-bone ma wo yɔnko a, wofa bi (:wofa tua).
If you incur a bad debt for your friend, you pay some
yourself.

3399. Wotwa brɔdeɛ na ɛfwe ase wabirim a, onse sɛ: wabirim,
ose: ɛwɔ ase.
If plantain is cut down it falls down "swish" it doesn't
say "swish", it says: "I am down."

3400. Wotwa brofere de yɛ atumpan a, ɛbɛyɛ ye; na wɔde ma damirifa
a, obi nte.
If you carve a drum from a pawpaw tree it will be all right
but when you use it in giving condolences to someone, he
can not hear it.

3401. Wotwa anyankama so gyentia a, na aka boba.
If the "anyankama" tree is cut for firewood, it remains
only a dry branch.

3402. Wutwa fiamparakwa (=nkontompo) na mempene.
If you tell a lie, I don't agree.

3403. Wutwa nkontompɔ a, wusuro Kumase.
When you tell a lie, you fear (the chief of) Kumase.

3404. Wutuwa no tenten a, na wunya no fow.
If you cut it long, you get it cheap.

3405. Wutwa asu wie a, na wuse: ɔdɛnkyeɛm ano pɔw.
Once you have crossed the river, you say the crocodile
has bumps on his mouth.

3406. Wotwa twem-mone to hɔ na woamfa so a, ɛmporɔw (da).
If you put a bad wooden bridge across the river and you
don't cross it, it never rots (until you cross it yourself).

3407. Wutwa wo tɛkrɛma so toto we a, wunnya nam. R. 123. Z. 24.
If you cut your tongue and roast it, you don't really have
meat.

3408. Wutwam' na obi serew wo a, wode ma Onyame.
If you become thin and someone laughs at you, you give it
to God.

3409. Ntwatoso sen makowa yaw.
False accusation is worse than painful pepper.

3410. Atwe abien boro wi. R. 105.
Two small antelopes can beat one big antelope.

3411. Ɔtwe di twe, ewi di wi.
The small antelope mates with a small antelope, and a big antelope mates with a big antelope.

3412. Ɔtwe dua yɛ tia a, nea ɔde pra heno are nen. (:nansoso ɔpra neho sa.) (Ɔtwe aduatia, ɔde sa na ɛpara ne ho.)
Even though the antelopes tail is short, nevertheless it drives the flies away with it.

3413. Ɔtwe nhoma suane nea ɛyɛ hare. =1419.
The antelope's hide splits where it is thinnest.

3414. Ɔtwe anko gua; ne nhoma kɔ.
The deer does not go to market, his hide goes.

3415. Ɔtwe ne ɔtwe ko na wohu gyahene a, na wokɔ afa na woguan.
When two deer are fighting and they see a lion, they run off together.

3416. Ɔtwe ani ansen a, na efi bommofo.
If the antelope is unhappy, it is because of the hunter.

3417. Ɔtwe nya nantu a, wokyi.
If you see an antelope that has thick legs you avoid it.

3418. Ɔtwe mporɔw adu kurom!
The antelope does not spoil (get killed) if it stands between the buttresses of a tree.

3419. Wotwe mu twe mu a, ɛtew.
If you keep pulling it breaks.

3420. Ntwemu nti na agyinamoa antɔ akoa. Z. 48.
Because of the act of stretching one's body, the cat did not buy a slave.

3421. Mentwɛn safo ansa-na manom nsa (mabow) (:maboro nsa).
I do not wait for a seller of palm wine before I get drunk.

3422. Twɛrebo nti na otuo di abaninsɛm. Cf. 3388. 1792.
It is because of the fling-stone that the gun performs wonderful deeds.

3423. Twitɔn ka kyerɛɛ otokoataka sɛ "nsa onyankerɛn yare" nti
na ɔda awiam! Cf. Gr. # 291.

The "twitɔn" plant advised the "otokoataka" tree not to
seek medical treatment for the "onyankerɛn" tree and that
is why the "twitɔn" plant is lying in the sun.

3424. Twɔtwɔ mu wɔ twɔ.

Among vaginas there is a preferred one.

3425. Etwow duru ansa-na 'yɛapɛ ne ntama.

Hydrocele comes before we look for a cloth.

3426. Nwa-kyɛm mu mpa tabiria.

There is always a gray snail in a number of black snails.

3427. Nwaw de neho sie, a, na wɔfa no tope.

If a snail takes care of itself, it will be taken as a big
snail.

3428. Nwaw hintaw neho a, na onyin yɛ ɔnwanini (:otope).

If the small snail hides itself, it grows into a big one.

3429. Nwaw nam ara ne nea etua n'ano.

The snail's food is what is in its mouth.

3430. Nwaw wu nkwan mu a, ɛmporɔw.

When a snail dies in the soup, it does not rot.

3431. Ɔnwansane nni afuo, nanso ɔwe nkuruma.

The antelope doesn't have a farm, yet it eats okra.

3432. Ɔnwansan anto nkuruma a, ɛwɔ ne tɔ-da.

If the antelope doesn't meet the okra, there is a day when
it will meet it.

3433. Aware rebɔ wo a, wonfwefwɛ mu yɛyere.

If a husband and wife want to get divorced, they don't look
deeply for the real reason.

3434. Aware foforo sa ɔde.

A new marriage picks out the good yam.

3435. Aware-gyae nnu kurow.

Divorce does not ruin a country.

3436. Owataku-aba na ɛkyerɛ ɔtomfo nna-bɔ.

The seeds of the "owataku" tree teach the blacksmith how to make a light blow with his hammer.

3437. Ɛwɔ obi a wofwɛ n'ahim su a, nsu ba.

There is someone who if you look into his face, you get tears when you cry.

3438. Ɛwɔ nea basin yɛ onu n'aso mu.

There is a way in which a one-armed person cleans his ears.

3439. Wowɔ ba-pa a, ɔsen nkwan-pa.

A good child is better then good soup.

3440. Wowɔ biribi a, na wudi ahantansɛm.

If you are rich, you act proudly.

3441. Wowɔ Boakye a, na wowɔ ayan.

If you have Boakye, you have drumming.

3442. Wowɔ ahyehyɛde na wuhyia ayɛforo a, wommerɛ.

If you have jewels and you go to a wedding, you are not tired.

3443. Wowɔ sika a, na wɔfrɛ wo nana (:nyansafo).

If you have money, you are called "nana" grandsire.

3444. Wowɔ sika a, na wɔkae nnyafin.

If you·have money, you remember and old grievance.

3445. Wowɔ aso na woka asɛm kyerɛ onipa a, ɔte.

If you are a good listener and you advise someone, he listens.

3446. Ɔwɔ de ahoyeraw (:ahometew) na ɔka. Gr. # 40a. Cf. 1358. 1399.

If a snake is disturbed, it will bite.

3447. Ɔwɔ aduru, wɔtew no ahoɔhare.
(Aboa no ad. wɔde ah. na ɛtew.)

The herbs to be applied to a snake bite are plucked quickly.

3448. Ɔwɔ nka onipa kwa.

. A snake does not bite a man without a cause.

3449. Ɔwɔ nkesua nko na ebesuw wuram' a, anka biribi ara-nsɛee ɛ.
If it were only snakes' eggs that got rotten in the forest,
then nothing would ever spoil.

3450. Ɔwɔ na obu bɛ se: ohiani nkyere hiani.
The snake gives his proverb: "A poor person doesnt' catch
a poor person."

3451. Ɔwɔ te sɛ hama, na (:nso) wɔmfa nkyekyere ade.
A snake is like a rope, but it is not used to tie up
things.

3452. Wo nko wudidi a, wo nko wugoru.
If you eat alone, you play alone.

3453. Wo na woma ɔsaman kɔn dɔ tɔ.   Cf. 3215.
It is you who made the ghost like mashed yams.

3454. Wo na wopɛ wo asɛm na woanya!
The trouble you like is the one you get!

3455. Wo na woayɛ oguan (:akokɔ) dɛn na dwensɔ abɔ no.   R. 240.
Cf. 3579.
What harm have you done to the sheep that it is sick of
disury?

3456. Wo ne bi (:nipa) nsɛ a, wo-ne no nni asrasom. (:nni asi.)
If you do not like someone, you are not close to him.

3457. Wo ne akokɔ da a, wompɛ ntɛm nkyere no. (:wompɛ no kita
ntɛm.)
If your chicken sleeps in your compound you are not in
a hurry to catch it.

3458. Wo ne kraman bɔ abusua a, nisu mpa wo ani ase da.
If you and a dog belong to the same extended family, there
are always tears in your eyes.

3459. Wo ne kwasea goru a, ne kwasea san wo.
If you play with a fool, you also become a fool.

3460. Wo ne wo agya akoa two abɛ a, ɔfrɛ wo awɛ.   R. 108.
If you tap palm wine with your father's slave, he calls you
friend.

3461. Wo ne wo yɔnko te dua-bone (:kontonkye) so na wobɛsɔre a,
wokae mo.

If you and your friend are sitting on a crooked tree and
you get up, you notify your friend.

3462. Wɔ-ne wo renna a, wɔkyerɛ wo wi.

The people who are not sleeping teach you to steal.

3463. Wowo ba-bone a, wofa ɔkasaberɛ.

If you give birth to a bad child, you will become tired
of speaking.

3464. Wɔwo nipa na woawo ne tamfo.

When a man is born, his enemy is also born.

3465. Wɔwoo Tafoni ba (no), na onkura ta.

When the man from Tafo was born, he did not hold a bow.

3466. Wɔwoo wo di amim Kwasida, na wɔwoo wo yi-adwow Dwoda.

The greedy person was born on Sunday, and the extortioner
on Monday.

3467. Mawo wo mabɛrɛ, wokyi.

I am weary of having born you is something no one should
say.

3468. Awo bone na ɛma wokum asonetakom.   Cf. 3034.

The birth of bad children makes people kill the small
sand worms.

3469. Awo te ho yi, ɛyɛ nkuku-toto.

Giving birth goes with the purchase of cooking pots.

3470. Ɔwɔbie yɛ na.

It is a rare person who always gets what he wants.

3471. Awonio! fi kɔmfo anom'.

My mother! comes from the fetish priest's mouth.

3472. Ɔworaworakɔtɔ (se):me na minim sika dabere.

The small crab says: "I am the one who knows where the
gold is lying."

3473. Awosawosaw kyɛn sika ntansa.   =3515.

Having plenty to eat is better than gold worth a hundred
and eight.

3474. Wowɔw ɔde-fufu ma obirebe a, odwumaba ara na ɔne. (:ma
kokokyiniako-ba di a, ɔne odwuma-aba.)

Even if you make yam fufu for the "obirebe" bird, he will
still pass the seeds of the trumpet tree when he goes to
toilet.

3475. Ɔwoo-wo te hɔ a, wɔmfrɛ woho agya-ɔba. =2275.

If your mother is alive, you are not called your father's
son.

3476. Owu a akum wo na akum wo agya se obekum wo a, wunnye no
kyim.

When a death which has killed your mother and your father
says, it will kill you, don't say it is not true.

3477. Owu a akum wo na ne wo agya wɔ hɔ a, wunnye din (:wunsu)
se: aka me nko.

If death which has killed your mother and your father is
there, you don't say to it; "I'm still here."

3478. Owu bae nkɔe a, wunse no se: aka me nko.

If death has come and not yet gone away, you don't tell it:
"I'm still here."

3479. Owu bekum wo se ne wo ni a, nsu sɛ: me se ne me ni awu!
na su sɛ: me-ne m'agya (ne na) bɛkɔ.

If death has come and killed your father and mother, do not
weep saying, "my father and mother are dead," but say,
"I will go with my father and mother."

3480. Owu bekum wo na wofrɛ no agya a, obekum wo, wofrɛ no ɛna
a, obekum wo.

If death is really going to kill you and you call it
father, it will kill you, and if you call it mother, it
will also kill you.

3481. Owu adare nnɔw fako. R. 228.

The hoe of death does not weed in only one place.

3482. Owu de ne pasua fa ofi mu a, ɔbosomfo aduru dan nsu.

If death passes through a house with its battle lines
the medicine of the fetish priest turns to water.

3483. Owu nhina yɛ owu.

Every kind of death is the same.

3484. Owu na wannya babi ankɔ a, na ɔkɔ asaman.

If death has no particular place to go, it goes off to the world of the spirits.

3485. Owu ne wo ase hyɛ wo adwuma-yɛ a, owu de na wokɔ kan.

If both death and you mother-in-law hire you for work, you go and do death's work first.

3486. Owu to wo a, wunse no se: fwɛ aberewa!

If death comes upon you, you don't say to it: "look, there is an old woman (take her)."

3487. Owu wo ɔkyekyefo adaka ano safe.

Death has the key to the miser's chest.

3488. Owu, wonwu no mpɛn abien.
(Owu, wowu no dakoro.)

You don't die twice. (You die only once.)

3489. Owu yɛ adewa a, anka Tafofo na esii kan.

If death were the "adewa" dance, then the people of Tafo would have been the declared the best dancers.

3490. Owu yaw nti na wɔde anhomaguan to gyam' a, ɛpompono.

Because of the pain of death, if a sheep's hide is thrown into the fire, it does not wrinkle.

3491. Owu yɛ anhomaguan yaw.

Death is painful to the sheep's hide.

3492. Owu nyɛ yaw a, anka wɔde anhomaguan to gyam' a, ɛmpompono.

If death were not painful, then when a sheep's hide were thrown into a fire, it would not shrivel up.

3493. Owu nyɛ pia na wɔadi mu ahyemfiri.

Death is not a sleeping room in which one can go to and fro.

3494. Mirewu kyena, mirewu 'nɛ, na 'yɛde yɛ ayie?

"I am going to die tomorrow, I and going to die today," do they begin the funeral custom because of this?

3495. Wurewu a, wunse sɛ: mirewu o, mirewu o!

When you are really dying, you don't say: "I am dying, I am dying."

3496. Wuwu ansa-na wo hia ana wo sika yi adi.
You die before your poverty or riches become known to others.

3497. Wuwu ntɛm a, wosie wo ntɛm.
If you die quickly, you are buried quickly.

3498. Wowu gyaw mpanyini kasa a, wonnyae nkasa mmofra kasa.
If the elders leave you a legacy of dignified language, you do not abandon it and speak childish language.

3499. Wura a ɛta nsu ani wɔ nea ne ntini wɔ.
The grass which floats on the surface of the water has a place where its roots are.

3500. Wo wura bɔ wo bo a, na wankum wo.
If your master throws a stone at you, he doesn't kill you.

3501. Owura ne akoa ntam' nni twe-ma-mentwe.
Between the master and the slave there is no pull and let me pull (no striving for the mastery).

3502. Owura pa yɛ ahode.
A good master becomes rich.

3503. Wo wura tan wo a, na ɔfrɛ wo akoa dehye. R. 63.
If your master hates you, he calls you a free born slave.

3504. Awuru rewea, (na) ba rewea: (na) hena na obegye wɔn tata?
If the tortoise is crawling, and his child is crawling, who will teach them to walk?

3505. Owusiw ne enim asase so kwan.
Smoke knows the way on the ground.

3506. Mawe atadwe, mawe afwerew: afwerew sen atadwe.
I have eaten tiger nuts, I have eaten sugar cane, but sugar cane is better than tiger nuts.

3507. Wowe wo se so dua na wunyiyim' a, ɛte sɛ wonwee so dua da.
If you clean your teeth with a chewing stick and you don't rub it back and forth, it is as if you never cleaned your teeth.

3508. Wekɔ sene prae animonyam.

An old pot, which contains a mixture of red clay and chaff used to rub the floor of native houses, is greater than the broom's praise.

3509. Nwera nye biribi a, eye nsunsuane-na.

If a silk cloth is nothing, it is a rare thing to the heavy rain running over the ground.

3510. Wo wers fi na wosan kɔfa a, wonkyi.

There is nothing wrong with giving back to get something if you have forgotten it.

3511. Were reporow a, wommisa bersbo.

If the hide of an animal is rotten, you don't ask about the liver.

3512. Awere na skɔfaa ntama-pa baa ofie.

A sack cloth went and brought a good cloth to the house.

3513. Nwerewerewa (:wera) na ete dampare kasa.

The cockroach understands the rafter's language.

3514. Nwerewerwa we ade (:we a, wɔde) hye akura.

If the cockroach chews on something, he blames the mouse.

3515. Owesa-mene kyɛn ntansa. =3473.

To be able to chew and swallow is worth more than a hundred and eight dollars.

3516. Ewi nkɔ na apurupuro nka.

If the antelope doesn't run, you don't hear the rustling noise of an antelope.

3517. Ewi ne wansan gyina hɔ a, yebehu nea ɔwee aberewa nkruma.

If the "ewi" antelope and the "wansan" antelope are standing there, we will see who has eaten the old lady's okra.

3518. Ewi nwo ba na ɔnkɔse ɔnwansan. F.

The "ewi" antelope doesn't bear a child that resembles the "wansan" antelope.

3519. Awi na eye aniwu, na ohia nye aniwu.

Stealing, not poverty, is disgraceful.

3520. Owifo mpaw dabere.

The thief cannot choose his sleeping place.

3521. Owifo se: 'nɛ 'nɛ nko (ɛnnɛ nko (n)ko)!
The thief says: "Only today (have I come here)."

3522. Owifo, wɔkyere no nsa.
The thief is caught by the hand.

3523. Awia mu nni aduɔson-anum.
There are not seventy five different sunshines.

3524. Owia wɔ soro na ɛhyehye sa ye (:sɛ), na menne sɛ ɛbɛbɛn
fam'. (...ɛhy. nnipa yi, na ɛba fam' de a, anka minnim nea
ɛbɛyɛ.)
Even though the sun is far away, it is burning; how much
more would it burn if it were close to the ground.

3525. Wiase wɔtra no banu banu.
People live in the world in pairs.

3526. Ɔyafunu mu nni pumpunu.
There is no store room in the stomach.

3527. Ɔyafunu yɛ botɔ, woahhu no hyehyɛ a, na apae.
The stomach is a bag, if it is loaded too heavily it will
burst.

3528. Wo yam' ye a, womfa wo yere nkyɛ. R. 37.
No matter how generous you are, you don't give your wife
away.

3529. Wo yam' ye a, na ɔhɔho bɛtra wo fi.
If you are generous, a stranger will live in your house.

3530. Ɔyamɔnwenefo nko nyi dɔm da.
A stingy person never gains the victory.

3531. Ɔyamɔnwenefo na ne fi gye apopobibiri.
Moss overtakes the stingy person's house.

3532. Ɔyamɔnwenefo na ɔtwɛn ade-kɛse ansa-na wayɛ ayɛ.
The stingy person waits for big riches before he presents
gifts.

3533. Ɔyamɔnwenefo wɔ ne yeyifo.
Even the stingy person has someone who praises him.

3534. Oyamonwenefo (wo ho yi, woyi no amo, na) wonyi no adwow.
You accuse the stingy person of stinginess, but you do not kidnap him.

3535. Ayamye, woye sie, na wonye nkye.
Kindness, is preserved, it is not given away.

3536. Oyamyefo a oso ne boto, wokyi.
The generous person who holds his purse is hated.

3537. Oyamyefo na okye ade-ketewa.
The generous person gives small gifts.

3538. Yanom a ekoo osa na obi nko ntoo o, na mense se samampow mmua nna. B.
My own comrades went to war and no one brought back anything, I can't say that the ghost should fast.

3539. Yanom e, yanom e, wogyee no.
You call to your friends saying: "Oh, these people, oh these people."

3540. Oyare a ebekum wo bo wo a, wonkae duruyofo.
When the illness that is going to kill you comes upon you, you forget the doctor.

3541. Oyare ebekum wo nnim aduru.
There is no medicine for the sickness that will kill you.

3542. Oyare afi yisa atifi! (Oy. kofi yisa atifi a, wokyi.) Cf. 2879.
Sickness comes from the upper part of guiena-pepper.

3543. Oyare woko no ahohora.
Sickness is driven off by insults.

3544. Oyare ne abew.
Sickness is a hindrance.

3545. Oyare nsae a, wonnye ayaresade. Gr. p. 162.
If you're not cured of your sickness, you don't pay the doctor's fee.

3546. Oyare see akyeafo.
Sickness changes the appearance of a handsome person.

3547. Ɔyare to wo mu a, ɛyɛ anyamesɛm, na ɛnyɛ wo abusuafo na ɛreku wo.
If you become sick, it is the way of Providence, and not your relatives that are killing you.

3548. Woyare anomdɛw a, na woyare ntotɔ. Cf. 392.
If you suffer from a compulsion to eat sweet things, then you also have a compulsion to buy.

3549. Ɔyarefo na onim nea ehia no (:nea ɔyare no wɔ).
The sick person knows what he needs.

3550. Ɔyarefo nni (:nyɛ) anem.
A sick person can not carry out anything.

3551. Ɔyaw yɛ mframa.
Insult is mere wind.

3552. Woyaw mpanyimfo a, wo fwene buruw (:tu).
If you insult the elders you nose gets smashed in.

3553. Wokɔyaw ɔpanyin bi na ɔfwe wo a, ansa-na wobɛka akyerɛ no sɛ "meyɛ abofra ɛna?".
If you go and insult an elder he beats you before you ask him, "Do you think I am a child?"

3554. "Yɛ ma yɛnfwɛ!" yɛ ɔyɛ-na. (Yɔ ..ɛyɛ ɔna).
"Let me see you do it," makes the performance difficult.

3555. Ɛyɛ fɛ, na ɛnyɛ anibere. R. 23. Gr. 251c.
It is beautibul, but it excites no desire.

3556. Mayɛ ɔdemerefua, me ho ayɛ ohuam. (Mp.)
I was a bush dog, I had a sweet scent.

3557. Mayɛ sɛ wo pɛn.
I was once like you.

3558. Woyɛ berɛberɛ a, woware ahenyere. Cf. 3299.
If you have patience, you can marry one of the chief's wives.

3559. Woyɛ obi ade yiye a, ɛka wo so.
If you do a good deed for someone, you benefit from it.

3560.   Woyɛ obi yiye na wanyɛ wo bi a, na obu wo aboa.
        If you do good to someone and he does not do good to you,
        then he considers you a fool.

3561.   Woyɛ biribi a, yɛ no ntɛm, na me nane tia adɛre so.
        If you do something do it quidkly, for my foot is stepping
        on the cutlass.

3562.   Woyɛ biribi na anyɛ yiye a, womfa nka-asɛm.
        If you are doing something and it doesn't turn out well,
        you don't talk about it.

3563.   Woyɛ abofra a, wuse: woyɛ ɔdehye.
        If you are a child you say you are a member of the royal
        family.

3564.   Woyɛ abofra a, nserew akwatia,   R. 6.   Gr. p. 170.
        If you are young, do not laugh at a short person.

3565.   Woyɛ adebone a, wo ani mpa ho da.
        If you do something bad, you never forget it.

3566.   Woyɛ adwuma na woannya mu sɛnkyerɛne a, wokyi.
        If you are working and you don't get any benefit from it,
        you hate it.

3567.   Woyɛ ofi koro mu kuna-perɛnsa a, wofrɛ wo busufo.
        If you are in the same house with three widows, you are
        called a wicked person.

3568.   Woyɛ hm-hm (hu bebrebe) a, wode wo sekan gua ɔnanka.
        Cf. 3128.
        If you are reluctant to say no, they use your knife in
        skinning a rhinocerous viper.

3569.   Woyɛ nkommomim a, wofwere sɛmodɛbofo.   Cf. 1700.
        If you are greedy in conversation, you lose the wisdom of
        your friend.

3570.   Woyɛ Kwakwa a, woyɛ woho.
        If you make the sound of a raven, you insult yourself.

3571.   Woyɛ me-nko-medi a, wunya asman nhui.
        If you want to have everything for yourself, you will go
        to the land of the dead.

3572. Woyɛ nnam bebrebe a, wotwa wo tiri so dwira.

If you are very brave, your head is cut off to celebrate the yearly yam custom.

3573. Woyɛ sika-nibere a, wuwu awusin.

If you are greedy for money, you die prematurely.

3574. Woyɛ asonkwa a, wɔsoma wo akyiri.

If you are a good for nothing person, you are sent far away.

3575. Woyɛ atiwase a, wo ho nnyae tan yɛ da.

If you are a spiteful person, you are always hated.

3576. Woyɛ yiye a, wɔde yaw wo mma; woyɛ bone nso a, wɔde yaw wo mma.

If you do good, you insult your children, and if you do evil, you also insult your children.

3577. Woyɛ yiye a, ɛwɔ ne mfaso.

If you do good, you are rewarded.

3578. Wokɔyɛ ha na wuse "gye akyekyere kɔma agya" a, enyɛ ahayɔ. Cf. 1262.

If you go hunting in the bush and say, "take the tortoise and give it to your father," it is not real hunting.

3579. Wobɛyɛ kɛse a, ennim adidi-dodow.

If you want to grow big you are not worried about eating too much.

3579a. Wo na woayɛ oguanten dɛn na ne twɛ bɔ ne to? Cf. 3455.

What have you done to the goat that her vagina is so near her anus?

3580. (Wo, de,) woayɛ kotoku-saabobe, onni ano na ɔhome. =1751.

If you have the flower of a certain vine "kotoku-saabobe), it has no mouth but it breathes.

3581. Woayɛ nea wɔnnyɛ a, anka woahu nea wonnhu.

If you do what you shouldn't do, you will see what you shouldn't see.

3582. (Sɛ) woayɛ wo proku a, yɛ wo dua.

If you have bad teeth, use your chewing stick.

3583. Nyɛ na minnyi wo Kwakyewa (mi)nnse wo!

If you are not good, I don't call you Kwakyewa.

3584. Ɛnyɛ ɔba a ɔbɛte fo nko ne nea ɔda fo nhoma so.
It is not only the child who hears the monkey, that lies on the hide of the monkey.

3585. Ɛnyɛ aba a wɔde bɔ wuram' aboa na wɔde bɔ fie aboa. Cf. 31. Z. 21.
You don't use the same stick to beat a wild animal and a domesticated one.

3586. Ɛnyɛ ɔbako na nsu kɔ ne turum' a, ɔta.
It is not only one person who farts when water it put into his anus.

3587. Ɛnyɛ ɔbarima a ɔbɛfwere yere ne Kwasi Nkromma.
It is not only Kwasi Nkromma who lost his wife.

3588. Ɛnyɛ ɔbea nko na ɔwo, na ɔbarima nso wo bi.
It is not only a women who bear children, men also bear children.

3589. Ɛnyɛ obi ne bɔmmɔfo na ɛkɔɔ wuram'.
No one went into the bush with the hunter.

3590. Ɛnyɛ biribi nko na wɔhyɛ mu kana (:kena, kra, na asɛm nso wɔhyɛ mu kra).
It is just anything that you mark (but an important case you mark.)

3591. "Ɛnyɛ biribi", na (ɛyɛ) biribi ara ne no. R. 46. Z. 199.
"It's nothing," but even that is something.

3592. "Ɛnyɛ biribi", wonse no abodwo.
"It's nothing," you don't say this calmly.

3593. Ɛnyɛ abopae nko ne adwuma.
The quarrying of stone is not the only thing called work.

3594. Ɛnyɛ Brofo nhina na wɔbɛyɛ sɛ James.
Not all Europeans will do things like James.

3595. Ɛnyɛ da(koro) a wofua ɔde (no) ara na wosi ne pam (:wosoa ho pam).
It is not the day on which the yam is planted that we fix sticks for its climbers.

3596. Ɛnyɛ aduan na ɛma onipa ho yɛ yiye.
It is not food that make people feel well.

3597. Ɛnyɛ aduan na ɛsono nya di kyɛn adowa nti na ɔyɛ kɛse sen no.

Ir is not the larger amount of food that the elephant gets to eat that make it bigger than the antelope.

3598. Ɛnyɛ adwene (:nam) dabere ne muka (bikyia, bukyia) so. Cf. 1053.

The sleeping place of the mud-fish is not on the fire place.

3599. Ɛnyɛ adwene ahonya ne gya so.

The fish's liberty is not on the fire.

3600. Ɛnyɛ fa a woabɔ nhina na ɛkɔ mu.

Isn't it the soil from which everything was made that you go into?

3601. Ɛnyɛ agoru ne "ma yɛnto aduru".

It is not a joke to say, "let us poison someone".

3602. Ɛnyɛ gua pa bi ne mpɛsɛwa-gua.

A good chair is not brought for one pesewa.

3603. Ɛnyɛ ohia nko ne ahohora.

It is not only poverty that is disgraceful.

3604. Ɛnyɛ ɔkafoni yɔnko ne defoɔ.

The debtor should not make the rich man his friend.

3605. Ɛnyɛ okisi nko ne ne bɛdɛw ni.

It is not only the rat who has a basket woven of palm leaves.

3606. Ɛnyɛ koko a wɔde ko dɔm na wɔde ko ntokwaw.

It is not the same boldness with which you conquer an army that you use in fist-fighting.

3607. Ɛnyɛ konkron na ebetumi dɔ.

It is not a waist cloth that can be made bigger.

3608. Ɛnyɛ "wonkum, wonkum!" nhina na wokum.

It is not always when they shout "kill him, kill him," that they kill him.

3609. Ɛnyɛ nkyempae (:nkyene berefi) na ɛbɛte Firaw mu.

It is not a bag of salt that stays in the Firaw river.

3610. Ɛnyɛ mmorɔsa dɛw nti na wotɔ.

It is not because the European brandy is sweet that you buy it.

3611. Ɛnyɛ nan-nodow na ɛma ani bere amoakua.

It is not his many feet that makes people desire the squirrel.

3612. Ɛnyɛ nantwi nko na ofi Saraha bae (baa ha, baa Kumase).

It is not only cattle that come from Salaga to Kumasi.

3613. Ɛnyɛ nea mmoa adi kɔ na ehia, na nea aka na wobɔ ho ban.

It is not the animals which go that need protection, but those that remain.

3614. Ɛnyɛ nea egu fam' yi na matɔ mantua, na nea egyina hɔ no na mantɔ mantua.

It is not that which is lying on the ground that I have bought and not paid for, but that which is standing there that I have not bought nor paid for.

3615. Ɛnyɛ nea n'ani ayɛ kɔkɔ nko na n'ani abere.

It is not only the person whose eyes are red that is serious.

3616. Ɛnyɛ nea Saforotwe akoa nhuu bi da ne manniamfrɛ ɔha.

The slave of Saforotwe has often seen a hundred mouth gags.

3617. Ɛnyɛ nea tan abɔ ne ti nko na asɛm yɛ no tan.

It is not only he who has hatred in his head to whom a palaver is hateful.

3618. Ɛnyɛ nea ɔtwe nhuu (:nhuu bi) da ne (sɛ) wonka ntware no.

"Go round this way to intercept and shoot it" is not what the antelope has never heard.

3619. Ɛnyɛ nnipa nhina na enim sɛ, osu tɔ a, wɔsɔre kɔ ɔdan mu.

Not all people know that when it is raining they should get up and go into the house.

3620. Ɛnyɛ ano a wɔde pɛ bosea (:fɛm) na wɔde tua (:tutu).
Cf. 3217.

The mouth with which one asks for a loan is different from that with which it is paid back.

-297-

3621. Ɛnyɛ ɔpanyin bi na okura adare dɔw.

It is not a real elder who carries the cutlass to the farm to weed.

3622. Ɛnyɛ sa nko na ɛyɛ kwae.

It is not only the "sa" trees that make up a forest.

3623. Ɛnyɛ sika bi akoa ne sika bi.

One man's money is not the slave of another man's money.

3624. Ɛnyɛ osisiriw na ebetumi akisikuru.

It is not the "osisiriw" tree that is able to withstand a sore discharging pus.

3625. Ɛnyɛ asu nhina mu na woguare gu.

It is not all rivers that you bathe in.

3626. Ɛnyɛ Ata nko na ɔtɔn atadwe.

It is not only the twin who sells tiger-nuts.

3627. Ɛnyɛ Ata anim a wɔta ade.

It is not in front of a twin that you place something.

3628. Ɛnyɛ tɛ a esi nipa ani so na wɔde bua no.

It is not only cataract that cuases a person's eye to close.

3629. Ɛnyɛ tɛkrɛma na ɛbɔɔ nantwi nti na wanhu kasa.

It is not because of the big tongue which the cow has, that he doesn't know how to talk,

3630. Ɛnyɛ "matɔ, matɔ!" na wɔde tɔ ade.

You don't say, "I have bought it, I have bought it," before you buy it.

3631. Ɛnyɛ ɔtɔmfo nko ne Adabraka.

It isn't only the seller that says, "reduce the price".

3632. Ɛnyɛ ɔtwea a ɔbɛfwere da ne Boasiare.

The female dog which will never waste things is Boasiare.

3633. Ɛnyɛ "maware, maware" na wɔde ware bea.

You don't say, "I have been married before, I have been married before," in looking for a woman to marry.

3634. Ɛnyɛ ɔwora-koro (:wura biako) mu na woyi (mu) daha.
It is not just from one pond that you pluck the leaves of
the "adobe" palm tree.

3635. Ɛnyɛ wo yɔnko ne nea ade kye a otumi bɔ wo ano akɔnhama.
The person who feeds you in the morning is not your neighbor.

3636. Menyɛ Simpa prako na mede maso mayɛ me mmɛn.
I am not a pig from Winneba that I use my ears as horns.

3637. Woanyɛ ɔhene bɔne a, wonkum wo da.
If you have not done anything bad to the chief, he will
never kill you.

3638. Woayɛ hu a, wonyɛ nnam.
If you are frightened, you are not bold.

3639. Wonyɛ prako na woawo ba(na wo)adi.
You are not a pig that when you gave birth you were
eating.

3640. Ɛnyɛ na wɔnkɔtow nkyene a, womfa nto fie.   Cf. 3351.
If it is not good, it should be thrown away and not kept
in the house.

3641. Ɔye-bone te sɛ ntama a aye fi: wode nam a, wo ho ntew wo.
A bad wife is like a dirty cloth; if you travel with it,
you are not clean.

3642. Ɔyɛ-dedaw na onim okunu kɔm.
One who has been a wife for a long time knows what kind
of food her husband likes.

3643. Ayefare sika nyɛ sika bi.
The fine for committing adultery is big.

3644. Ɔyem nyɛ ɔde na abɔ akɔ fam'.
Pregnancy is not like a yam that grows downward.

3645. Ɔye-pa sen sika.
A good wife is more precious than gold.

3646. Ɔye-pa yɛ ahode.
A good wife is personal wealth.

3647. Wo yere a onye no (:Wo yere ho nyɛ fɛ a,) na ɛte sɛ obi
aguaman (:mpra).
If your wife is no good, she is like someone's concubine.

3648. Wo yere kɔ asu ba na ose "soɛ me" a, soɛ no, na da bi
wobɛkɔ bi anom a, wunnim.
When your wife goes to fetch water and returns and asks you
to help her put the bucket down, help her, for you don't
know when you will have to fetch water for yourself.

3649. Wo yere anyin a, wuntutu 'mirika na ɛkohyia no.
If your wife is old, you don't run to meet her.

3650. Wo yerenom anum a, wɔ tɛkrɛma anum.
If you have five wives, you have fine different tongues.

3651. Wo yere apem a, wo asɛm apem.
If you have a thousand wives, you have a thousand troubles.

3652. Ɔyere te tɛ kuntu: wode kata wo so a, wo ho keka wo; wuyi
gu hɔ nso a, awɔw de wo. (Sal. Salforo)
A wife is like a woolen blanket, if you cover yourself
with it, you itch; if you take it away, you feel cold.

3653. Ɔyere nyɛ nam na wɔakyekyɛ amana.
A wife is not meant to be sent to someone as a gift.

3654. Wo yere nye a, ɛnte sɛ wo nko (wo) da.
Even if your wife is not good, you don't sleep alone.

3655. Ayere-dodow yɛ ohia na ɛnyɛ five. Cf. 26.
Too many wives cause poverty but it doesn't matter.

3656. Yerɛw-yerɛw wɔde se onipa anim.
Something glittering is said of a person's face.

3657. Ayɛyi di nya-ma na enni kyɛm-ma.
Benevolence is performed with "let us all eat" and not
with, "let us eat in his absence."

3658. Ayɛyɛ akatua ne nnase (:makye meda-ase). Cf. 852.
The reward of benevolence is gratitude.

3659. Wuyi dadu wɔw brɔde a, ɛnnan de da. (Nkoa bɛ.)
If you set apart ten people to pound fufu, four are still
left.

3660. Wuyi wo ahina ayɛ a, ɛbɔ.

If you praise your water pot, it breaks.

3661. Wunyi me ayɛ a, nsɛe me din. R. 16.
(Enyi m ayɛ a, mma nsɛe me dzin. (F.) G. p. 193.)

If you do not praise me, at least do not spoil my reputation.

3662. Wonkoyi mmusu a, wɔde koto ɔkɔmfo nkɔmman mu.

If you don't protect yourself from evil, do you go and
prostrate yourself inside the fence within which the
fetish priest performs his practices?

3663. Wonyi atɛn a, wɔnto ntam.

If you are not accused of having done something wrong, you
don't transgress an oath.

3664. Ayi, wɔso no abaw-abaw.

The corpse is carried on the arms of the carriers.

3665. Oyimforo fata Ɔkwaku.

A young person and a monkey suit one another.

3666. "Ayisa, woame ana?" Ose: "woma me sɛnea woma wo ba a,
anka mame."

Orphan, are you satisfied?" He replies, "If you gave me
as much food as you gave your own child I would be satisfied."

3667. Ayisa, pere were, na mpere 'merɛbo!
Orphan, fight for the skin, but not for liver!

3668. Ayisa su a, ɔmmerɛ nusu ho.
If the orphan cries, tears come easily.

3669. Ayisa yi wo ani; wo de ne kyɛmfɛre mu!
"Orphan, give ignorance to everything." this is said while
his hand is in a dish.

3670. Yiyeyɔ nti na nsiammoa kaa nam mu. =3678.
Because of doing good, maggots got into the meat.

3671. "Yɔ ma memfwɛ!" ɛyɛ ɔna. =3554.
  .   "Let me see you do it!" makes the doing difficult.

3672. Wo yɔnko da ne wo da.
Your neighbour's day (of death) is you day (of death.)

3673. Wo yɔnko di wo amim na wunni no bi a, na ɛte sɛ wusuro
no. Cf. 417.
If your neighbour cheats you and you don't cheat him,
it means you fear him.

3674. Ɔyɔnko mu wɔ yɔnko.
Among many friends there is one true friend.

3675. "Yɔnko, yɔnko" na ɛma asɛm terɛw.
Friendship spreads the news.

3676. Ayɔnkogoru nti ɔhɔho kɔ kurom a, ɔfa abarima.
It is because of playing with friends that when a stranger
goes to town he engages himself as a servant.

3677. Ayɔnkoguru nti na ɔkɔtɔ annya ti. R. 74.
It is because of playing with friends that the crab has
no head.

3678. Ayɔnkokogoru nti na nsiammoa kaa nam mu. =3670.
It is because of playing with friends that maggots got
into the meat.

3679. Ayɔnkogoru yɛ fɛ kyɛn ɛna-mma.
Friendship is more beautiful than brotherhood.

3680. Nsɛm nhina ne Nyame.
All wisdom is from God.

STUDIES IN AFRICAN LITERATURE